Peter Ross has written for newspapers and magazines including *The Guardian*, *The Times*, *Scotland on Sunday*, *The Big Issue*, *National Geographic Traveler* and the *Boston Review*. He is an Orwell Fellow and a six-time winner at the Scottish Press Awards. His first book, *Daunderlust*, was also published by Sandstone Press. He is married with two children and lives in Glasgow.

You can read more of his work at
www.peterross.scot

THE PASSION OF
HARRY BINGO

Peter Ross

SANDSTONEPRESS
HIGHLAND | SCOTLAND

Published in Great Britain by
Sandstone Press Ltd
Dochcarty Road
Dingwall
Ross-shire
IV15 9UG
Scotland.

www.sandstonepress.com

The publisher acknowledges support from
Creative Scotland towards publication of this volume.

ISBN: 978-1-910985-81-6
ISBNe: 978-1-910985-82-3

Cover design by Mark Ecob
Typeset by Iolaire Typesetting, Newtonmore
Printed and bound by Totem, Poland

For my mother – and for my father

Acknowledgements

Many people made this book possible. I am grateful first and foremost to those who appear in these pages, in particular to Mr Henry Calderhead – Harry Bingo, who gives the book its title – and to his family. Thanks also to Ally Palmer, editor of *Nutmeg: The Scottish Football Periodical*, whose enthusiasm for the title story is the reason that particular tale exists.

Thanks to the editors who commissioned these stories and gave permission or blessings for their inclusion here. Ian Stewart, then editor of *The Scotsman* and *Scotland on Sunday*, has been especially accommodating in this regard.

My thanks, too, to Robert Davidson and the team at Sandstone Press.

Val McDermid has been tremendously supportive of my work. It means a lot that she took the time to write a foreword to this book.

Siobhan Lynch gave her blessing to my quoting from a very kind letter, which I cherish, written to me by William McIlvanney.

George Gunn read my story Whaligoe Steps and gave permission to quote from his book *The Province of the Cat* and his unpublished play *Camster*. I thank him for that, and wish to express my gratitude to his publisher The Islands Book Trust.

There are a number of friends, acquaintances and colleagues whose support, example, suggestions and comradeship have been important to me before and during the writing of the stories in this collection. They include: Kelly Apter, Archie Bland, Robbie Coltrane, Melissa Denes,

Brian Donaldson, Kenny Farquharson, Dani Garavelli,
Jane Graham, Alison Gray, Ian Jack, Jamie Lafferty, Barry
Leathem, Fiona Leith, Damien Love, Kathleen Morgan,
Stephen McGinty, Paul McNamee, Robert Perry, Stephen
Phelan, Kevin Pocklington, Ian Rankin, Alison Stroak and
Graeme Virtue.

Love, as ever and forever, to Jo, James and Jack.

Contents

Foreword

Scotland's first great novelist, Walter Scott, summed it up:

> Breathes there the man, with soul so dead,
> Who never to himself hath said,
> This is my own, my native land.

For we all know our own country. We know its landscape, its history, its culture, what makes us different from everywhere else.

Or at least we think we do. We all fall into the trap of thinking that what is familiar to us is what there is to be known. But every now and again, someone comes along who points out the richness that exists beyond our knowledge, often right on our own doorsteps. Who reminds us that curiosity is one of the cardinal virtues, a gift that never stops giving.

Peter Ross is such a man, and the book you're holding is a route map to the strange, the bizarre and the wonderful that exists out there on the edges of our everyday. But these are not the stories of the kind of eccentrics who build follies just for the sake of it. These are the stories of extraordinary men and women who dedicate themselves to tradition, to maintaining elements of our collective history that can warm the heart and take the breath away. They're not just doing it for themselves. They're doing it for all of us. They've found passion in the most unexpected of places and they've dedicated themselves to the unusual that often lurks behind the most unpromising of surfaces.

Whether it's the Clavie King leading the fire ritual in Moray where a large barrel of tar is set alight and paraded through the streets to mark the Julian New Year; or the Burryman who is covered with prickly burrs and walks the streets of South Queensferry all day fuelled only by whisky; or the exotic patrons of the Drag Queen Ball in Glasgow, the commitment of the participants to stepping outside daily life and making something happen is as strong. These are people who often take risks to pursue what matters to them and it's impossible not to feel delight as we share their stories.

Peter Ross gives them all space to tell their tales. This is the best kind of journalism, where the interviewer gives the interviewee time and space to relax into their stories, to forget 'A chiel's amang ye takin notes. And, faith, he'll prent it.' There is an art to this kind of conversation between student and subject, where the journalist is there to learn everything he can then distill his new knowledge into a tight, coherent piece that tells us what we want to know without ever slipping into self-indulgence. It's the kind of writing where the writer makes himself almost invisible, pretending simply to be a conduit while actually being a master craftsman who shapes the narrative into something irresistible. It is sometimes a celebration, sometimes an elegy, sometimes a memorial. It is always a pleasure.

This is a book of delights to dip into and savour. Except that once you start dipping, you won't want to stop. As I read it, I caught myself making mental notes of the dates of extraordinary events and the locations of places I wanted to witness for myself. The abandoned terrain of the Bass Rock. The terrifying cliffside pitch of the Whaligoe Steps. A Half Man Half Biscuit gig. The small town festivals of West Lothian. The obsessive players of chess and crazy golf. The extravaganza of Christmas lights in Port Glasgow. I'm charmed and entranced by these entrées into secret worlds.

If you truly want to feel the heartbeat of this strange and diverse country, look no further.

Val McDermid
Edinburgh
2017

Introduction

On the day of the US Presidential inauguration, a day on which journalism felt like a fruitless and possibly futureless occupation, I was hard at work in Edinburgh. It is unlike me to take any time away from a story when I am in the thick of reporting it, but such an inauspicious occasion, heavy with dread, called for a counterbalance of solace and beauty. So I chucked it for a while and walked over to the Gallery of Modern Art for the Joan Eardley exhibition.

Her paintings of seascapes and stairheid weans were, indeed, soothing. I recognised one – 'Sweet Shop, Rottenrow' – that I'd last seen on a wall of Edwin Morgan's home when I had visited his Glasgow flat almost seventeen years before. They corresponded, the poet and painter, but never met, and even though they were much the same age, she died long before him. She was very shy, he told me: 'I saw her once, sitting on the steps of the Royal Scottish Academy in Edinburgh as I was passing along Princes Street, and I almost stopped. I wish I had done so but I was too shy myself to talk to her.'

There was a film playing in one of the rooms of the exhibition. *Three Scottish Painters* had been broadcast in 1963, the year of Eardley's death. We see her working in the studio, making a pastel drawing of one of the Samson children, her urchin muses. She does not shy from showing mucky faces, spindly legs, jug lugs, a wee girl's squint – the paintings are unsparing in that way, yet no one who sees them can doubt they were done with love. 'Thus the eye and the heart of Joan Eardley,' the narrator drawls in his BBC voice. 'Observation that is keen yet kind.'

1

Keen yet kind. Those words struck home. It could be a three-word manifesto for a certain sort of journalism, the sort that appeals to me. The sort I want to write. When my first book, *Daunderlust*, was published in 2014, I read from it and spoke about it at a number of book festivals. I very much enjoyed hearing people laugh, or say afterwards that they had been moved, but best of all was when they told me that they found my writing kind. Reporters are sometimes celebrated for being fearless, sometimes condemned for being heartless, but kindness is a quality that seems not to be much valued or even considered. I think that may be because no journalist wants to be thought of as soft, or bland. But empathy is not weakness. Understanding is not sentimentality. We need these things if we are to access other lives and report back.

There is a moment early on in *The Road to Wigan Pier*: George Orwell is on a train, leaving the town, passing through the 'monstrous scenery' of the industrial north, when he notices a 'slum girl' in her twenties, kneeling on slimy flagstones, trying to unblock a drainpipe with a stick. Although the train goes by in a flash, Orwell tells us that he 'had time to see everything about her' – her face, her clothes, her tragedy. She wore, he writes, 'the most desolate, hopeless expression I have ever seen', and he senses, in an instant, that she herself is quite aware of the 'dreadful destiny' of a life in poverty. This brief encounter – not even that, just a glimpse of a life – may be my favourite passage in all of Orwell. His ability to observe and describe with great penetrating sharpness is a gift, but it is his humanity which whets it. Keen yet kind. Eyes and heart.

Close observation is itself a form of compassion – to pay intense attention to a person or place or situation, with no more end than writing about them accurately and insightfully, there's something loving in that. Not altruistic, though. Out on a story, using all my senses, forced into conversations with strangers, I feel alive in a way that I do not at most other times. When someone asks me, as they often do, 'What's the angle to your article?' I rarely know what to say. I almost never have an angle. I just want to describe what's out there, so that I might know it better, and because writing about what I find in the world makes me feel I have a place and purpose within it.

This basic function of journalism – telling tales, describing people and places, getting lives down on paper – is too often overlooked during discussions of the crisis in the industry. The emphasis is always on journalism's social and political role; that reporters ought to speak truth to power, reveal corruption and lies, and cover the day-to-day functioning of democracy from community council meetings and local courts to great matters of state. Society is ill served, the argument goes, when cuts and declining sales make it impossible for the media to do this effectively.

All of that is true, but I would argue that journalism also has a vital task in simply recording life as it is lived. Each day goes by in a blur of impressions, emotions and events; people are born and die, they laugh and cry, they fall in or out of love; they suffer or prosper; endure or give up. None of this would make a headline, necessarily, but it is worth trying to record and fix because it is the daily business of being alive. Let us not forget to beat the drum for the humdrum.

Recently, I went to a friend's birthday party in Glasgow. The pub was full of journalists, men and women in their thirties and forties, some of the smartest, funniest, most culturally engaged people you could hope to meet. They should, by their age, be star writers or senior editors on our national newspapers. But most had left staff jobs in one of the endless rounds of redundancies and were now scraping a living as freelancers, or they had quit the industry altogether, finding the daily hustle for scraps of work no longer tenable or indeed bearable. There is sorrow in this for each individual, of course, a dream that didn't

3

work out. But what I sensed in that pub, very strongly, was all the stories untold, the photographs never taken, the sentences unformed. You could almost see the wasted ink seeping out of the door and running down the gutter of Hope Street. It would be an exaggeration, but not too great an exaggeration, to say that the life and lives of Scotland are in danger of going unwritten.

I feel very fortunate to have been able to write the stories in this book, to have had the excuse of the writing to meet the people who are their subjects, and to have had them published by editors who saw the value where others might not. The Eagle's Bairn, the Burryman, the Naked Rambler, Harry Bingo and the Herring Queens: I have a strong sense of us all crammed on to a raft, clinging to the mast; hopefully, George Parsonage – the Riverman – is at the oars.

If you enjoyed *Daunderlust*, I hope you will like this collection. If you are new to my writing, welcome; I hope you will not regret picking up this book. The great majority of these stories remain more or less as they first appeared in print. A few have been reworked substantially. Most were written between 2013 and now, but one – the final piece, on the murder of Angelika Kluk – dates from 2007. That story has always been important to me. It was the first time that ideas of redemption and resurrection and a kind of spiritual endurance came together in my writing. Writers of fiction are able to weave these themes into their creations. I don't have that skill, but seem to be drawn to the lives and stories of people who embody them.

Although I think of myself as essentially a comic writer, there is, I think, a sadness in the world, in me, and subsequently in these stories that was not in *Daunderlust* to the same degree. Yet I trust that the dominant note remains hope, and a celebration of the extraordinary in the ordinary.

Not everyone in these pages is still alive. Some have

passed since first publication. I would like to think that these stories honour their memories. It has been my pleasure to catch a glimpse of their lives, and I hope it will be yours, too.

Peter Ross
Glasgow
2017

After the Referendum

THE WHOLE DAY felt diseased. Stillborn, malformed, a thing of smirr and haar, hard words and soured dreams. Dawn on Friday, 19th September 2014 broke grey and uncertain; a false dawn for those who nurtured hopes of a new nation.

Alex Salmond, in Edinburgh, had just acknowledged defeat in front of a few hundred supporters. The Scottish independence referendum had been lost and there were tears on the cheeks of the faithful. Fourteen hours later, in Glasgow city centre, tears streamed down the snarling faces of the First Minister's most bitter foes, provoked by smoke from the flares around which they danced and chanted. I saw the weeping of both sides, those hurting and those hating, a sight to sear the soul of anyone who loves Scotland.

It began at first light as we left Our Dynamic Earth, the science centre in Edinburgh, across the road from the Scottish Parliament. This was supposed to have been the scene of what had been reported as the SNP's 'victory party'. Despite the convivial presence of the spliterati – Irvine Welsh, Brian Cox et al – it did not take long to become a wake. The crying began at Inverclyde and by the time Fife declared was in full flow. To ask, 'How do you feel?' seemed an intrusion on private mourning. 'Torture,' replied Catherine Ratter, an elderly lady and long-term supporter of independence. 'This has broken my heart,' said the actor Martin Compston. Neither seemed to be speaking metaphorically.

'A once in a lifetime opportunity and the people of Scotland didn't want it,' said Brian McDermid, a forty-four-year-old from Dunfermline with AYE on his T-shirt. 'They blew it.'

Outside, it was damp and dim, and the Union flag hung limp above Holyrood Palace. A sign over the science centre entrance advertised an exhibition of geology: 'Change,' it read, 'is the only constant.'

Grief has five stages, they say: denial, anger, bargaining, depression and acceptance. The Yes campaigners in Glasgow, later that day, appeared to have skipped the first and gone straight to the second and fourth. Bargaining can be left to the politicians as they negotiate Scotland's new powers. Acceptance is still a long way off.

In George Square, or Independence Square as it had become known, only a few bleary, weary revellers saw in the commuter hour, huddled together on benches, wrapped in Saltires. Here they were, pale and stunned, as the cleansing men swept away the slogans – 'Glasgow says Yes!'; 'Too many sheep in Scotland' – chalked on the ground.

A tourist coach held up in traffic displayed a Red Hand of Ulster banner. The driver yelled through a window as it moved away: 'Ya Yes wankers! Ah'm Scottish, too, and ah voted no!' A young man, angrily waving a Saltire, chased the bus. This was a sign of things to come.

Later, a few dozen, a mere rump in comparison with the thousands of recent days, gathered around a man with a guitar and sang a frail, lamenting 'Flower of Scotland'. 'But we can still rise now and be a nation again' – many choked on that line.

Schaun Shirkie, and his friends Ruari and Claire Gordon, all in their twenties, had travelled to Glasgow from Arran full of hope and now found themselves in despair. 'People say this isn't the end, this is progress,' said Schaun 'but I don't believe that. This is never going to happen again.' He had returned to the square that morning for reasons he didn't quite understand: 'I feel a bit displaced. It's like our journey's been in vain.'

For Claire, seeing the Western Isles vote no made her feel the meaning of Scotland had been lost. 'That just broke me.'

This sort of thing, in print, can look melodramatic, but to regard it as such is to misunderstand the impact the referendum campaign has had on pro-independence activists. Although the political transformation they sought has not come about, many feel a huge personal change. They are engaged with society in ways they were not before. They feel, finally, that they have managed to get some purchase on life. Many also feel a deep cynicism, even paranoia, about mainstream politics and media. Those who work in public life, and those of us who comment upon it, will struggle to win them back.

The Yes Bar, a pub on Drury Street, is a convivial hub for independence supporters, but has barred the BBC on the grounds of bias. Outside, three new pals, young working-class guys in their twenties from Stirling, Penicuik and Port Glasgow – 'We're the United Nations!' – explained that they had been politicised by the campaign. Yet they felt betrayed by the result; by a more prosperous older generation whom they perceived had sold them out.

Also out on Drury Street, twenty-nine-year-old Zara Gladman, who, as the performer and activist Lady Alba, has become one of the breakthrough personalities of the referendum, agreed that faultlines between rich and poor, young and old, had been prised open. She cried as she spoke. It was the thought of those living in poverty who had come out to vote for the first time in the belief that it could change their lives for the better. She worried that hope would dissipate. The voter turnout had been incredible, but who would now bet against a more profound disenfranchisement than before? Yes had been a people's movement, 'but, in the end, the politicians won'.

The dream of independence is not entirely dead. Many campaigners point to a combination of possible scenarios

– including the UK leaving the EU – which could sharpen the appetite of the Scottish public for future separation. Yesterday afternoon, members of the activist group The Hills Have Ayes hiked up into the Campsies, just outside Glasgow, and wrote the defiant message 'Aye'll Be Back,' in geotextile letters eight metres high, on a steep slope visible for miles around. 'The message is: stay political,' said Dave, a spokesman for the group. 'Don't let the feeling that has been alive through this go away. The no vote won, but 45 per cent is a huge number.'

Unquestionably there is division in Scotland. To call this a country divided against itself is to overstate the case, but the fact that 1.6 million people voted yes, while 2 million voted no tells its own story. There is a wound. The danger is that it becomes infected by bitterness.

Already, this weekend, there have been attempts at healing. The Arches venue in Glasgow hosted a 'What Now?' brunch, dishing out bacon rolls, hugs and consoling chat to all who needed them. St Nicholas Cardonald, a church in the south-west of the city, opened its doors for prayer, conversation and reconciliation: 'Scottish people are resilient,' said Rhona Boyle, a retired school secretary. 'We knew there weren't going to be any winners in this. But we will pick ourselves up. We've come through worse.'

It was a fine sentiment which brought comfort later as the flares and punches flew. The trouble began in early evening when hundreds walked into George Square holding Union flags, intent, they said, on a victory party. Immediately, there were confrontations with the outnumbered independence supporters already there. The police struggled to hold both sides back. A young man with a beard and woolly hat climbed on his pal's shoulders and brandished a sign with an image of a newborn child and the slogan, Scotland's Future In Scotland's Hands. 'Stick your Union Jack up your arse!' he shouted.

A forty-something called Steven found himself isolated.

He held up the Saltire he had bought for his boy at a football game and was thumped in the face. 'I wish there had never been a referendum,' said Colin Quintin Young, a furious thirty-nine-year-old ex-serviceman who had exchanged angry words with Steven. 'Alex Salmond and the SNP are tearing this country apart.'

'Rule Britannia', one side sang. 'Flower of Scotland' was heard from the other. But it would be a terrible error to mistake this for the mainstream. Those with the Union flags and the odd No Thanks placard appeared to be Loyalists. Confronting them were not only some of those Saltire-wavers who had been in the square earlier, but hooded newcomers with dark scarves across their faces, throwing objects and chanting anti-fascist slogans. It mutated into a sectarian confrontation, a fight over territory. It was not really about the referendum, but it was its misshapen offspring.

The truth is that Scotland has been administered a jolt of pure wild energy by this referendum. On the occasion of the 1979 vote, William McIlvanney observed that the Scots were apathetic. The national flag, he wrote, 'might be a lion dormant, with mange'. Well, no longer. This has been the Scotland of the last whisky at last orders, the one that crowns the night and sometimes ruins the morning. There has been a feeling in the air – a sort of euphoric reckless-ness. It is tangible in the pubs and public squares, audible in lecture halls and libraries. It echoes from red sandstone and granite, tenement and tower block and suburban semi. The lion is not dormant. It does not have the mange. It is rampant, roaring and set upon change.

How that change will be made manifest is the question no one, yet, can answer.

The Clavie King

'WE,' SAYS THOMAS, his face all soot, 'have creosote in our blood.'

In their blood, on their hats, on their boots, down their backs; Thomas Ross and the other men of the Clavie Crew have creosote everywhere, with the exception of their whisky. They take that with water, a substance which they otherwise disdain as being fine for quenching a thirst but a terrible thing to allow near a bonnie flame.

I am in Burghead on the Moray coast for the Clavie, an annual fire ritual in which a large wooden barrel full of creosote and tarred staves is set on fire and paraded through the crowded streets. This takes place in the town on 11th January to mark the end of the old year and the beginning of the new. When Scotland switched from the Julian to the Gregorian calendar in 1600, the people here, known as Brochers, refused to change, meaning that their 'Hogmanay' comes eleven days after the rest of the country. Once a large Pictish fort, this is the only place in Scotland where ancient carvings of bulls have been found, and this feels appropriate. No better beast could represent Burghead folk – born to be thrawn and refusing the yoke.

The barrel is built and carried by the Clavie Crew, led by the Clavie King, a position of great honour and responsibility which has been held since 1988 by Dan Ralph. At sixty-eight, he has no thoughts of giving up. Popes, it seems, may retire; Clavie Kings do not. 'Oh no,' he says. 'You go until you die.'

Ralph has an Ancient Mariner beard and is five foot four or so. He used to be taller, but a near fatal accident more than twenty years ago – he fell off the pier – resulted in compression fractures of the spine, costing him an inch and a half. That it did not cost his life may, he likes to believe, be due to the Clavie – it is considered good luck to take home a piece of the charred black wood each year. 'I think it's powerful magic,' he says.

As Burghead's undertaker, Ralph sees the local people at their lowest; as Clavie King he sees them full of joy and hope. His father Jock, a Royal Navy veteran, was one of three men who revived the Clavie tradition in 1946 after a period of abeyance during the Second World War. The others were both called James Mackenzie – distinguishable by their nicknames, Peep and Lichtie – and had been in the thick of the fighting.

That first post-war Crew was made up of men returning from service and close relatives of those who had not survived. Burghead's war memorial is carved with Ralphs and Mackenzies and other stalwart Clavie families, but it could be argued that the annual burning is a more meaningful memorial to the spirit of those men and the town, symbolising continuity and home. What must it have felt like to come back to Burghead from the darkness of war and light that first Clavie? Peep, Lichtie and Jock tossed a coin to decide who would be King; Peep won and reigned until his death in 1987 after which Dan Ralph was asked by the Crew to take over. He had served a long apprenticeship. 'I mind being able to carry it at about fifteen, and thinking, "That's me, I'm a man". It's an initiation, aye, and the young ones noo are feeling the same thing.'

The finished Clavie is, essentially, a six-foot tall torch. One can imagine some Doric Statue of Liberty holding it aloft at the entrance to the town's harbour: 'Give me your fire, your stoor, your Burghead masses yearning to breathe fumes.' The Crew reckon that when the Clavie is full it may be as much as 130 kilos. But no one is quite sure, and in any case the question of precise weight is academic. 'It's heavy and it's on fire,' Lachie Ralph, Dan's son, explains. 'There's aboot an inch of oak between yer heid and the flames.'

I had witnessed its construction on the previous evening in the Ralph family workshop. The Crew had gathered: twenty men, young and old, crammed inside the rough stone walls, wood shavings softening the sound of their boots on the floor as they stamped against the cold. Rusty barrel hoops hung from the ceiling like an ogre's bracelets. To become a member of the Crew, you must be related to current or former members. It is an exclusively male affair. 'Women have a role,' Dan explained. 'Pouring the odd dram and dressing burns.' The future was represented by two of his nine grandchildren, just wee boys but already taking their turn with the tools.

Lachie had started to build the Clavie just before Christmas, and this was the ritual of the finishing touches. The barrel was circled in chalk and sawn in half. Donald Tolmie – retired from the sea and 'a great Free Kirk man' – climbed atop the work bench to bang in the nail that connects the remaining half-barrel to its pine pole, or 'stack'. He used as a hammer the ceremonial round stone which, according to the legend, was thrown by Picts in their trials of strength. The nail, too, has a long history; it is a boatbuilder's nail which each year is picked from the embers and reused.

'Anither dunt, Donald,' called a member of the Crew, encouraging Tolmie as he worked. 'An' anither ain yet.'

'Wob's watchin' ye,' said someone else. 'Big shoes tae fill.'

Wob is the nickname of Gordon Robertson, a great old character who had died three months before at the age of eighty-nine. It was, by tradition, his task to hammer in the nail. Tolmie, an ingenue at seventy-one, was taking on the role for the first time. The nail and the stone, venerated objects, have passed through the hands of generations of Clavie men. As one man falls another takes them up.

Not that they fall easily. Brochers are tough. 'I'll tell you about Wob,' Dan had said. 'Probably twenty years ago, he foolishly wore nylon trousers for the Clavie. They got covered in creosote and flared up on one leg. My wife, who was the nurse in attendance, quickly pulled off his trousers, and with them came all the skin.' He ended up in Aberdeen's burns unit for three-and-a-half months; bed-bound, his leg muscles wasted and he returned home, eventually, on crutches, which he was still using when 11th January came around again. One might expect that he would stay, chastened, at home. But no. He was right there in the Clavie's glow, using his crutches to push out bits of burning stave from the fiery barrel so that onlookers could get their lucky piece. 'That was Wob,' Dan recalled with a fond shake of the head. 'He lacked fear.'

The night of the burning is not a night for fear. Unquestionably, it is perilous, especially for the Crew, but there is a strange air of protection that hangs over the whole occasion as if the town were enclosed within a charmed circle. Oh, it's wild, though. Sleety gusts of sixty-five miles per hour. Waves bursting over the sea wall, spending themselves in spindrift. But there's no chance that the Clavie will be cancelled because of poor weather. After all, it went ahead during the hurricane of 2005 when slates were pinging off all the roofs and the Crew could barely stand up. 'A calm night is more dangerous,' Dan insists. 'The wind swirls aroond and ye get yer beard singed.'

He is dressed for the occasion. No ermine for this king. He wears a dark peacoat, around a century old, inherited from a great-great-uncle; the back and shoulders are blistered with warty daubs of tar, marks of Clavies past. His crown is a felt hat, cloche-shaped, of similar vintage. A cotton rag tucked inside his collar keeps sparks from falling down his neck, and lends him a parsonish air. Fireproof gloves protect his hands.

At ten to six, he leaves his house and walks to a near neighbour to take a piece of peat from the fire. This will be used to light the Clavie. 'The eternal flame,' he says, as the wind howls down Granary Street and blows it into life. The crowd parts to let him through, and he places the peat inside the barrel. There are about five gallons of creosote in there already, and it soon roars into life.

Creosote, by the way, is not easy to get these days. The European Union, concerned that it may cause cancer, passed a law to prevent its purchase and use by the general public. The Clavie Crew voted for Brexit, the joke goes, in order that this iniquitous legislation be overturned.

It takes three quarters of an hour for the Clavie to be paraded through the grid of streets. There are brief stops along the way for refuelling and to hand pieces of burning stave in at those honoured houses which have a historic connection to the ritual. It is a mark of the Crew's obsession with continuity that it is the address which matters, not the person who lives there; regardless of flittings or passings, that house will receive a burnt offering. 'I'd better take this inside,' says one Brocher, lifting his piece of Clavie from the doorstep as calmly as if it were an extra pint of milk and not a hefty chunk of wood on fire.

The thousand-strong throng following the Clavie are bridesmaids bearing a train of sparks and smoke. The full moon is all but eclipsed. You could choke on the reek. Each member of the Crew takes a turn carrying the barrel, taking on his head and shoulders the physical burden and the weight of tradition. 'One-two-three-*woooooarghhh!*' they cry as they bend and lift.

It would not do to drop it. 'If you drop the Clavie, disaster will befall,' Dan Ralph had told me, summing up a belief widespread among Brochers. It had been dropped in 1913, he said, and, soon afterwards, the *Prominent*, a local herring drifter, had sunk with all hands; the dismal balance sheet arising from this tragedy had nine men in the debit column, six widows and twenty-eight fatherless children in the credit.

'My father's uncle was the last to see her lights,' Ralph recalled. 'When daylight came, he picked up the body of the boat's dog, removed its collar, and took it back to the skipper's widow. Aye.'

That 'Aye' – it slipped out, a sigh full of regret. Ralph doesn't go so far as to say that he believes the boat sank because the barrel was dropped, but he doesn't disavow the notion either. The Clavie is coated in layers of belief, superstition, meaning and personal resonance thicker than any tar. You can feel it in the air, hear it in every cheer of the crowd as it passes through Burghead. Firelight dances on the low stone houses, casting a sign on King Street – 'If the Lord will, the Word of God will be preached on Sunday' – in an orange glow that does not feel entirely Christian. The Clavie is thought to be rooted in paganism, a casting out of wicked spirits. Its purpose these days has more to do with affirming Brocher identity, but there remains something ancient and uncanny about it, too.

'Burning Clavies was perfectly well accepted until the Reformation, when Protestantism came in and they took a dim view of anything they thought was idolatrous,' Ralph had told me earlier. 'The Kirk gave a lot of trouble before my day.' There is a famous story in his family concerning his Uncle Dan, who was badly burned at a Clavie during the early 1930s and had to attend church the following morning with his head bound in bandages. The minister took as the subject of his sermon 'the sins of fire-worship', preaching directly at the injured man. Uncle Dan, stubborn even by Broch standards, got up from the pew and walked out while the minister was speaking, causing a family schism as his own father was an elder. In modern times, with religion no longer such a power in the land, threats to the Clavie have come more often from the police and health and safety officials. Informed by one councillor that she had the power to prevent the event from going ahead, the present Dan Ralph retorted: 'I guess you must be considering bringing in the army. I know you have insufficient policemen to stop us.' His uncle, one imagines, would have nodded his sore head with approval and pride.

At around quarter to seven we reach the top of Grant Street, and the Crew cut up an alley for Doorie Hill, a small steep rise overlooking the sea on three sides. On the top stands a round stone altar, about four feet high, with a hole in its centre into which the pole of the Clavie is wedged. I had visited earlier, in daylight, and was struck by the primeval presence of the place. It is said that the hill once formed part of the ramparts of the Pictish fort, and I can well believe it. Blackened and greasy-looking, the altar gave off a thick clotted stink of smoke; it resembled one of those giant prehistoric tree trunks that sometimes emerge, semi-petrified, from peat bogs. Now, at night, it's just a black shape yet, for all that, the cradle of the whole town's hopes for the year ahead.

The Crew set about their business, throwing another fifty gallons of creosote over the Clavie with explosive effect. Part of the hill is on fire. One fancies shapes in the flames: a ship, an eagle, the devil. The firkin, a small barrel within the large one, falls out and hits Lachie on the back. He does not hesitate; lifting and placing it back inside. Later, he will show his sister Ruth the burn on his left hand, dismissing it as 'a war wound'. Exactly so: an injury sustained in the service of the Clavie. Round here, they wear their scars like campaign medals.

As a rising wind tosses the flames and sparks around, I notice Dan Ralph standing up on the stone, grasping the side of the barrel, like a look-out clinging to the crow's nest in a storm; like a king surveying his realm from the battlements; like Prospero using rough magic to bind the people to the place. Pick your simile, he embodies it. The locals cheer as the flames burn higher than ever until, finally, burning out, and then push in for a prize – a piece of the still-glowing embers, to take away and bless their homes. None of this has been done for the benefit of tourists, or journalists, or to boost the local economy. It happens because it has always happened and must always happen. It is for the Broch by the Broch.

Afterwards, I wish happy new year to Donald Tolmie, who has been burning Clavies for about as long as I have been alive. His face scorched red and black, his white hair smutted dark, he looks exhausted but happy.

'Och,' he says, wiping his brow. 'Once a year is enough.'

A Night with the Naked Rambler

AT A QUARTER to ten on Saturday, after a leisurely breakfast of porridge and sugarless tea, Prisoner 81590, also known as Stephen Gough, better known as the Naked Rambler, is getting undressed to go to work.

In a field just off the B7026, not far from Penicuik, the fifty-three-year-old bends to tie his hiking boots, and one of his bare knees sinks into the damp autumn ground. He stands and puts on his floppy green hat and heavy rucksack. His lean body is pale after more than six years of prison, and dotted with insect bites after a day out of it; his pubic hair dark, chest hair white. Varicose veins make a river delta of the back of his calves. 'Right,' he says, squinting at the rising sun, 'if I can do twenty miles today, that'll be good.'

We had spent the night together. On Friday evening, we found a spot in a field, sheltered by a fallen fir, with incredible views towards Salisbury Crags. He offered to let me sleep beside him in his tent. 'As long,' he joked, 'as you don't get naked.' There was no chance of that.

Released that morning – Friday, 5th October 2012 – before dawn had broken, from Saughton prison in Edinburgh, he had walked naked out of the gates and headed south for the Pentland Hills. Since 2006, he has spent most of his time in custody in Scotland, usually being arrested very soon after release. During his court appearances he refuses to wear clothes, and refuses to wear them in prison, which has meant that he is kept in segregation from the other prisoners. When taking exercise in the yard in Saughton, he was hidden from the overlooking windows by a wooden frame on wheels known as the Rambler Scrambler.

His rambling had begun in 2003. He walked naked from Land's End to John O'Groats, and did it again in 2005, this time accompanied by his then girlfriend, Mel, also naked. As Gough became famous, a tabloid favourite, the police seemed to pay him more attention. The frequency of arrests increased, and Gough became 'a bit hardcore' in the way he responded. In 2006, on a flight from Southampton to Edinburgh, travelling to Scotland for a court appearance, he took off his clothes in the toilet of the plane and emerged naked into the cabin. He was arrested on landing and has only briefly been out of custody since. His most recent conviction for breach of the peace – the crime he is judged to be committing as his actions could cause the public 'fear' or 'alarm' – followed his arrest this summer in Dunfermline, three days after leaving Perth prison.

His intention now is to walk naked home to Eastleigh, near Southampton, to see his family and live naked in the community. He suspects that if he can just get over the Border, English police will treat him with greater lenience.

I met him in the Midlothian village of Auchendinny. He had been in the hills all day but was now back on the roads, eating an apple like the biblical Adam. A six-foot three-inch former Marine, he walks fast, a great yomping lope, never slowing even as traffic slows and peeps at the sight of him. A man in a white van shouted 'Get your fucking clothes on!' but Gough ignored him. Road workers in hard yellow hats asked him to stop so they could have their photos taken together. He smiled when they told him to enjoy his freedom. 'Yeah,' he said, 'as long as it lasts.'

The Naked Rambler has not been rambling alone. There is a film crew making a documentary about him, and he is also accompanied by members of the public impressed by his cause. George Cavanagh, a courier from Musselburgh, has created a board game based on Gough's travels.

Another of his supporters, John Hamilton, a retired civil servant, though not a naked one (he is wearing an anorak) uses satnav on his phone to find a suitable route. Hamilton had met Gough following his release from Perth prison. 'I believe the Scottish system has been totally unjust to him,' Hamilton says. 'It's not illegal to be naked. His being sent to prison is an embarrassment for Scotland.'

But Hamilton does feel, as do many people, that Gough would do himself a favour if he just put on some clothes, went home, re-established contact with his teenage children and saw his elderly mother for the first time in years. There is a growing sense that his story has gone from comic to tragic and that he is ruining his life for the sake of a point about civil liberties which he made long ago.

The truth is, though, that it's hard to maintain a feeling of pity for Gough when you are walking along at the side of him, close enough to smell his musky sweat, and listening as he orates – there is no other word – on personal freedom. He does not come across as a pitiful figure. He says his walk is a mixture of public statement and inner journey. He says that he is the word made flesh. He considers this to be his job. 'If you compromise your truth,' he insists, 'you compromise yourself.'

As a result of all the attention paid to his penis, which varies in shade from ruddy to pallid depending on the reaction between body and air temperature, it is never remarked that he has an extraordinary face – long, lean and lined, with soulful brown eyes and a mouthful of crooked teeth. His nose bends slightly to the right, the result of a beating he received on one of his early walks. A great grey beard spills like a waterfall from the crag of his chin. He has the look of some intransigent philosopher, or dissident from the salt mines: Socrates, Solzhenitsyn, Stephen Gough.

In the early evening, we had turned off the road, looking for a place to camp. Gough negotiated a barbed-wire

22

fence. 'I've never snagged meself on one of these yet,' he said, stepping over, 'and that record still stands.'

The midges were bothering him, so Gough got dressed, pulling on a fleece and green trousers. That old joke – 'I didn't recognise you with your clothes on' – sprang to mind. George handed him a phone: 'Steve, ABC Radio in Australia want to talk to you, live.'

He took the phone. 'Hello? This is Steve. Yeah, it's nice to see a big sky. I'm standing in a field at the moment and I can see some sheep.'

The radio presenter asked what he was wearing, and seemed disappointed that he wasn't naked. 'It's because I've stopped walking for the day,' Gough explained. 'I'm not actually a naturist or a nudist. I'm for freedom. I want to wake up in the morning and not feel I can't go naked because people don't like it.'

It was just as well he had dressed. As darkness fell, so did the temperature. We built a fire and watched the stars. We drank some whisky. 'This,' he said, 'is the opposite of prison.' Not seeing his kids is hard, but he feels he is setting them an example of how to live a life of integrity. He dislikes the idea that anyone would believe he was insane, and told me that even if he had to spend the rest of his life in prison, he wouldn't give up what he is doing. He explained the roots of his naked rambling go back to a walk he took when living in Vancouver and burst into tears at the epiphanic realisation that human beings are essentially good; how, then, his argument goes, can the body be bad?

He phoned Mel, his ex. He phoned his mother, who is in her eighties and seems to be hard of hearing. 'No,' he corrected her, 'I'm not in Kent, I'm in a *tent*.' He belched and farted with gusto. He sniffed his socks. He snored.

Now, as the sheep look on, Gough hits the road again. He is making for the Borders village of Walkerburn, via Peebles. We walk along the A701 and, in Howgate, a young woman called Regan Drew, walking two poodles, blushes as he passes. 'Is this actually happening?' she asks.

Gough passes the village hall, where a bake sale is being held. He waves to the middle-aged ladies peering through the windows. 'My goodness, that was a vision to behold,' says Jan Stewart. Is she offended? 'Oh God, no. Not at all!'

'I'm just damned disappointed,' says Cheryl Wilkinson, 'that I didn't have my glasses on.'

My night with the Naked Rambler. It has the air of a scandalous confession, and yet was more enlightening than erotic. I learned a lot from our time together. I came to believe that he is a more rational, more focused individual than the media portrayal of him has led us to believe, and to feel certain that the public are more tolerant than the legal system which is supposed to protect us from the sight of his nude body.

I leave Gough just outside Leadburn, but can't resist asking, one last time, about the purpose of his journey. He has talked quite a lot about religion. Is this, then, some sort of pilgrimage?

The Naked Rambler mulls this over. 'But I'm not going anywhere am I?' He rubs musingly at his beard. 'Well,' he says. 'I suppose I'm going to my mum's.'

The Storm

At 7 a.m. on 12th January 2005, Neil Campbell woke in a spare room of his father's croft house on Benbecula, one of a chain of Hebridean islands known as the Uists. A BBC television director, he had agreed to deliver a live report for Radio nan Gàidheal, the Gaelic station, on how the community had been affected by the storm of the night before.

It had been the worst in living memory, and by first light it was clear a great deal of damage had been done to roads and buildings. What Campbell did not yet know – and was about three hours away from knowing – was that the words with which he concluded his broadcast had a dreadful personal resonance. 'I think,' he said, 'there will be a lot of people waking up to a day they'll never forget.'

As soon as Campbell finished the report, he went out to look for his father, Calum, who hadn't come home the night before. He might have stayed with his daughter, Murdina, but Campbell couldn't reach her either. With a growing sense of foreboding, he called the police to report his father, sister and her family missing. The phone operator – who clearly knew something – said 'Oh, my God' and hung up. This was not reassuring. Every passing minute felt like an eternity. Then a relative, calling round, whispered to him, 'They have found a body at Creagorry and they think it is Archie.'

Archie MacPherson was thirty-six. He had grown up on South Uist but left for Glasgow, where he worked as a joiner and married Murdina Campbell, and where their children, Andrew and Hannah, were born. In 2003, they moved back to the island, buying a croft in the coastal township of Iochdar, near Archie's parents. Murdina found work as a secretary in the local primary school. This was the Hebridean dream: returning to the island of your birth, bringing the generations together, continuing the traditional way of life that modernity does its best to erode.

Photos discovered later in Murdina's camera reveal the tender mundanities of a loving family celebrating what they have no idea will be their final Christmas together. Andrew is seven, Hannah five; smiling kids in pyjamas and Santa hats. It is a sweet photo soured by the menace of the pictures that follow, the last pictures of all. These show the view west through the rain-smeared kitchen window, the coming tempest – a rising, hungry sea under a darkening, angry sky.

The killing storm of 11th January 2005 had begun two days earlier as a shallow depression off America's eastern seaboard, developing rapidly in intensity as it moved north-east, zeroing in on Scotland, South Uist, a darkened road, two cars, five lives. The Met Office chart shows its progress as a writhing tangle of fanged spirals, a diagram which serves as a pretty fair representation of the rage and grief the wind left in its wake.

All across the island that night, mobile phones were down, electricity out. A driver passing through Iochdar at around 6.30 p.m. had seen Murdina and her family standing framed in the window of their home, holding candles. There's something haunting and haunted about that tableau; something about it that brings to mind those glass-fronted roadside shrines to Our Lady which are dotted all over South Uist, and which are lit, some of them, at night. You drive past, in the immense darkness, and glimpse a blurred blue dress, a swaddled child, hands raised in prayer.

This was the last time anyone saw the five of them alive.

At some point during the next half-hour, the family made a decision to flee. The combined power of wind, tide and low air pressure had driven the Atlantic up over the beach and machair (the strip of sandy grassland characteristic of the Hebrides) to the threshold of their house. Waves crashed against and around the building with such force that rocks were thrown into the front garden. They left for what seemed the greater safety of Archie's parents' home – David and Mary MacPherson lived just a mile and a half along the coastal road. Calum went in front, in his car. The others followed in their red Saab. On this narrow single-track, the two vehicles appear to have been swept off the road by the storm surge and swallowed by the flood.

Three generations lost at once, a grievous blow anywhere, but one felt with special keenness in such a small community. As a local woman remarked in the aftermath, 'This is an island of tears.'

* * *

The Uists, as seen by God or Google Earth, look as if some great landmass has been dropped from heaven, shattering into shards. A five-hour ferry trip north-west from Oban on the mainland, the islands are connected by a series of causeways, large and small. Were Bonnie Prince Charlie to land today on tiny Eriskay, as he did in 1745, he could travel sixty miles, all the way north to the tip of Berneray, stopping only for sheep on the road.

Around 5,000 people live here, mostly on the west coast, facing the Atlantic. Gaelic is spoken widely. The three main islands are quite different in character. North Uist is Presbyterian, although the Sabbath is not observed as strictly as it once was. South Uist is largely Catholic. Benbecula feels quasi-military: it is home to the headquarters of a missile-testing range; the slopes of Rueval, its largest hill, are made strange by the juxtaposition of a radar tracking station's white domes and a twenty-five-foot granite statue of the Virgin and Child.

The causeways have their genesis in the 1975 establishment of a single local authority with responsibility for the whole of the Western Isles. Depopulation had long been a problem, and it was felt that life on the islands would be made sustainable, economically and culturally, if transport between them could be improved. The South Ford Causeway, from Benbecula to South Uist, was built in 1982. For the previous forty years, a bridge had linked the islands; before that, you took your chances at low tide with a horse and cart. Not everyone made it. One memoir of island life recalls, 'The South Ford was a dangerous place. Ghosts of people who had been drowned made frequent appearances. They were to be recognised by traces of sand in their hair.'

The Campbell and MacPherson families believe this causeway was a significant factor in the deaths of their loved ones: the wind-driven Atlantic, unable to pass through this blocked channel, became like water overflowing a basin, spilling out onto the surrounding land and submerging the coastal roads to a high-watermark of almost two metres. Now, ten years on, the families are calling for a fatal accident inquiry, the Scottish equivalent of a coroner's inquest, into exactly what happened that night. They expect it would establish the culpability of the causeway as a legal fact, putting pressure on the council to remodel it. Flooding will end more lives on Uist, they fear, if lessons are not learned. This is why they have decided to speak for the first time about the storm that blew into their lives a decade ago: 'We want that causeway opened up,' says David MacPherson, Archie's father, 'so no family will suffer what ours has.'

* * *

There were eight Campbell children, four girls and four boys, growing up in a three-room thatched cottage in

Benbecula. Marybell, the eldest, was born in 1962. Murdina came along five years later.

It was to allow their own children to experience the island life they had known that Murdina and Archie chose to return home, swapping the big city for the big sky. 'They moved back only two years before the accident,' says Marion Campbell, who was three years older than her sister Murdina. 'They wanted to give their kids a safer, happier way of life.' She smiles grimly at the irony.

We are talking in Marion's flat in Glasgow three days after what would have been Murdina's forty-seventh birthday. These anniversaries – the would-have-beens, the should-have-beens – are especially painful. The Uist tragedy is almost an experiment in grief. It takes an awful hypothesis – if you lose your father, sister, brother-in-law, niece and nephew all at once, surely it isn't possible to carry on? – and puts it to the test.

Marion was at work when she learned about the accident. A phone call. She remembers screaming.

At that point, only Archie's body had been found, washed up by the side of the road. Marion and others in the family who lived on the mainland made the long journey north in several cars, a cavalcade of fear. 'My first thought when I got to Uist, because I was in shock, was, I'm going to wade into the sea and swim out and find Murdina,' she recalls. 'My husband was physically holding me back. I just so wanted to go into the sea. It was drawing me to it.'

It is strange to talk about this in a city flat, on a sunny day, with the sound of children at play rising from the street. It all seems so far away, yet Marion, as she talks, is right back there again: in the eye, on the shore. She and the others were met by those siblings already on the island, Marybell and Neil. There followed a blur of days. 'All I remember is a whirlwind of people in and out the door. Priests, ministers, the doctor. The seven of us that were left would sit in the sitting room and every now and then the police would come in and say, "We've found somebody else. We've found somebody else. We've found somebody else." And the last person was Andrew.'

Neil Campbell identified the bodies, all but one. 'I saw it as a duty,' he says. 'I didn't want anybody else to do it, to see them like that. But I couldn't do it with Murdina. Just too close to her.'

He had seen her on the day she died. Neil lived in Glasgow at the time, but had travelled to the island that morning for work. He popped over to visit. 'I told her, "You look beautiful. You look radiant" and gave her a big hug. I'd never said that to my sister before. These are the things you think about afterwards. I had a wee chat with her, played with the kids. I even took photos ... I have these perfect final memories. It was like I got the perfect opportunity to say goodbye.'

Neil almost lost his own life in the storm. Murdina had invited him to her house that evening, for a drink and some food. He set off from the village of Balivanich at about half-past six, but, after three miles, hit flooding and his car began to float away. A rock smashed the back window and the wind roared in. He couldn't see anything for water. He panicked, shouting, 'Help me, God! I'm dead!' over and over. Somehow, he managed to get the car under control and returned home.

He knows he was fortunate. What would have happened had he reached Murdina's home as planned, and left with them? 'There would have been six members of the same family killed.'

There were a number of lucky escapes that night. In Benbecula, at around 7.30 p.m., a five-man fire crew were responding to a call-out when the engine became water-logged. The men abandoned their vehicle and, in wind gusting at over a hundred miles per hour, made for a house a short distance away on the brow of a hill. The Atlantic, on a normal day, is a few hundred metres to the west of the road at that point, but it had surged over the fields and was rising fast – to waist height in a few minutes and growing deeper all the time. A tidemark inside the twelve-tonne fire engine, which was shifted by the water from one side of the road to the other, showed that it reached two metres.

'You'd think you were in the middle of a rapid river,' a firefighter told me. Debris was being swept past: planks of wood, beach rubbish, a dead seal. 'We jumped out, linked arms. The tide was trying to take us away, but we inched our way up. When we got to the top of the hill, because of the wind, we couldn't stand up, so we crawled on our hands and knees. Slates were coming off the house and slamming into the ground, four inches deep.'

The bill for repairing damage – to roads, causeways, a school – has been estimated at between £15 million and £20 million. That does not include the cost to individuals (few roofs were left intact that night) nor the losses suffered by farmers. One crofter alone gathered seventy-two dead sheep the next day. 'If this had happened in the south of England, it would have been declared a national disaster,' says Uisdean Robertson, a local councillor.

Perhaps, though, the most destabilising effect of the storm was invisible – the way it brought a sense of vulnerability to the island. Born into a culture where gales are common, Hebrideans can be blasé about the weather. 'We thought it would be just another storm,' says David Muir, who is recently retired from a senior flood risk-management role with the council. 'Tie down the henhouse, that sort of thing. But it turned out to be vastly different.'

Now, there is a real fear of bad weather. 'There is a loss of confidence in travelling in the evening, between islands especially, if there are storms forecast,' Muir says. 'People are conscious of what happened in 2005, and what could happen to them. Community events, ceilidhs in village halls, are often poorly attended or cancelled because people are worried about going out. This was once considered a very safe place to live, but there's this threat from the sea now.'

Marybell MacIntyre knows that when the wind blows hard on Uist now, people think of her, of what happened, and she is grateful for that association and the compassion that comes with it. 'It's like, "OK, so I'm not alone in this. That's so good, that you feel the same horror." When a colleague puts their hand on my arm and says, "Marybell, I think about you on these bad days", I feel like hugging them, because they're acknowledging that it hasn't just gone away.'

Marybell, a teacher of English and Gaelic, and her husband Angus still live on Uist. They feel that being on the island has helped them cope. 'Facing up to it makes you stronger,' she says. 'I drive past the place where Murdina's body was found on my way to school: if I wasn't doing that every day, I couldn't work. So I just end up doing it and not thinking about it. Whereas my sister who lives in Inverness, when she drives across that causeway, she's a wreck.'

Their religious faith has helped, as it has many on the island. Father Roddy McAuley was the priest who tried to comfort them, and believes the islanders' reaction was a manifestation of faith. 'I would say God was in the countless people calling to the homes of the "broken" with baking and gifts of hospitality,' he says. 'God was in the people searching for the bodies, God was in the solidarity of the community. God was in the people gathering to pray. God was in the uniting, suffering and the pain of the families who had lost their loved ones. In the midst of this tragedy, God was there.'

While faith is a comfort for some, for others action will be the only solace. 'It would bring us peace if they sorted that causeway out,' David MacPherson says. Now in his seventies, he still lives close to the spot where his son's family were swept off the road. The kitchen window looks out on the sites where his grandchildren's bodies were found.

The causeway has a fifteen-metre opening at its northern end; according to a plan obtained by MacPherson, it was designed to have an identical opening at the southern end, but this was not built. A study of the 2005 storm, carried out for the council, suggested that it would not have made a significant difference to the flood levels, but he can't help wondering. Would his son and the others have survived? He is angered, especially, that the decision not to have that second opening appears to have been made to save money: 'It cost our family a hell of a lot more.'

The study proposed instead that a 250-metre bridge be built to replace part of the causeway. At a meeting earlier this year, this proposal was rejected on the grounds of cost (an estimated £20 million), opting instead for a £2 million set of flood-risk measures. Amid local fury, that decision was overturned a week later; the flood-risk measures will go ahead, but the council now plans to seek additional funding from the Scottish Government to enable the creation of the bridge.

Lawrence MacEachen, sixty-nine, owns the croft on which seven-year-old Andrew was found three days after the accident. 'I saw a man carrying the body of a child out of that dirty, filthy water,' he says. 'If people had seen that, maybe they wouldn't be thinking of the money that causeway is going to cost.'

The house where Murdina and Archie and Andrew and Hannah lived, the house they left that night, is small and white, with a narrow road in front and the Atlantic at its back. This is South Uist's exposed western flank. The water is perhaps sixty feet away at high tide, an inviting shade of pale blue, separated from the house by the machair and a strip of white sand. 'It's so disconcerting,' says Angus MacKinnon, looking out at the waves, 'to think that beautiful thing can turn into this absolute monster.'

Angus is Marion Campbell's son. He is twenty-nine and lives in his aunt and uncle's former home with his partner

Gemma and their five-year-old, Ewen. He was very close to his family, the loss 'flattened' him, and it is upsetting for him to talk about. He was living in Glasgow at the time and felt he would never return to the island, but he and Gemma decided, like Archie and Murdina before them, that Uist would be a better place to raise a child. They moved back in September last year.

'I found it hard to be alone in the house at first, because I would remember everything,' Angus says. 'There's Andrew's room, there's Hannah's room. But my auntie would have loved my son, she would have loved Gemma, she would do anything for me, so I feel a connection with them now. It is amazing that we are getting to experience this life that they experienced, because I know they were happy.'

In January, when winds were recorded at ninety miles per hour, Angus felt for the first time what it is like to live on the Uist coast in a storm. The whole house shuddered. Windows bulged. The sea came within a few feet of the garden. And all the time there was this enormous growling, the wind a wild beast. He can well understand why his family left the house that night, a decision of which some have been critical.

Lately, Angus has taken to working in the garden, as his aunt once did. A rockery, a vegetable patch and other features Murdina had created were buried with sand and earth by the force of the storm and ten years of coastal drift. Digging down, he has uncovered signs of work and life. Daffodils and tulips – that hadn't come up since the storm – bloomed this spring. Beneath a foot of topsoil, he found a toy car, and remembered that he and Andrew had once played with it. In grass long uncut, he discovered a toy watering can that had belonged to Hannah. His son picked it up, delighted, and asked where it had come from.

'I didn't know what to say,' Angus says. 'I'm not going to hide anything from him. I'll let him know what the dangers are. But it was such a strange experience, seeing him holding it. Ewen doesn't look like Andrew, but I sometimes see Andrew in him.' He pauses, tearful, fearful. 'I don't want anything to happen to him.'

Whether the family will get the official inquiry they desire remains to be seen, as does the future of the South Ford Causeway. What is certain is that life on the island changed that night, and as winter arrives, so the season of anxiety and bad memories will return.

'Every time there is a storm here,' Marybell says, 'people will always think of us.'

The World Crazy Golf Championship

IT IS THE six hundredth anniversary of the Battle of Agincourt when Michael Smith, a moon-pale young man, leaves his guest house and makes the short walk to Hastings seafront, intent on winning the World Crazy Golf Championship. After the first day's play he is well in the lead but now faces another four tough rounds, so it is once more down to the beach, once more into the company of that band of brothers (and a few sisters) – Britain's competitive crazy golfers.

The emphasis is, or should be, on competitive rather than crazy. The few dozen Brits who play crazy golf at elite level may sometimes call themselves 'nutters with putters' but they take the sport – which they insist *is* a sport – very seriously indeed. They are devoted to it; obsessed by it. They have, all the time, windmills on their mind.

'I don't think anyone will ever know how much the sport has meant to me,' Smith says. 'When I learned that I was about to become the British number one, that was probably the best moment of my life.'

In 2016, crazy golf celebrates its centenary. Possibly. The origins of the game are disputed. The prim Scottish town of St Andrews has some claim to having invented it, in 1867, with the undulating ladies' putting green known as The Himalayas. However, it was in 1916 that the first artificial miniature course, Thistle Dhu, was commissioned by the American steamship tycoon James Barber for his estate in North Carolina. This was the beginning of a craze, and it is estimated that by 1930 there were up to 50,000 courses across the United States. It became part of

American culture. The silent film actress Mary Pickford had a beautiful art deco course built in Los Angeles. Al Capone loved the game, too, and invested his ill-gotten dollars in crazy golf construction companies, one of his hoods claiming that it was 'more profitable than rum-running'.

Now, in the US, crazy golf – or minigolf, as they call it – is seen as a sport worthy of respect. The tournaments with the largest prize pots in the world are played there. In mainland Europe, too, minigolf is mainstream. But in the UK it remains regarded as an entertainment for children, a seaside diversion, something to do between donkey rides and downpours. The tragedy for Britain's best players, therefore, is that they have achieved supremacy in a discipline which brings neither cash nor kudos. If you won every single tournament in Britain over the course of a season, you would earn about £3,000, barely enough to cover a year's B&B and fish 'n' chips. Nevertheless, they love it, and especially in Hastings. 'This,' one player says, sweeping the head of his putter around the vista of the course, 'is crazy golf's spiritual home.'

The crazy golf scene is clustered in the south-east of England but Hastings looms especially large. Its three seafront courses host a number of major tournaments, including the World Crazy Golf Championship, known as the World Crazies, which take place under the auspices of the British Minigolf Association. It is usually played outwith the holiday season so the course does not miss out on tourist business at the height of summer. Elite crazy golfers are used to playing in the wind and the rain. None is a stranger to a kagoule.

'Of all my wins, the most memorable was the 2008 World Crazy Golf Championships. Horrendous conditions, waterlogged course,' recalls Tim 'Ace Man' Davies, who has won the event more often than any other player and is now retired in France. 'How did I feel? Sheer elation and a deep sadness. My mum had passed away the previous year, this one was for her. No one could have beaten me. It was never about the money, titles and all that. It was about being the best. And I was.'

The World Crazies offers a top prize of £1,000 – the largest in Britain – and is played on a lovely eighteen-hole course of the classic sort: windmill, lighthouse, water wheel, smartly painted in white and green. By first light, most of the seventy-five entrants are already out practising. There is a faint pink glow above the English Channel. Union flags flap in the morning breeze and the leaves of palm trees rustle like the pages of old books. A man and his daughter, azure with cold, paddle a disconsolate swan across the boating pond.

Hastings is odd. The thirteenth-most deprived town in England, according to recent statistics, it has a careworn beauty; the ghost of affluence past. Across the road from the course, within the elegant Ionic portico of the church on Pelham Crescent, a man is sleeping rough. Yet, as the High Street full of antiques and boutiques seems to suggest, there is money here, too. The general air of atrophied bohemianism is best summed up by the shop on Wellington Place offering, as a two-for-one deal in its closing-down sale, Joy Division T-shirts and batteries for mobility scooters. This, in Hastings, is not as niche as would be the case elsewhere.

Hastings, remember, is where Aleister Crowley, the occultist known as 'the wickedest man in the world', moved in his final fading years, taking health treatments at the Riposo Hydro and staying in room number 13 of a local guest house, where he enjoyed snacks of sardines sprinkled with curry powder, and frequent injections of heroin.

The town has a historic weirdness, a sense of strangeness at some deep geological level. People must have felt this even in its days of wild popularity, back in the 1930s when 3 million visitors a year were drawn to attractions including a giant D-shaped open-air pool that cost £60,000 to build. This lido was the creation of Sidney Little, known as the Concrete King, the civil engineer whose work transformed Hastings during the 1920s and '30s. Much of it is gone now, as declining levels of tourism negated the need for leisure infrastructure on the epic scale he favoured.

Still, pleasure-seekers are abundant in Hastings, even on a cold day in October. There they are, wandering along the front, daring each other to try a tub of jellied eels from one of the seafood shacks. The town is home to the biggest beach-launched fishing fleet in Britain, and the Stade, the historic fishing area, is notable for its Victorian-era 'net shops' – a cluster of black wooden towers used by generations of fishermen to store their gear. Built very tall and very narrow for the most pragmatic of reasons, a lack of space between sea and cliffs, these now appear mysterious and fairy-storyish; one imagines some mermaid version of Rapunzel letting down her seaweed hair from a top-floor window.

You can stand in the shadow of the net shops and watch the world pass. Fishmongers, Morris dancers, a young curate cycling past on his way to perform Holy Communion for an ailing parishioner. The miniature railway chuffs its way along the half-mile track, as it has since 1948.

John Napier plonks a pair of blue-sequined stilettos – size nine, vertiginous heels – on the counter of his shop, Cobblers to the Old Town, on the High Street. These, he says, belong to a loyal customer, a handsome South American man who works in the film industry and whose partner, a New Zealander, is a big noise in oil. They are part of a new affluent gay crowd visiting and even moving to the town. Napier, who is sixty-six and bald with a white goatee beard, believes that his shoe repair business tells the story of the renaissance of the seaside; that the soul – or sole – of Hastings is somehow here. So, he gets the high heels and party shoes, but also fixes split wellies for thrifty fishermen, tap shoes for nifty showbizzers and expensive brogues for hipsters DFL (down from London).

'I do love that mix,' he says, Glaswegian accent peeping out, like scuff through polish, after almost half a century in the south. 'On Saturday afternoons in here we all have a glass of wine and a chinwag. Musicians, a private investigator, a newsreader, actors, a lord; Harold Bishop from *Neighbours* came once, when he was doing panto. Oh, yeah, Hastings is picking up.'

Up at the clifftop castle, with its long views to Beachy Head, magpies and jackdaws rattle and churr over the ruined battlements, disputing this territory just as the Normans and Saxons once did. From this height, the crazy golf course is pleasantly toytownish. Up close, though, you can feel the tension and meet the characters.

Take Tiger Pragnell. The crazy golfer formerly known as Alex, he changed his name by deed poll in honour of his hero Tiger Woods. 'As soon as I changed me name, I won me first tournament – the Hastings Winkle Club Challenge. So there's obviously something in it.'

Pragnell is thirty-six, dressed from head to toe in Tiger Woods-branded sports gear, and lives in Hastings, having moved from Bexhill-on-Sea so he could be closer to the course. 'I wish to surpass Tim Davies and Michael Smith as the greatest minigolfer in England,' he declares.

A popular figure on the tour, Pragnell has the learning disorder dyspraxia and found school difficult, which has made his success at crazy golf all the sweeter. 'I struggle to play sport as naturally as some other people,' he says, 'but all credit to me, I've stuck at it and I'm going to keep going until I achieve my goals.'

He practises three days a week for up to eight hours at a time. He still thinks ruefully of the time he was about to get a hole-in-one when a seagull swooped down and took the ball, mistaking it for a chip. This is his one regret. He has no wish to change his name again in the light of

40

Woods' fall from grace, perhaps calling himself after a certain Northern Irish phenomenon.

'No,' he insists. 'Rory Pragnell doesn't have a good ring to it. I'll stick with Tiger.'

Crazy golf differs from regular golf in several ways. The novelty obstacles are the most obvious difference. Less apparent is the fact that while crazy golfers use only one club, a special rubber-faced putter, they carry a large number of different sorts of ball, sometimes fifty or more, which vary in terms of weight, hardness and bounce. Choosing the right ball for a particular hole in particular weather conditions is one of the delicate arts of the sport. The qualities of balls can be affected by heat and cold, so in order to maintain stability of temperature it has been known for players to carry them inside their trousers or even under their armpits.

The World Crazies, incidentally, is one of the very few tournaments where this doesn't apply. All competitors are issued with the same type of ball. What matters most, therefore, is knowledge of the course. The competitive game is nothing like the family holiday version where everybody laughs when Auntie Morag takes umpteen strokes to get the ball under the sails of the windmill. If you can't complete each hole in two putts then you are a failure who is never going to win anything. A hole-in-one – or ace, as they call them – is what's wanted.

'It is an obsession,' says John McIver, one of the all-time greats of the game. 'One man or woman armed only with a putter taking on eighteen holes and the English weather, striving for perfection, for a flawless creation of beauty – a sub-thirty round.'

The top players turn up several days before a tournament in order to familiarise themselves with every inch of the course. They talk of 'the joy of finding the perfect line' – knowing exactly where to hit the ball, at which angle it must bounce off the side wall in order to roll serenely

THE PASSION OF HARRY BINGO

holewards past the miniature obelisk. Each player carries a well-thumbed notebook full of densely arrowed diagrams, plotting the options for each hole, and often stops to consult this before a shot. 'There's about three or four courses in here,' explains McIver, flicking through his notes. 'That's London. That's Margate. That's hole number seven here.' He gives a low whistle of dread. 'There's some quite nasty second putts on that one.'

John McIver, known as Big Top Ted, is one of the real characters of the sport. He is fifty years old, a Hastings native and co-author, with Tim Davies, of the book *Nutters with Putters*. With his longish greying hair, crushed velvet jacket and psychedelic trousers, he has the look of a prog-rock dandy in semi-retirement, although still too young, perhaps, to be looking for a deal on mobility scooter batteries.

'Crazy golf does attract obsessive people,' he nods. 'My girlfriend would probably say I'm in that category. A few years ago there was a big influx of new players from London, and it could have become a sport for hipsters. But that didn't happen.'

Good. Crazy golf shouldn't, one feels, be played with an arched eyebrow. Its keynote is sincerity, and they don't come much more sincere than Michael Smith, the British number one. His Blackburn Rovers beanie hat is stitched with the club motto *Arte et Labore* – skill and hard work – two qualities Smith embodies. He is thirty years old, a first-year student of criminology, and has an earnestness of manner that suggests steeliness overcoming shyness.

Smith, 'a minigolf machine' according to one fellow player, has been playing the sport since 2010. 'I was at a point in my life when I really needed something to motivate me. I needed a fresh start,' he recalls. 'I was a late starter. I got into writing for a few years with the aim of becoming a published novelist but that wasn't working out and I gradually got more and more – I hate using the word but it's true – depressed. I needed a buzz of adrenalin, and this turned out to be it.'

Minigolf – he never calls it crazy golf – suited him. It was cerebral and creative and intensely competitive. He didn't find it undignified. From being someone who lacked confidence and had a certain fragility, he developed the 'exceptional mental strength' he believes gives him the edge. He became the British number one on Valentine's Day 2011, and has held the position ever since. What did that mean to him? 'It was kind of everything. I had not achieved a huge amount in life, so to be the best at something in the whole country was a great feeling.'

It is worth pointing out that Smith, despite being the best British player by some distance, is, at the time of writing, only sixty-third in the world. Above him are hordes of Germans, Swedes, Czechs, Austrians, Swiss and Finns, umlautering with intent in the ranking table. In many countries of mainland Europe, minigolf has, for decades, been regarded as a 'normal' sport, with players able to access coaching and finance. There are only a hundred or so players in the UK who play competitively, compared with around 4,000 in Germany.

'We struggle because Sport England won't recognise us as a separate form from golf,' says Sean Homer, chairman of the British Minigolf Association, 'but then the Royal and Ancient say minigolf is nothing to do with them. It's a catch-22. Until we get recognised as a sport, lottery and local authority funding isn't open to us.'

The only professional player in Hastings is Olivia Prokopova, the Czech equivalent of a wunderkind, who is twenty years old but has been travelling to compete in this English seaside town since she was eight. Prokopova won the championship in 2012, the first and only female winner, adding it to her US Open and US Masters titles. She is a celebrity in her native country and has played with the president. She is reputed to travel with a manager, coach, masseur, physical therapist and nutritionist, but the 99 cone she enjoys between practice rounds suggests that the last role, at least, is hyperbole.

It seems more believable that she employs a manicurist, going by the long, perfectly buffed pink nails that she insists do not interfere with the way she holds the putter. Watching Prokopova hole balls gives the spectator that woozy feeling of witnessing a magic trick familiar from watching Muhammad Ali punch or George Best score. Her English is not up to detailed analysis of how she does this but seven shrugged words suffice: 'It looks easy but it is hard.'

It looks easy but it is hard. That sums these championships up. This is a wonderful spectator sport. Punters peer awestruck over the privet as golfers strike past, or else settle on benches by the first hole, puffing on vapes and gaping at putts. Everyone is in the zone. Players block out the noise of keening seagulls, screaming children, barking dogs and – hard by the eleventh hole – the whoosh of the hand dryer in the ladies toilets. All they are thinking is ace, ace, ace.

Those of us able to take a step back can appreciate the beauty – yes, beauty – of the course. Crazy golf courses are a sort of folk architecture in Britain, as much a part of the aesthetic of the seaside as a Donald McGill postcard or the particular shade of pink your dad's nose goes when he falls into a super-lagery sleep in the Blackpool sun.

One couple with a true appreciation for the visual allure of crazy golf are Richard and Emily Gottfried, a husband and wife from Luton who, since 2006, have been on a quest to play every course in Britain and have, so far, visited more than 650. They believe there are around 700, but new courses are opening and old ones closing all the time. Richard gets 'goosebumpy' on the discovery of a new course but has an appreciation, too, for those heritage courses which have brought pleasure to generations of holidaymakers, such as England's first crazy golf course, in Skegness, which opened in 1926. He enjoys, too, 'the melancholic, haunted feel' of abandoned, overgrown courses. Connoisseurs of crazy golf feel about such places much as the nineteenth-century poets felt for medieval abbeys and classical ruins – the sweet ache of the sublime. 'Oh yeah,' says Emily, 'you can get really romantic about minigolf.'

Poets aside, it is Michael Smith, the wannabe novelist, who wins the tournament in the end, writing himself into the crazy golf history books with an eighth career major. We might offer the last word, though, to John McIver, Big Top Ted, who shoots 41 – a disaster – in his last round. Out there on the course, under scrutiny and pressure, all his fancy clothes meant nothing.

'I've gone from crushed velvet to just crushed,' he says, mournfully, as the sun sets over the Channel and the moon rises, like a great golf ball, above the castle.

Shine on you crazy golfers, shine on.

The Sikh Pipe Band

Beneath a Saltire blue sky, with Irn-Bru in their bellies and an old Punjabi war cry on their lips – '*Sat Sri Akaal!*' – the men and women of the Sri Dasmesh pipe band march out into the grassy arena of Glasgow Green, the first time a Malaysian group has competed at the world championships, and give their medley laldy. 'Gaun the Sikhs!' shouts a turbaned fellow in the crowd.

The World Pipe Band Championships, known as 'The Worlds', is the Olympics of piping. Some 230 bands from sixteen nations, adding up to around 8,000 pipers and drummers, are taking part this year. The championships date back to 1906, but they have never seen anything quite like Sri Dasmesh.

There are about forty of them, ranging in age from early teens to early sixties, tricked out in a manner that makes the uniforms of even their gaudiest rivals appear drab. Over white robes they wear a bright sash, a plaid in Royal Stewart tartan, and a faux tiger-skin apron, combining in one outfit the distinctive styles of Mason Boyne, Mary Doll Nesbitt and the Bay City Rollers. All of this, mind, topped with a turban and pink plume, or kalgi, bearing the symbol for 'One God'. They look amazing: Glasgow fabulous; Kuala Lumpur dead brilliant.

That's the city from which they have come, travelling 7,000 miles from the banks of the Klang to the banks of the Clyde. For many, this is their first time in the country from which the music they play originates. A homecoming of sorts.

'This is an almost thirty-year dream coming true,' says

Sukdev Singh, the band's founder, a tall, aquiline man with a silver beard and sovereign air. 'When we set up the band, we would dream of one day just coming to Scotland. We had no idea there was such a thing as a world championship.'

His younger brother Harvinder, the fifty-two-year-old pipe major, takes up the story. 'We were living in a world with no pipe bands. We didn't even know what strathspeys or reels sounded like.'

Sri Dasmesh – named after the tenth guru of the Sikhs – was formed in 1986 by Sukdev, a commercial pilot. He had remembered, in childhood, hearing the skirl and drone coming from the police parade ground, back in the days (he considers them the good old days) of British rule. The sound and feeling stayed with him, and he decided, on graduation from university in the UK, to reintroduce bagpipe music to Malaysia. An instrument store was closing down, so he bought drums cheap, later adding Pakistani bagpipes which, Harvinder laughs, proved impossible to tune.

Harvinder, in 1990, was dispatched to Glasgow for a week of lessons at the piping college, returning to Kuala Lumpur with the band's first proper notation books, and a handful of CDs by some of the great bands. Here was treasure. The present generation of Sri Dasmesh – many of them the sons and daughters of original members – have grown up with this music from the cradle, and thus consider, say, the Shotts & Dykehead Caledonia Pipe Band to be hugely glamorous figures.

To visit Scotland and actually meet the likes of Jim Kilpatrick, Shotts & Dykehead's drum major, has been overwhelming for the Malaysians. But they, too, have had their taste of fame. Everywhere they go on Glasgow Green, they are mobbed by members of the public wanting selfies. 'Ah wis *drawn* tae them,' says Jean Campbell, a sixty-one-year-old from Cumbernauld, enjoying a contemplative fag in the smoking area. 'Thae turbans ur a magnet fur me.'

The last maharajah of the Sikh empire, Duleep Singh, sometimes known as the Black Prince of Perthshire, was deposed by the British in 1849 and exiled to Scotland, where he was petted and fêted by high society; Queen Victoria is said to have particularly admired his eyes and teeth. Yet even the Black Prince did not reach the benchmark of Scottish celebrity achieved by the Sri Dasmesh band – being interviewed for the lunchtime news by Jackie Bird.

During their fortnight in Scotland, the band have travelled around the country, competing at Highland games, and connecting with people of their faith past and present. Scotland is home to around 9,000 Sikhs. Sri Dasmesh have performed at gurdwaras – temples – in Glasgow and Edinburgh, and travelled to Kenmore, Perthshire, to pay their respects at the grave of Maharajah Duleep Singh's infant son. They laid flowers and played 'Highland Cathedral'; a moving and complex moment, a Sikh band from Malaysia playing Scottish music in a Christian kirkyard in tribute to the heir of a lost Indian kingdom.

There is something about the majesty of the music Sri Dasmesh plays that transcends the dark history from which it has emerged. 'We should be a bit embarrassed by our colonial past, but if any good has come out of it, there it is,' says Joe Noble, a Royal Scottish Pipe Band Association adjudicator and former world champion drummer, nodding towards the Sikhs. 'The music was good and the music's stayed. That's our culture, and it's brilliant that they are prepared to play it.'

Not just prepared, eager. Sri Dasmesh do not regard bagpipes as the instrument of the oppressor, but rather as an emblem of a shared history. 'This is our mechanism for creating a bridge between our society, religion and community with the Scots,' says Sukdev. More, they simply love the sound. Priya Kaur Kesh, an eighteen-year-old tenor drummer, was raised on Indian classical music, the daughter of a tabla player, and recalls the impact of hearing bagpipes for the first time six years ago: 'I was shocked. Stunned. I had goosebumps. I thought, "I need to learn that asap."'

On Saturday, after early prayers at the gurdwara on Berkeley Street, Sri Dasmesh travelled by coach to Glasgow Green for their heat. They were accompanied by their tutor Barry Gray, a no-nonsense middle-aged Australian who spotted the band in an Anzac Day parade three years ago and promptly 'adopted' them. Gray is a veteran musician well known for performing with whichever big rock and pop acts find themselves in Sydney and in need of a piper. He is no stranger to 'Mull of Kintyre'. The good thing about working with a Sikh band, he says, is that they don't get drunk. The bad thing is that their timekeeping is dreadful; he fines latecomers twenty pence a minute, and during one rehearsal in Kelvingrove Park raised twenty quid for the kitty.

Following their performance, the band wait anxiously for the results of the judging, damping down nerves with trays of chips 'n' cheese, a Scottish delicacy for which they have developed a taste. The announcement, when it comes, is a triumph – they have qualified for the finals. They leap in the air, hug, tears rolling down cheeks; they get on their phones to home, breaking the news in excited Malay, Punjabi, English and Chinese. Later, their second performance will not go as well, but that doesn't matter. Qualification was their goal and represents victory, as indeed does this whole journey.

I ask Tirath Singh, the eighteen-year-old pipe sergeant, how it feels, but he can hardly speak for crying. 'This is my dream,' he says, as the silver dagger at his waist glitters in the Scottish sun.

The Passion of Harry Bingo

IT WAS THE first day of the new season, an hour till kick-off. The curtain had not risen; those heroes and villains, strolling players and strutting fools who make up Scottish football's dramatis personae, were yet to make their entrance, and so this moment of expectation belonged, as always, to that loyal audience, the fans.

One of these fans, perhaps the most dedicated of all, sat in the supporters' bar at Firhill, sipping a bottle of lager, one of two he allows himself before each game. A ritual within a ritual. Henry Calderhead, better known as Auld Harry, better still as Harry Bingo, is ninety-seven years old and has been going to see Partick Thistle, known as the Jags, since the end of the Second World War. How extraordinary to think that Harry's brown eyes – not as sharp these days – have watched Thistle play for more than seventy years, since Clydebank was rubble, and his voice – not so loud these days – has urged on players now old men themselves. To be a supporter for so long, to give your life to it, requires us to accord that word 'passion' its older, deeper meaning; that of endurance, even suffering. The Passion of Harry Bingo was what I had come along to witness, in the hope that this old, rather frail man, swathed in a scarf of gold and red, could teach me to care like he cares, could help me to understand why the suffering is worth it. I wanted, in short, to learn to love football.

Don't get me wrong, I *like* the game. I like it, but I don't feel it in my guts. This, I say without resentment, is down to my father. He was, in theory, a Stirling Albion fan, but I never knew him to go. He'd had a bad experience at

Ibrox or Parkhead, something to do with urine streaming down the terracing steps, and had vowed never to return. The idea that I might be taken along to a match and thus exposed to those *animals* was out of the question. So, although we lived in Glasgow in the era of Dalglish and Greig, although we lived near Aberdeen at the time of Alex Ferguson's Gothenburg miracle, none of it registered. I wore a Scotland strip to the Primary One fancy dress party, a white ribbon seven stitched lovingly on the back by my mother, but I might as well have gone as Kenny Everett for all that number and shirt meant to me.

This has turned out to be a problem. A passion and knowledge of the game seems to be a basic entry quali- fication for Scottish manhood. It's so much part of the national conversation. Oh, I can fake it for a few minutes with a taxi driver, a barber, or a stranger at the bar. I can talk pidgin football, but I'm not a native speaker, and I've long felt this as both a lack in myself and something that excludes me from the easy society of other men. I don't have a team and I don't have a clue.

At the age of forty-three, have I left it too late? Perhaps not. On Monday 28th September 1931, the author C. S. Lewis was travelling to Whipsnade Zoo in the sidecar of a motorcycle being driven by his brother Warren when he found that, all of a sudden, he was a Christian. 'When we set out I did not believe that Jesus is the Son of God and when we reached the zoo I did,' he recalled in his memoir, *Surprised by Joy*.

I would dearly love to go through something of the same, but with football rather than faith. I want to be sur- prised by Moyes. Or Mourinho, or McInnes – the manager doesn't matter, nor the team. What I want is a conversion experience. I want to believe. In fitba.

'Naw, naw,' said Harry Bingo, 'you're never too auld.' If I was to start going to Firhill now, he winked, I could fit in another fifty-odd years. 'One thing about Thistle, you'll always get a good day out. Once you start following them, there's no other team. There's no going back.'

This was a particularly good day for him. He was the recipient of a golden ticket, presented by the manager Alan Archibald, which gets him into games for free for the rest of his life. It is a reward for his loyalty. 'Just think of all the pain he had to go through to get that,' said some wag at the next table. Harry ignored him, or perhaps didn't hear, his hearing aids being a great filter of cheek, especially when it comes to his beloved team. The Jags, well known these days for their joyously unsettling mascot Kingsley, designed by the artist David Shrigley, are often the butt of jokes; even their own supporters are quick to remind you that their full name is 'Partick Thistle nil'.

Harry was here with his family. His granddaughters Mary and Heather, and Heather's wee girl, Cara, who is seven. What, I asked, does this club mean to him? 'Everything. Everything. My life goes around Partick Thistle. And the bingo. See when Thistle get beat, I go home and I lie in bed and I can't sleep.' And when they win? He stuck up his thumbs. Those thumbs contain multitudes.

It was at the bingo that I had first met Harry. A few years ago, at the Carlton Hall on Dumbarton Road, which he still called the F&F, as it had been known back in the days when it was a Palais de Dance. He was already a nonagenarian, and had thus gone beyond the scope of the bingo books, which only go up to ninety. He was there every day, he had explained, except for when the Jags were playing.

'If we were going to an away game in maybe Perth or Dundee, we could get back in time for him to go to the bingo,' Heather had told me. 'He'd be sitting on the edge of his seat making sure that driver was going as fast as he possibly could. He wouldn't miss the football to get to the bingo, but if he could do both in the same day then that was the best day ever for him. If we had a new driver who didn't know about the bingo, he'd be up to high doh.'

Heather is thirty-six. Mary is fifty. They are both committed fans of Partick Thistle, having been introduced into the true faith, in childhood, by their granda. They had the experience I lacked – a love of club handed down the family like an heirloom, or, depending on how you look at it, a hereditary disease. As wee girls, they'd sell programmes, making pocket money from tips. 'I used to rope in some of my friends from school,' Heather had said. 'I'd say, "If you sell programmes with me, you'll get in for nothing *and* you'll get a free pie." But most of them fell away eventually.'

She herself fell away in her mid-twenties for six or seven years when her partner, not a Thistle fan, didn't want to go to the games. 'But then we split up, and it was a place where I could go back to and felt, "This is where I belong."' It was a bad break-up and her confidence had taken a knock. Football offered a familiar embrace. 'I knew I would fit in. That was very important. A lot of the friendships that I had together with my partner, I didn't want to continue, and I had to cut ties. So it was nice to go back to having my football pals, or to make good new pals on the bus.'

Why does football mean so much to so many people? 'That's a very simple question which has many answers,' says John Williams, a senior lecturer in the sociology department at Leicester University. Williams is a Liverpool supporter and a specialist in fan behaviour. 'It is still substantially, for many people, about family and place. The world changes very quickly these days. Lots of people feel quite alienated about their relationships and connections with place, and football is a kind of anchor.' Football as a provider of identity has strengthened, Williams believes, as other traditional providers – work, religion, the stable family unit – have declined in influence. 'I think for a lot of post-industrial towns in England and Scotland that is precisely what is going on.'

Harry Bingo was born in 1919. He's from Port Dundas originally, but now lives in Bishopbriggs; his first job was as a 'trace boy' – leading the heavy horses that helped pull carts loaded with beer barrels from Speirs Wharf to town. He's had lung cancer and skin cancer. A cold in the winter can go into his chest. The week before this season-opener against Inverness Caledonian Thistle ('the fake Jags' as Heather calls them), he had keeled over while watching his team take on Queen's Park in the league cup. 'Low blood pressure,' he explained. 'Conked me oot.' Yet here he was back.

'Right, come on boys,' said Mary, taking her granda by the arm, and the supporters seated by the stairs in the Jackie Husband stand leaned out their left shoulders so that Harry could rest on each as he made his way down the rows to his seat. There was no sense that they pitied him. This was a guard of honour.

Three o'clock approached. Constant drizzle. Floodlights in early August. Just shy of 3,000 people here. There was a minute's applause for a sixteen-year-old fan who had been stabbed to death not quite two months before. 'Once a Jag,' said the voice on the tannoy, 'always a Jag.'

It wasn't much of a first half, but a Chris 'Squiddy' Erskine goal in the thirty-sixth minute brought things to life. I've rarely seen anyone look happier than Harry Bingo when Squiddy scored. It was a look of pure transcendent joy, the sort of expression you might find on a stained glass window to illustrate the adoration of the magi. 'He cannae shout,' Mary explained. 'He husnae got the voice any more.' But he didn't need to. His feelings were clear. 'I'm happy,' he said.

Last season, Mary explained, her granda had informed her that he wasn't going to go to the football any more. 'I'm a burden,' he'd said. Well, she wasn't having that: 'No, you're no'.' She would get no pleasure from going to the football, she told me, knowing that he was at home. It was not a thing to be countenanced. His commitment to the club, after all, is greater than that shown by any player or manager. Harry Bingo *is* Partick Thistle in a sense. As Nick Hornby wrote in *Fever Pitch*, 'Football is a context where watching *becomes* doing,' and Harry's seventy-plus years of watching football at Firhill, of bearing witness, made him the most senior, experienced and representative figure in the ground that day. He had celebrated his seventieth, eightieth and ninetieth birthdays there, and the director Jacqui Low hoped to host his centenary. That day will come, God willing, but for now he'll settle for a decent season.

'We're looking for a win the day,' he had told Alan Archibald sternly as the manager presented him with the golden ticket, and a win is what he got. The lanyard around Harry's neck, I noticed, said Thistle Forever and Ever.

* * *

We were somewhere along the A9 when an idea took hold. 'Here,' said Shep, 'that's us going past Stirling Castle. Is the bar no' gettin' opened?' And suddenly the air was full of rustling as poly bags were produced, their contents taken out and offered round: pre-mixed vodka in two-litre bottles of own-brand fizzy orange, lemonade and cola (diet for health). 'Pretty classy,' said Keith. 'Nae Buckfast on this bus. This is Queen's Park.'

Stirling Castle, high on its rock, has had many noble functions over the years – royal palace, besieged fortress, army barracks – but today it served as a beacon for a coach-load of football fans heading north from Glasgow so they'd know when was a decent moment to get the booze out.

It was nine in the morning on Saturday, 10th September 2016 – a massive day in British football. A day of derbies, grudges. Manchester United versus Man City was being talked up as a personal battle between Pep Guardiola and José Mourinho. In Scotland, all the focus was on the Old Firm as they met in the Premiership for the first time since Rangers' return. The action, clearly, was elsewhere. Yet it felt good to be driving almost 200 miles with around twenty Queen's Park fans – the entire travelling support – to an away game in Peterhead. There was a slight air of 'we few, we happy few' about the occasion. No one was unaware, nor did they seem to mind, that there was something tragicomic about it all. 'Epic scenes,' Martin had observed when we stopped for passengers on the High Street, 'as five folk get on in the toon.'

Martin, Keith, Shep, Higgy, Ian, The Vicar – I was getting to know these fans. I'd been to a home game the weekend before, an unexpected 2–0 win against Morton in the Irn-Bru Cup, and had been introduced to a few of them. Higgy is Michael Higgins, a fifty-three-year-old railway worker who has been going to see this team since he was a boy. In the social club, before the match, I had explained about my quest to learn to love football. 'I'll give you a challenge,' he had said. 'Go and watch Queen's for five games on the trot, and that'll be you. Folk talk about Barcelona and Real Madrid and all that, but if we bludgeon out a 1–0 win the day, that – for me – is better.'

Queen's Park, known as the Spiders, is my local team. I can walk to their ground from my house in twenty minutes, so it makes both practical and a kind of moral sense for me to support them. I also enjoy the oddness of their history: that they are the oldest club in Scotland; that they invented the passing game; that they have chosen to remain amateur, their players unpaid, which keeps them true to the purity of the sport's roots, but is also a form of masochism and self-debasement as it means that they will never again compete at the highest level. Those famous black and white jerseys, which the players wear untucked to signify their amateur status, are hairshirts of sorts, and all of that begs the question – who supports a team like this? 'Freaks and weirdos,' said Gordon McCallum, a middle-aged fan in a black Harrington and oxblood Docs, who lives in a flat in Govan with six parrots. 'I fit in perfectly.'

We had been talking at the Morton match. It is one of Queen's Park's pleasant absurdities that home games are played at Hampden, the 52,000-seater national stadium, in front of crowds of 500 people. There is no atmosphere, except when a burst of 'Enjoy Yourself' by The Specials blares over the tannoy to mark a Queen's goal. This tradition is a nod to the Two-Tone movement with which Queen's, in their monochrome hoops, and with their cohort of ska-loving fans, are associated. Home game aficionados might also find themselves in idle moments playing 'Vicar bingo' – mentally ticking off the repertoire of shouted insults from Stewart Hendry, known as The Vicar, a seventy-six-year-old supporter who has been going to see the team for so long that he witnessed the debut of a sixteen-year-old Alex Ferguson in November 1958. Each outburst from The Vicar comes wafting across the crowd, fragranced by the Clan tobacco which he favours in his pipe, a suitable perfume for heckles from a gentler era. 'Intae these chanty-wrastlers!' is about as fire and brimstone as he gets.

All of which is by way of explaining how I found myself en route to Peterhead. Ian Nicolson, a zealous convert to Queen's Park after a lifetime following Hibs, had emailed to say that the supporters' bus was the best in Scotland. 'To really get being a football fan you need to experience an away day,' he had written. 'I'd like to think that we're civilised drunks. While a bevvy is taken, we can still discuss the finer points of Marxist philosophy, alongside the collected works of Mark E. Smith.' This, it turned out, was the case, although he might have added that the conversation would likely also touch upon Tony Benn's diaries, Nick Cave's music, and which is the best episode of *Columbo*. Opinions on these matters varied widely and were the subject of spirited debate, but a touching moment of unity occurred when, while passing the entrance to Donald Trump's golf course, everyone rushed over and gave the tongs to the sign.

In some ways, this journey was the point, rather than the match itself. Queen's were not expected to win against Peterhead. This is very different from supporting a big club, where defeats are regarded as intolerable humiliations. Everyone on this bus was used to getting beat, had experience of relegation, had known the black moods that accompanied losses. Yet there was an awareness that this was part of what it meant to support the team – trial by ordeal. 'We've had more bad years than good, and you just thole it,' said Keith McAllister, a fifty-nine-year-old accountant with a Shakespearean beard and a Stoic bent who has been head of the Supporters' Association since he was fifteen. 'Win or lose, I enjoy the day. But there have been certain games we've lost where I've felt absolutely dreadful.'

The worst was a 1982 quarter-final of the Scottish Cup against Forfar in which they conceded a last-minute goal. Had Queen's won, they would have played a semi against Rangers at a time when that team was in poor form. A place in the final was so close Keith could taste it. 'So that was probably the worst day of my life. I was absolutely devastated. But then I've had moments that will live forever. There was one game in 1981 when we were 3–0 down at Stenhousemuir and we won 4–3. I can still remember the feeling. In fact, look at that.' He lifted his left arm to show me the hairs standing up at the memory of the winning goal. He could see it, in his mind's eye, replaying in slow motion some thirty-five years after it crossed the line.

Keith hasn't missed a game, home or away, since 1979. 'Three o'clock on a Saturday, this is what I do. I've told my daughter, "If you get married on a Saturday, I might not be there."'

He is quite serious about this. He seems like a reasonable and thoroughly decent man, yet he has this monomania, this compulsion at the centre of his life. Does he really get any pleasure from football? Isn't it more like a burden? 'No, I don't see it as a burden. I know exactly what you mean, though. There are days when I've woken up, when we're playing really badly, and it's Ross County in February and it's pissing down, and I think, "Oh shit, do I really want to do this?" But I know that if I don't go, I would really regret it. There have been a few times when I've felt like death, and I didn't want to go to the game, but I went anyway.'

He showed me a tattoo on the inside of his left forearm – a white rose and a few lines of romantic verse by the poet Hugh MacDiarmid. This reminds him about a particular love affair, about his feelings for Scotland, and about what it is to follow Queen's Park. 'You know it's going to break your heart, but that's okay,' he said. 'You're happy to take the lows because you know you're going to get the huge highs. That's football. That's my team. That sums it up.'

'Suffering following your club is a very necessary thing,' John Williams of Leicester University had told me. 'It's crucial and central to what being a fan means. To experience real suffering demonstrates your support. You don't lose faith in your club even though they perform badly. For real fans who feel they have a deep and authentic connection with their clubs, they have to suffer in order to be able to enjoy what you hope in the future might happen. Somehow, suffering earns you the right to be happy and successful with your club. You can't really know how that feels, or how important that is, unless you've been there in the dark times.'

Or, as C. S. Lewis puts it in *The Problem of Pain*, 'tribulation is a necessary element in redemption'.

We arrived at Balmoor about an hour before kick-off. It

was a bright day. Seagulls ghosted overhead. Stovies were on sale in the clubhouse at 50 pence a helping. Scottish country dance music came lilting over the PA, lending a romantic air to the views of pebble-dashed houses and the power station. Percussion was provided by the home fans banging pitchside advertising hoardings for a funeral director and the *Press & Journal*. Here, perhaps because they were away from the civilising influence of The Vicar, who no longer makes these long trips, the Queen's support were less genteel. Shouts of encouragement ("Mon the Spiders!') mingled with rhetorical enquiries directed at the referee – 'How's he offside, ya fuckin' walloper?' – and the keening of the gulls.

After the long, boozy trip north, the game itself went by in a flash. Queen's missed an early penalty and were punished for it, conceding two goals in the second half. The fans, loyal to the last, applauded their team off the pitch, but the mood on the bus home was subdued and reflective. I admired these men, their commitment and companionship, but I could not yet share their faith.

'Sometimes,' said Higgy, 'I take a walk to what's left of Cathkin Park, Third Lanark's old ground.' Third Lanark were one of Scotland's great early teams, but went under in 1967. Remarkably, the Glasgow ground is still there, and it's a melancholy, haunted place. The stone terraces are mossy, and slippy with fallen leaves, broken in places by great thrusting groves of poplar, hornbeam, sycamore and ash. Hunched in the branches, magpies prattle like football rattles.

'I'm an athiest, ken,' Higgy continued, 'but it's kind of like a church for me. It's quiet and there's naebody aboot, so I do a lot of thinking there. I'll sit on the bit terracing that's left and think, "This could be my team. This could be Queen's just disappeared. What would I dae?" Imagine that happened. It would be a huge part of my life just taken away.'

He spreads his hands, shakes his head, clearing the dark thoughts. 'I don't know, maybe we're aw just nuts.'

* * *

Driving down from Glasgow, I passed the spot. On a sloping grass verge of the roundabout where, in newspaper photographs, the bus lay tipped on its side, there was now a shrine. Flowers and football tops. The red, white and blue. Two weeks before, here on the A76 between Mauchline and Kilmarnock, a coach carrying Rangers fans to a match against Partick Thistle came off the road and overturned, injuring several and resulting in the death of one man, thirty-nine-year-old Ryan Baird.

He was from the village of Magheramorne in Northern Ireland, and the funeral would be held there; an Orange ceremony was planned, with regalia worn, and the Rangers manager in attendance. I was on my way to the memorial service, in the Dumfries and Galloway town of Sanquhar, where Baird had made his home. He worked as a joiner, had two sons, and was engaged to be married.

Outside St Bride's, a pretty nineteenth-century church, Billy McLeod was shaking hands, welcoming folk. A stocky man of fifty-five, McLeod had played for Ipswich Town, Partick Thistle and Queen of the South in the late seventies and early eighties. These days he is a stalwart member of Nith Valley Loyal, the Rangers supporters club which had been travelling on the bus that day. He wore a dark suit and a Rangers scarf. His face bore an expression of grim compassion. It seemed clear that he was suffering, but you had no doubt that he would do his duty by the friend he had lost and the fellow club members whom he considers a kind of kin.

A banner tied to a fence outside the church displayed the red hand of Ulster and the words Prod Boys on Tour. Inside, the pews were full. A couple of hundred people at least. Country music played on the PA and some of the mourners sang under their breath, tapped their feet softly on the wooden floor: *We love to see the lasses with the blue scarves on, we love to hear the boys all roar...*

The public response to the crash had been remarkably ecumenical. Rival football clubs and fans offered condolences, and Rod Stewart, one of Celtic's best-known supporters, made a donation to a fund set up in the aftermath. Yet in St Bride's there was a sense of a distinct people grieving for one of their own. Almost everyone was wearing Rangers colours over their funeral clothes. One woman, I noticed, wore an orange scarf on which the words No Surrender were written in Gothic script. That, of course, is a contentious slogan with a particular historical and religious context going back to the seventeenth century, and many people would consider it anti-Catholic, a provocative and inappropriate thing to wear. But here, in Sanquhar, it seemed to take on another, better meaning – defiance in the face of tragedy and a refusal to give in to grief.

Large windows on the north side of the church showed the Lowther hills. The music ended and the Reverend William Hogg, a kindly looking man with a grey beard, began his sermon. 'You are wondering and I am wondering,' he said, 'where are the words of comfort in the face of such a painful loss? Someone you have cared about and respected has had his life ended in a moment of utter disaster. We cannot and must not avoid saying that.'

The minister wore a blue stole over his vestments. Not quite the right shade, he admitted, but it felt like an appropriate gesture. 'In modern Christian thinking, blue is the colour of hope, of the sky, of heaven above. I assume that any football fan knows everything about hope. You can experience it minute by minute during a match or season. When things are a bit rough and disappointing, there's the hope that things will get better, that difficult times can't last forever ... It is on that hope, that promise that we rely this morning, as we commend Ryan to God's safe keeping. And we have, as a reminder, the blue.'

Football fans in Scotland, Rangers supporters in particular, often get a bad name for their behaviour and attitudes. While this may, at times, be well deserved, what I saw in Sanquhar was a side of fandom that is less often acknowledged and discussed. Football is tribal, which can be problematic because tribes define themselves against other groups and cultures, hence sectarianism, violence and all that rank rottenness. But a tribe is also a kind of family, which means solidarity, sticking together, us against whatever the world throws. It means a scarf around the neck, an arm around the shoulder. 'We are the People', the Rangers fans sing; another contentious phrase, yet it has become clear that – come the darkest hour – 'we' is the important word.

There were a lot of people in that church who had been hurt, physically and emotionally, in the bus crash. But they had come together, based around a shared love of football, of club, to offer each other comfort. This is passion. Harry Bingo feels it. Higgy and The Vicar feel it. Ryan Baird, surely, felt it too.

I don't. Not yet. Maybe not ever. But perhaps it is not such a small thing, a privilege even, that I am able to sense it in others and can write here Billy McLeod's words when he told me what it has been like to return to Ibrox in the aftermath of the crash. It has meant getting back on a coach and passing the crash site, which cannot be easy, but it has meant, too, a feeling of unity and love; the embrace of something bigger.

'It's comforting,' he said. 'People at the games see our Nith Valley badges on our tops and jackets and instantly recognise that we were the club that were in the crash. It was a tragedy, it was an accident, it was an ill-fated day. It's been difficult for the boys that were on the bus, and difficult for some that weren't and feel terrible guilt about not being there and able to help. This supporters club has been put on the map for a reason we didn't want, but the tragedy has brought our community closer together, and the big Rangers family has been absolutely amazing.'

Afterwards, after the hymns and prayers, the dark vale and falling eventide, we walked outside and lined the mossy kirkyard path as the coffin was carried shoulder-high to the hearse. It was a bright autumn day, and, in the mourning hush, the noise of kids playing football drifted up the hill from the school. Shouts and whistles; sniffs and sobs; death and life. No surrender.

Herring Queens

AT THE STROKE of seven on a bright June morning, sunlight bouncing off the buttons of their cheerful scarlet jackets, the Linlithgow Reed Band start to play 'Crimond', the old Scottish musical setting of the 23rd Psalm, and several of the dozens of men and women who have assembled to hear this, as they do each year, begin quietly to weep.

'Oh, it's emotional,' says one old man afterwards, dabbing his eyes with a paper hankie. 'I think of my wife that I've lost and the friends that I've lost.'

This is the Marches, the annual festival which has taken place in the town for hundreds of years. The people of Linlithgow, who are pleased to call themselves Black Bitches after an ancient legend involving a loyal hound, have a great passion for the Marches – named for the practice of riding out to inspect the March Stones which marked the boundary of the town land. It is a thronging celebration of kinship and belonging, home and heart, a grand, noisy occasion fuelled by long draughts of pride and a few whisky chasers, and at the very start of it is this moment of reflection when locals think of those dear to them, now gone, who loved and shared days like this. The Lord may be their shepherd, but what Linlithgow folk celebrate is their joy at being part of a flock.

Every summer, from Ayrshire to Fife, you'll find these fairs and gala days. They don't get much attention beyond a few photos in the local papers but they mean a great deal to tens of thousands of people. There are around seventy such events in Lanarkshire and the Lothians alone. The heartland is in post-industrial working-class communities;

pit villages which no longer have a pit, mill towns without mills – these are the places where fairs and galas flourish, expressions of identity that have come to replace the togetherness once offered by shared employment.

Yet, in comparison with the Common Ridings or the Highland Games, fairs and galas are paid little mind by both media and academia. They are regarded, somehow, as trivial. Alan McLaren, stalwart of Loanhead Children's Gala Day and author of a history of Midlothian's local festivals, believes there is a widespread misunderstanding that such events are recent inventions when, in fact, their roots go much deeper.

'There's a lot of ignorance,' he says. 'Galashiels, Kelso, Jedburgh, Coldstream, Duns – all are relatively modern inventions. But if an event involves adults riding about on horses then that's seen as culturally more important than those where children play the principal parts. That's a mistaken view. You're basically writing off the tradition in a large part of lowland Scotland.'

Quite right. A central Scotland summer can be a dazzling, almost trippy spectacle of pomp and pageantry. Bo'ness, for example, is home to what claims to be the biggest children's fair in Europe. Beginning in the eighteenth century as a drunken celebration of the end of indentured labour among coal miners, it has developed into a colourful ceremony in which one local schoolgirl is chosen to be Queen, while other children become the royal retinue – page boys, heralds, fairies, flowergirls and the like. Most extraordinary are the frontages, known as arches, which many Bo'nessian families build in front of their homes.

Palaces, medieval fortresses, magical grottoes – anything goes. 'This has just gone up today,' says Claire McComb, pointing across the street at the thirty-foot tall wooden castle standing in her garden. 'The crane is just away.'

Her eleven-year-old son Jamie is Champion, the main boy part, at this year's Bo'ness Fair. Parents of a child elected to one of the principal roles enjoy a few moments of hyperventilating pleasure on receiving the phone call from the school, but then the realisation sets in that only a few months hence they will have to build an arch and it will have to be fabulous, costing anything from £2,000 to £10,000. Families fundraise to pay for this, but there is also a massive investment of time and energy. In June, the streets echo with the sound of hammering and sawing, while smoke machines and spotlights are fetched down from lofts. It is the Las Vegas strip made manifest on the Firth of Forth. And each year the arches seem to get bigger. It is as if the gargantuan industrial architecture of the nearby Grangemouth oil refinery, with its belching cooling towers and dragonish gas flares, had influenced both the scale and aesthetic swagger.

The great night for arches is Fair E'en, the evening before the big day, when Bo'nessians saunter through the streets, from showy villa to roughcast council terrace, admiring what has been made – and all that work for just a couple of days. 'Yeah,' laughs Claire McComb at the thought of this, 'I'm threatening to keep ours up till Christmas.'

The Bo'ness Fair is modelled, in part, on Lanark's Lanimer Day, thought to be the first fair in Scotland at which a local child was crowned Queen. That goes back to 1893, though Lanimers itself dates from 1140 when the town was made a royal burgh. It takes place over the course of a week in June, the main day being the Thursday. It is a splendid scene, the whole town packed onto the steep High Street for the grand parade, bunting bright against the blue sky. 'This,' as one local woman puts it, 'is a Scottish Mardi Gras.'

In Lanark, rather than arches, the big thing is floats. You can't call them floats, though, without attracting hoots of derision. They are known as Lanimer lorries. There are twenty-four lorries in the procession this year, each competing for the coveted grand prize, the Silver Bell Trophy.

There are, in addition, awards for different categories of lorry, depending on its size and whether it is powered by an engine or shoved-and-shoogled along by hand. There are just two in the Motorised Large category this year: both gigantic; one inspired by the culture of Thailand, the other by Japan; and each decorated with tens of thousands of handmade paper flowers. These have been constructed by rival teams of lorry builders – the Kranal Club and Kilninie Club – who, between them, have dominated the competition for decades. This is the Old Firm, the El Clásico, of Lanimer Day.

For two reasons, there is even more of an edge this year. One, 'A Glimpse of Japan' is the last ever Lanimer lorry of Beth Brown, sixty-six-year-old head of the Kranal Club. Two, there has been quite a stooshie, with the Kilninie Club accused of cheating by incorporating into their lorry a large model elephant which had been made in Jersey for that island's annual carnival, 'The Battle of the Flowers'. Kranal members are certainly unhappy about this – 'Their Buddha's smaller than ours and their elephant's bought in,' harrumphs one.

Loraine Swan, the retired teacher who heads the Kilninie, insists there's nothing in the rules to say that everything has to be made from scratch. The accusations have been hurtful for the Kilninie, she says, and don't take account of all the hard work that has gone into making their lorry, 'Treasures of Thailand'. 'There's a chap called Keith who's been in our group for years. He's eighty-seven. He made the Buddha in his garage.'

Unquestionably, the Lanimer lorries are remarkable. It feels inadequate to simply applaud as they pass along Lanark's narrow winding streets. Mississippi paddle-steamers, pirate ships, giant golfers, a zombie apocalypse – each a haund-knitted masterpiece in its own way. The Kranal and Kilninie lorries, though, are something else. Both have been built up around old tractors to the approximate size of a long-distance truck, and together are a Far Eastern phantasmagoria of pagodas, peacocks and golden boats as well as Lanarkians dressed as samurai warriors and Thai royalty. The Kranal lorry, one must add, blasts out 'Japanese Boy' by Aneka as it rolls along at a stately five miles per hour, prompting one young man with Big Sexy printed across the back of his Chelsea top to raise his Buckfast bottle in a toast of heartfelt, glaikit admiration.

'We've made a few masterpieces. I know before it leaves the shed whether it's a contender,' Beth Brown says. She is dressed as a geisha, a look she carries off with brassy aplomb. 'A Glimpse of Japan' is her fifty-third lorry. 'Valhalla', 'Caesar's Palace', 'The Moulin Rouge' – she and her crew have made them all. They are built in the barn of a sympathetic local farmer by a small team who only occasionally feel the urge to put their hands around Brown's throat. Planning starts immediately following Lanimer Day and building begins over the winter. Each of the tens of thousands of paper flowers must be cut and shaped by hand, the most crucial stage in the process, known as fluffing. 'Ah've been fluffin' since October,' groans one Lanarkian, Wee Karen, the numbness in her arms soothed somewhat by winning the Non-Motorised Large category.

Beth Brown, perhaps inevitably, is victorious in this valedictory year. The Silver Bell is, for the last time, hers. She leaps up when the announcement is made. 'I always take off,' she says later. 'I remember the first year that I won, I lifted my hat and threw it in the air. This auld woman in the crowd caught it, and she went, "How much have ye won?" Well, it was a fiver. So she says, "Pit yer bloody hat back on yer heid, hen!" She didn't realise how much this means to me. Oh, we're going out on a high.'

People in Lanark, in Bo'ness, will tell you the local fair is the best day of the year. We hear so much these days about fractured, purposeless towns. Well, the fairs offer a once-a-year jolt of civic unity. They are, therefore, not just pleasant but relevant, even vital.

In Eyemouth, many would agree that the annual Herring Queen festival is the backbone of the town. Like too many Scottish fishing ports, Eyemouth has seen a steep decline in the industry around which it first grew. There were once so many boats in the harbour, it is said, that you could walk right across from deck to deck without getting your feet wet. Now, as a result of various factors – EU policies; decline in fish stocks; young men seeking more lucrative and steady work in the oil industry – there are few fishermen left. 'It's important that folk know that places like Eyemouth are living on a pacemaker,' says Johnny Johnston, a retired skipper and former harbour master. 'The harbour is the heart of the community, and if that heart stops beating the toon's dead.'

Against this backdrop, one could detect a certain grim irony in persisting with a festival intended to bring luck and prosperity to those at sea. They don't even fish for herring out of Eyemouth these days; it's mainly prawns.

The first Herring Queen was crowned in 1939 but there followed a hiatus during the Second World War. The girl chosen is always fourteen or fifteen. Wearing a cloak decorated with fishing net, she sails the short distance down the coast from St Abbs, coming ashore at Eyemouth and being crowned by the queen from the previous year. The idea is that she has been plucked from the seaweed, a silver darling in the form of a girl.

Remarkably, some sixty-four of the sixty-nine former queens are still living, and many still live locally, as, of course, does this year's queen-to-be, fifteen-year-old Ailsa Landels. You can go to the town and talk to a Herring Queen from each decade since the 1940s. You can ask them what they remember and they'll tell you about the noise of the crowds, the tears of pride, the chill of the haar against their skin, and the way Eyemouth emerged from this sea-mist like Brigadoon.

The first queen, Mary Craig, died in 2010 at the age of eighty-seven. It meant a lot to her that she had been Herring Queen. Her daughter Muriel discovered her pink silk dress while clearing the house and has made a long-term loan of it to the local museum; it is a delicate relic which shows its years, and there's something moving in the thought of the lass who wore this on 22nd July 1939, on the cusp of womanhood, the cusp of war. It must have been an act of tremendous optimism and faith to inaugurate the festival when everyone knew that the barbed wire and bombing raids were just up ahead.

Anne Collin, now eighty-two, was the first Herring Queen after the war. She was called Anne Rosie back then, in 1946, but she married James Collin the following year, at sixteen. She and her husband had been born in the same room in the same house, hard by the harbour. When his family moved out, hers moved in. They grew up together. Their marriage, which lasted almost sixty years until his passing, was preordained, she says, laughing. He saw her being crowned, and they saw their daughter, Margaret, crowned in turn in 1969. Although she was a shy teenager rather stunned by the noise and excitement of the ceremony following the dreary years of the war, Anne was conscious that she was emblematic of Eyemouth's desire to get back to normal and fill their nets with herring.

She herself needs no lessons in abundance, having had four children, ten grandchildren and nineteen great-grandchildren, a veritable shoal. The twentieth is due shortly after this year's ceremony. Her time as queen shines as bright in memory as the silver brooch she wore for the first time on the day and still owns. 'It lingers on,' she says, 'in your mind forever.'

Back in Linlithgow, at the Marches, the ceremony is reaching its climax, the procession circling the old town well three times. All day it has been fiercely sunny, but now the rain begins, falling in great sultry drops on women in summer frocks, worthies in ermine, and red-faced men in deerstalkers and tweed. It falls on the trilby of Peter Henderson, a sixty-nine-year-old known as 'Zoom', in his mobility scooter decorated with a giant cardboard cut-out of his hero Elvis Presley, and it falls on the peaked cap of Eddie McKenna, eighty-three, a founder member of the Linlithgow Reed Band back in 1956 and on the saxophone still. He is playing 'Auld Lang Syne' as the Linlithgow folk join hands and sing with rain on their faces.

Scottish public life has, of late, been dominated by the independence question – the whys and wherefores filling every newspaper and news channel. Yet to travel around the country's towns and villages on these fair days, each high street tricked out in Saltires and Union flags, each town band playing 'Scots Wha Hae' and 'God Save the Queen', is to realise that what matters to people as much as and perhaps even more than national identity is local pride. Yes, we are Scots, but we are, too, Bo'nessians, Lanarkians and the rest. We are the streets on which we grew up, every gable, cobble and pebbledashed semi.

That is why there is such happiness and a sense of belonging to be found by involving oneself in fairs and galas, whether as a crowned head or simply making sandwiches for the picnic. Blessed, then, are the piece-makers; blessed are the riders of marches and builders of arches; blessed are the Herring Queens, the Black Bitches and Beth Brown, the grand lady of the Lanimer lorries – for they shall inherit that small Scottish corner of the earth which they call home and which, for them, is heaven.

Whaligoe Steps

'AYE,' SAYS DAVIE, peering into the wind blowing off the Moray Firth. 'A fine breeze to keep the midges away the day.'

Davie Nicolson is a small, wiry man of fifty-four with a white horseshoe moustache, his Harley-Davidson cap pulled tight and low, lest it be blown out to sea. A fading tattoo on his left forearm shows a cartoon devil encircled by the words 'Born to Raise Hell'. In truth, Nicolson is more of a guardian angel, and if he was born to raise anything it is the heavy slabs of flagstone which he hefts up and down the steep stone staircase built into the near-vertical cliff face at the foot of his garden here in Ulbster, in the far north-east of Scotland.

These Whaligoe Steps, as they are known, were constructed in 1792 to allow the wives of fishermen to carry loaded baskets of cod, haddock, herring and ling up almost 250 feet from the natural harbour to the village, and beyond. The local fishing industry is long gone, but the 337 steps remain, zigzagging up the cliff, a symbol and reminder of that heritage. Nicolson, whose grandfather was one of the last fishermen to use the harbour, has spent much of his life as the staircase's unofficial custodian and caretaker, resisting with muscle, sweat, and a rough Caithness tongue, the destructive forces of waves, wind and local vandals. He keeps a set of stocks in his garden as a warning to the latter. 'I put them in there and throw eggs at them,' he grins.

This place is one of Scotland's secret treasures, a remnant of an industrial past which has developed a fairytale, or mythic, air. Rapunzel's tower, Daedalus's labyrinth, the Whaligoe Steps. Unsignposted and unphotograph-able, even if you find them, you can't keep them. No lens can capture the experience of walking down the narrow, uneven, sometimes slippy path, kept from the plunging gorge to your right by no more than a low wall, and enter-ing stage right the sandstone amphitheatre of the harbour. On the horizon: the Beatrice oilfield, a haze of rigs upon the deep green. In spring, says Davie, the rocks are yellow with primroses; in winter, icicles, forty feet long hang from the cliffs like organ pipes.

Here is what the novelist Neil Gunn called 'The Grey Coast' and which his namesake, the poet George Gunn, describes in his book *The Province of the Cat* as 'a cavern-ous, honeycombed, geo fractured, craggy altar, massive and beautiful by varying degrees. The sea smashes its salt head against its feet in a perennial ceremony. From the sea you can fully understand what Caithness is: a rock plateau upon which people struggle to live.'

If this coast is an altar, then Davie Nicolson is its priest. He can chant the litany of Norse place names: Haster, Thrumster, Ulbster, Lybster, and has a parable or two for each. Few visitors leave without a sermon, and sometimes a cup of tea. He is in high demand among producers making films about the area – 'Och, we've had aw the telly here' – and, although he is always glad to give the history of the steps, he refuses to appear on camera, even when it is Billy Connolly doing the asking. 'I says, "No, Billy, I wouldna go on *Coast*, and I'm no' goin' on yours either."'

He has a wonderful voice, full of grit and mischief. I wish you could hear him speak. I wish you could run a fingertip along his words on this page and hear them rise up, ring out. He would tell you all about this place. 'The steps got the name "Whaligoe" because whales were washed up on the shore dead. They had a crane on top of the cliff there, and they pulled the whales up and used them whenever they got one. But if the whales were over a certain size, they belonged to royalty. Royal fish, aye. If they were over sixty feet, they werena allowed to touch them.'

One imagines that quite a few came in at fifty-nine feet then? 'Aye! "Cut a wee bit off the tail!"'

This harbour, known as The Haven, seems to have been used for as long as there have been people, although the way down would originally have been a dangerous path. Davie's cousin Iain Sutherland has written a history of the steps, and notes that the mussel and limpet shells found in middens beside Neolithic settlements in the area would, most likely, have come from Whaligoe. The development of commercial fishing in the late eighteenth century led to the steps and a curing station being built. There were twenty boats fishing out of Whaligoe at one time. Fish were gutted at the foot of the steps, in an area known as the Bink, and carried up by women in creels – willow baskets – that were roped to their backs. Davie estimates that each basket would have weighed two or three stone, and points out the large flat rock, about halfway up, where they would lay down their burden and rest. I place my hand upon it, imagining the rough strong hands, red with rope and cold, now just bone or dust, that had touched this place in centuries past. Once at the top of the cliff, they would either take the fish to a shed for salting or walk seven miles north to sell them in Wick.

The industry began to decline from the 1880s, and by the 1950s there were only two fishermen left. John Miller, known as Red Jock, was Davie's grandfather, and kept a boat called *Morning Star*. Willie Sinclair, called Willie B., was Miller's brother-in-law; his boat, the *Windward*, was pulled from the water for the last time in 1970. It is to preserve and celebrate this family and community heritage that Iain Sutherland and Davie Nicolson have spent decades caring for this place, keeping it in as good repair as they are able. 'It's cos I love the steps,' says Davie. 'My grandfaither, he was one of the last fishermen, and if we didna do it, nobody would do it. Och, it would be sad to loss the harbour.'

Davie attends to the steps twice a day, morning and evening, making sure all is well. He cuts the grass on the Bink, does the weeding, and makes such repairs as are necessary. He has a terrible time with teenagers and young men coming out of Wick and Thurso to push over walls and smash steps – 'It breaks your bloody heart' – and is forever peching up and down with replacement flagstones, rebuilding what is broken or lost. In 1992, he and his cousin manhandled twenty-two tons of stone down the stairs to repair damage. Nine years later, when a section of the Bink collapsed into the sea, a further fourteen tons were required. Perhaps it is the thrawn spirit of those old fishwives taking possession of living muscle and bone, but the steps seem to summon such feats of strength. A small plaque near the top of the steps pays tribute to the memory of Etta B. Juhle, the local postmistress, a misleadingly slight woman who, in the winter of 1975, singlehandedly cleared a large landslip of earth and clay, which had blocked the steps, using only a shovel and coal scuttle.

Davie hopes that one day a similar plaque might honour his own contribution. 'But I'm no' dead yet, though some days I feel like I am.' A dedicated biker, road accidents have cost him two broken legs, a bust ankle, smashed knuckles, a broken shoulder, and serious back injuries. 'Heavens,' he says, 'everything's sore.' Nevertheless, he goes on, day upon day, step upon step, stone upon stone.

* * *

Early that morning, before meeting Davie, I had made a small pilgrimage to the Grey Cairns of Camster, wanting to see them at first light. This part of Scotland has a large number of ancient sites – hill forts, brochs, mysterious rows of mysterious stones. 'Even more impressive,' writes George Gunn, 'are the many burial cairns which rise up across the Caithness flatlands like swollen bellies pregnant with the reverence the builders gave to the lives of their ancestors.'

New discoveries are still being made, putting us in touch with the texture of ancient lives. Six years ago, at Nybster, the excavation of an Iron Age broch uncovered a fragment of bangle made from cannel coal; one thinks of Donne's Relic – 'a bracelet of bright hair about the bone'. The two cairns at Camster are much older, built more than 5,000 years ago, and were first excavated in 1865. They are just down the road from the Whaligoe Steps, and a few miles inland. Davie Nicolson brought his wife Isla here, on the back of his motorbike, when they were in their late teens and first courting; she had recently moved to the area from Vancouver, which left her vulnerable to his wind-ups. This, he told her, pointing to the first cairn, is where they would live when they were married. 'The winds are that strong here,' he said, 'we've all got to build houses like this. But at least you won't have to bother with cleanin' windows.'

Both cairns are huge and set in a brown landscape of peaty moorland between a conifer forest and the ribbon of the single track road. I had hoped for a beautiful sunrise, but the sky was grey with smirr. Sheep looked on with mute cuddish blankness, a bright blue streak across their backs denoting ownership. An information board explains that the people who built these tombs were farmers. The land would not have been boggy then. They probably grew crops, herded cattle and sheep. It does not say if they fished. To expend time and strength building these struc-tures, when life was already a hard struggle for survival, must have been exhausting, which suggests it was also deeply meaningful. You would not do this unless your life, or perhaps your death, depended on it.

'They're just a pile of stones, you know,' says Seoras, a character in George Gunn's play *Camster*.

'No, Seoras, they're like life,' replies Helen. 'Like our life. It's as if you have to understand every single hand-carried stone in order to understand the total cairn.'

The igloo-like round cairn closest to the road is about eighteen metres across and four metres tall; the other, a great humped spine, is almost sixty metres long and twenty metres wide. You can go inside both cairns, which I never do without a sense of low-level dread, always aware that I am entering a grave. Gated doorways – small iron grilles, about three feet high and painted black – are held closed by pins, presumably to keep animals from sheltering inside.

I opened the gate of the round cairn and forced myself into the darkness. You have to bend and shuffle along on your hunkers. The passageway at its narrowest is only about a foot across, but soon widens. There are a couple of alcoves that you look at and think, 'This must be where they found the skeletons.' Excavation in the nineteenth century revealed two bodies in a sitting position, but missing their leg bones. There is a strong sense of a taboo being broken by coming in here. This may be my overactive imagination, but I felt unwanted, unwelcome, resented, detested. It has been suggested that access to these ritual places, and through them access to the bodies and spirits of one's ancestors, was granted only to a chosen few high-ranking individuals, perhaps some sort of priest class.

The stone walls were so thick that I could no longer hear the wind. The only sound was the drip of trapped rain coming through the roof. The inner chamber is about fifteen feet tall. A small window in the corbelled ceiling, partially obscured by moss and dirt, threw dim light on the large stones that form part of the interior walls. George

Gunn, who feels this place is full of love, suggests in *The Province of the Cat* that gently touching these stones offers a form of communion with the past:

'The blood beats through your own hand in the same way as it did in the hand which laid that stone on its neighbour as it did in the person whose charred remains were put into the clay beakers, after the bodies had been brought down from their place of public and sacred exhibition and ritualistically burned, then respectfully positioned onto a shelf in the burial cairn.'

Despite this otherworldly atmosphere, there was no doubt we were in Scotland. Someone had pushed a sprig of purple heather into a nook between two stones, and had left a crumpled can of Tennent's lager on the damp dirt floor. I removed the can, left the heather.

Such places have fascinated me since I was a wee boy. My grandparents were amateur archaeologists and would sometimes take me with them on digs. In 1984, when I was ten, my grandfather – Eric – got wind of a discovery in a quarry near Blair Drummond. A workman's mechanical digger had bitten into a sandbank and bones had come tumbling out. Unnerved by the sight, he downed tools and, soon after, pints. That night in the pub, as Eric listened, he gave up the whole story, including the location. We went there the next evening and were able to find the smashed remains of a Bronze Age cist – a small stone box in which, for 4,000 years, a body had lain crouched.

Over the next few days, we trowelled away at what remained. Shards of pot, of skull. I picked up a tooth, its smooth dry curve cushioned in the palm of my hand. It was a strange feeling, exciting yet solemn, a mixture which I was quite unable to convey in a report for *Discovery and Excavation in Scotland*, the archaeology journal. Clanking it out on an old manual typewriter, this was the first time

I had ever tried to write anything for publication, and my first experience of being rewritten by an editor. I remember the thrill of seeing it in print, quickly followed by disappointment at this bald statement of what we had done: 'Salvage excavation produced human skeletal remains and fragments of a beaker.'

Reading that again now, I'm aware of all that it doesn't and couldn't say. Those activities – the trowelling, the typing, the time spent with my grandparents – were likely intended to keep me busy and give my mother a break. Her belly had been swollen that summer with new life, a new son. He was born by the time the journal was published, but survived just fourteen months. Between the cist of her body and the cist of the earth, not long.

* * *

At the foot of the steps, on the Bink, Davie Nicolson is showing me the remnants of the fishing station: lengths of rusty chain; metal eyes for mooring; the pot where they boiled their nets and lines in a brew of oak bark and cow piss. The wall beneath the final flight of steps has a tall narrow recess for holding a mast, and three niches where crusie lamps – fuelled by fish oil – would have lit the landing of catch in the dark. This was all built in the late eighteenth century, but looks Stone Age, bringing to mind the shelves of Skara Brae, or – nearer to hand – the alcoved tombs at Camster.

'You're descended from the people who built and used these steps,' I say to Davie, 'but probably also from the folk who raised the cairns?'

'Oh, no doubt!' he replies, brightly and at once. 'Aye!'

It's quite common for people to have their ashes scattered at the foot of the steps, and there have been a few weddings, too. 'There was one lassie, the photographer was taking pictures of her up there on the steps, and when she went like that with her arm' – a sudden expansive gesture – 'her lovely golden bracelet came flying off.' It tumbled over the side of the steps and came to rest on a steep grassy bank of the cliff. Davie reassured the distraught young woman that he would get it back, and went off to fetch his fishing rod. After several casts, he hooked the bracelet, reeled it in, and handed it over to the bride at the reception in Wick. Had he not been at hand? It is easy to imagine that bracelet sinking into the earth for centuries before being dug up, a prize relic, by some future archaeologist puzzled that such treasure should be found on a bleak edge of Scotland.

As we walk back up the steps, Davie points out carvings in the rock wall: names, dates, anchors. Some still alive, most not. He knew them all. Davie's family have always been Caithness. He himself was born on a farm just down the road, and he has been coming to the steps since he was eight years old, delighting in the stories of Willie Sinclair, Willie B. The reason Davie knows so much about local history is that he has made a point, throughout his life, of talking to old 'mannies', and now carries their stories within him, a shining shoal caught in the net of his mind.

At the top of the cliff, he suggests we go for a drive. He'll show me a few things. That ruined cottage was the home of a poet; this field here was where, in the 1970s, Davie spotted a puma. He seems a cheery man, so maybe it's just what happens when you live in this unforgiving landscape, but his stories often tend deathwards. So-and-so lost his life while kayaking, such-and-such walked into the sea, leaving his wallet and a note on a stone by the shore; these are the rocks where his cousin fell and broke her back; that is the pool where his auntie drowned. Davie has a job cutting the grass in the small clifftop cemetery at Clyth, which suits his taste for conversation. 'I know a lot of the folks that's in there. I'm working away and talking to them: "How are you daein' the day, John?"'

We pull into a private road near the harbour of Sarclet

and trudge up a muddy track past a derelict farm. Caithness seems full of tumbledown farmhouses, no doubt built with materials recycled from earlier structures, and now themselves fit for scavengers. 'There are plenty of ruined buildings in the world,' as MacDiarmid wrote, 'but no ruined stones.' One senses in these farm buildings, swallows shooting starlike from the blackness of their windows, generation upon generation of human presence.

Davie leads the way to an old burial ground and we climb the dyke. The place is badly overgrown, all bracken and lichen; in the corners are great drifts of snowdrops, heads bowed and cowled. The grave-markers span the centuries from the 1700s to our own age. 'That's my Uncle Frank,' says Davie, nodding to what seems the most modern – a naval memorial dated 17th January 1945. 'He was torpedoed. He did survive, but ach, he was badly burnt, so ...'

A sad story, one of many, but not what we have come here to see. 'This is it,' says Davie. 'The Sinclair Mausoleum.'

The Sinclairs were powerful local nobles, descended from the Norman St Clairs, a force in this land since the fifteenth century. Their mausoleum, as Davie calls it, is also known as St Martin's Chapel, and is a striking building quite unlike anything else around. It has an odd harsh beauty, a dissonant chord within the symphony of the landscape. A weathervane bears the date 1700, which would mean it is older than the Whaligoe Steps by almost a century. Entirely square, seven by seven metres below a flowing curve of a roof, its slates are jaundiced with lichen, its harled walls a tubercular grey. Ten steps lead up to a wooden door high in the otherwise blank southern wall. Inside, there is a fireplace, its grate piled with bracken, like a nest for some dour Highland phoenix. A queer and suggestive thing, that fire. What gatherings, what partings did it heat? One can imagine a few cold mourners in rough black clothes; a sheeted body colder still. Over by the eastern wall, a slab in the flagstone floor marks the entrance to the crypt. It is sealed now, but when Davie was a boy, he and his pals made this place a playground. They would dare each other to open what was then just a trapdoor and climb down the ladder. 'The place,' he recalls, 'was full of bones.'

Full of bones. One might say the same about Caithness as a whole; or, of course, anywhere at all, but there is a strong feeling in these parts of the past being close to the surface of the present and the present sinking into the past. There are some people, Davie Nicolson being one, who seem to move between these worlds as easily as going up and down a flight of stairs, and if we pay them enough mind then maybe we can walk with them for a while and see what they see: the human continuum within which each of us is carried for a while and then laid down. Life upon life, our story piles up. The years stack like stones.

It's hard to see beyond one's own life, its births and deaths, joys and sorrows. But sometimes, squinting into the wind just so, it is possible to catch sight of the total cairn.

Barrowlands

TEN LETTERS. THIRTY-SIX stars. Two hundred and forty volts. Put like that it does not sound much, but the neon sign of the Barrowland Ballroom is so much more – a gaudy, gallus pleasure beacon which for generations has shone out into the Glasgow night, reflected in the mirrored windows of rock band coaches, in rain-choked Gallowgate gutters, and in the eyes of music fans intent on the good time to end all good times. 'What can ye say, darlin'?' shrugged one young woman, standing in the queue for Biffy Clyro. 'The Barrowlands *is* the Barrowlands.' Put like that, again, it did not sound much, but it was a statement of pure love and everyone who heard it understood exactly what she meant.

It was 1934 when Maggie McIver, 'the Barras Queen', did a stately pleasure-dome decree. She had founded the famous market some years earlier, and now had the idea that her stall-holders ought to have a room of their own for conviviality and dancing, a place to slake throats parched by long days hawking wares – everything, as they say here, from a needle to an anchor. It opened on Christmas Eve, was known at that time as the Barrowland Palais de Danse, and soon had a house band, Billy McGregor and the Gaybirds, whose showmanship attracted a clientele far wider than that of the market traders. It entered Glasgow's bloodstream and, all these years later, is part of the city's pulse.

The Gaybirds were still playing by 1958 when a fire destroyed the original ballroom. On reopening at Christmas 1960, it looked much as we see it today. Foxtrot,

84

jitterbug, swing, twist, jive, whatever makes you feel alive – the hall has seen the dance crazes come and go, decades of joy and lust and heartbreak worn into that wooden floor, those emotions rising now, every show night, sensual and spectral in the air, just as the faint scent of resin rises on opening an antique jewellery box.

Since 1983, the ballroom has been a pole star for touring bands, many of whom regard their first concert there as a rite of passage and every subsequent show as a homecoming. Shirley Manson has performed here on seven occasions, the first with Goodbye Mr Mackenzie in 1987 and more recently with Garbage. 'The Barrowlands is the talisman of my entire career,' she says. 'That sounds so dramatic, but, then, life is short, why not be dramatic? It's a place that began my adventure, and every time I come back I'm reminded of that. Actually, I made a little speech to my band the last time we were there, backstage before we went on, saying how privileged I felt to be able to keep coming back thirty years from the first time I played.

'I've performed all over the world, in venues of all sizes, and still look forward to coming back to the Barrowlands because there's something incredibly magical about it. And it's not just me who has this view. You travel the world and the minute you meet a musician who knows you're Scottish, one of the first words out their mouth is "Barrowlands". Everyone connects with that place. It's the quintessential venue of our entire nation.'

Manson refers to the ballroom as 'she' – 'I always attribute greatness to women.' Does she, then, wish to send a sisterly greeting? 'Barrowlands already knows how much I love her. There's nothing more that needs to be said between me and her, other than I just hope coming generations understand the value in her and safeguard her future.'

Going to see a band here is different from seeing them anywhere else in Glasgow, or indeed in the whole of

Scotland. The energy and atmosphere; the smell of booze and burgers and perfume and anticipation. Dust and dry ice drift through blue, orange and pink lights. The ceiling is set with diamonds and stars; the latter being sought-after souvenirs for the musicians who play here. David Bowie was said to have one framed in the toilet of his Paris home.

At around 7 p.m., when the doors open, the crowds pour in like a swift half down a drouthy throat. Above them, hanging from the ceiling, is a cart wheel encircled in red neon. This is what remains of a model – a market trader pushing a barrow – that used to be on the roof. When the original ballroom burned, all that survived was this solitary cart wheel, so, on rebuilding, it was given pride of place above the stairs. Few, in their excitement to get in and see the band, even notice this holy relic, but it is the heart of the place, and to pass beneath is a sort of benediction. 'It almost feels,' says Nuala Naughton, author of *Barrowland: A Glasgow Experience*, 'that when you are walking up those stairs, the mantle of permission to go mental comes down and covers you.'

In the downstairs bar, punters sup in the glow of neon treble clefs. A stern sign warns Anyone Caught Throwing Drinks Will Be Immediately Ejected With No Refund. Some hope. The flung pint, love it or hate it, is one of the signature sights of this place, lager sparkling in the spotlights as a band take the stage in Lowry silhouettes. It may be to do with the location of the ballroom, the fact that it is earthed in the ancient centre of Glasgow, connecting it to some primal wildness, some Weegie leyline, which gives gigs here their reckless, outlaw air. Whatever the reason, there is at times a profound connection between that electric trinity – band, crowd and place. One thinks, perhaps, of Dylan in 2004, grinning and shaking his head at being barely able to hear himself sing 'Like A Rolling Stone'. One thinks of Big Country doing 'Chance' at Hogmanay. And one thinks, most of all, of The Pogues.

It was 11th September 1985. The previous night, as Scotland played Wales in Cardiff, Jock Stein had suffered a heart attack and died. Now, halfway through The Pogues' set in Glasgow, Cait O'Riordan dedicated 'I'm A Man You Don't Meet Every Day' to the late Celtic manager's memory. The crowd, as one and at once, begin to chant his name and did not stop for a long time. It was a perfect moment, gruffly tender, more moving than any speech at any wake.

'The Barras defined the band,' says Spider Stacy of The Pogues. 'It seemed a perfect fit: the band for the venue and the venue for the band. It's been a real regret to me that we haven't gone back and played there for a long time. Some rooms just have something in the air. When the room is full of people and the right band is on stage, there's an alchemy. The people who are there watching are the ones that make it happen. It's a testament to the audience's ongoing ability to transform the evening from just another gig into something that sears itself onto your memory.'

Spider talks about 'The Barras', a term which, if one is being pernickety, should be used only in reference to the market. The Barrowland Ballroom is the proper name of the dancehall. But, of course, everyone calls it Barrowlands. This is a pet hate of the manager Tom Joyes, who insists on 'Barrowland', singular, but he's fighting a losing battle. The plural sounds more natural, and for good reason – those of us who love this place each carry a slightly different personal version of it within our hearts and memories. The Barrowlands, regardless of title deeds, belongs to us all.

We should be honest about the things we love, and honesty requires an acknowledgement of the darkness of the Barrowlands. Nearly 2,000 fans going daft for 'Chelsea Dagger' or 'Chocolate Girl' tends to dampen the feelings of melancholy and even faint dread, but they are always present in the place, and especially apparent earlier in the day or in the small hours when the ballroom is quiet. One can speculate about the causes of this. One can talk about the serial killer Bible John, for whom the ballroom became a hunting ground between 1968 and 1969, his tenebrous footprints part of the patina of that floor. Whatever the reason, the feeling is real. The dancer and choreographer Michael Clark detected 'an amazing atmosphere of romance and violence' while working alone through the night, creating his Barrowlands Project in the ballroom in 2012. 'You can sense the history of the place,' he recalls. 'I love it. Glasgow has got this glamour to it, but it's quite brutal as well. There's a frightening aspect to the glamour and there's something very attractive in that.'

The broadcaster Tom Morton believes that part of the appeal lies in what the French call 'nostalgie de la boue – that desire to get back to an earthy notion of what rock 'n' roll ought to be about; back to the streets, down and dirty, smuggling quarter bottles in your socks through a toilet window.

'Barrowlands,' he says, 'is like an interactive industrial heritage park, only for music.'

During the 1970s and into the early '80s, Barrowlands struggled. The fear and disruption caused by the Bible John murders and investigation, and the simple fact of changing fashion, disco usurping 'the dancin', meant its popularity nosedived. In 1983, however, one single creative decision kickstarted its future. Simple Minds decided to film the video for their new single 'Waterfront' there – tapping directly into that association with Glasgow's industrial heritage.

Pop and rock musicians had performed in the ballroom before, but only the odd couple of songs squeezed between Gaybirds sets. No one had ever considered putting on a whole show there. 'Waterfront' was inspired by the thought of Glasgow being eternal, a sort of prayer for the resurrection of a once proud city. The pulse of the song – *dum de-dum de-dum de-dum* – was the beat of the tidal river. Bruce Findlay, the then manager of Simple Minds, had a concept that the video for 'Waterfront' should be filmed in an abandoned warehouse by the Clyde. Logistics made this impossible, so when the promoters Regular Music suggested that this old, half-forgotten dancehall in the east end might be available, his ears pricked up.

He walked in. It smelled a bit foosty, but looked perfect. Those stars on the ceiling, that bounce in the floor. He shouted into the emptiness and liked the sound. Not too echoey; not completely dead. 'Waterfront' was filmed there on 20th November 1983, a video which established an idea of Barrowlands as a place where band and audience could make profound communion. Through a song about rebirth, Barrowlands was reborn. It also proved a turning point for Simple Minds.

'Yes,' says Bruce Findlay, still excited at the memory, 'that was the breakthrough. The Apollo was owned by The Who, by Alex Harvey, by The Rolling Stones. The Barrowland was ours. We'd already had a big hit record with *New Gold Dream*, but in terms of becoming the people's champions, that opened the doors. And I love the fact that we were party to that place being revitalised. We made a no-go area into a "go" area.'

Since that Simple Minds show, there have been nearly 2,000 headline performances at the venue. Many of these are commemorated in the Album Pathway created, in a nearby park, by the artist Jim Lambie – one hundred metres of coloured concrete strips, each set with the name of the act and the date on which they performed.

To walk along this path, in the pouring rain, in the company of the Barrowlands' greatest fan is to understand just how meaningful the place can become in our lives. 'Been to that one,' he says, nodding at the path. 'That one. That one. That one.'

Campbell Stewart, a fiftysomething from Airdrie with a

Hobbit belly and a Gandalf beard, reckons he has attended more shows there than any other paying punter. Like, *hunners*. His first, Motörhead in 1984, was appropriate for such a hard rock aficionado, but his taste is eclectic to say the least. He is surely the only person in Scotland to have enjoyed concerts by both Simply Red and Sepultura. EMF, INXS, SLF – he has seen them all.

As we're talking, a middle-aged woman walks over. 'Brings back some memories?' she asks. This is Carol, out walking Bo, a black Lab, and Randy, a Labradoodle. She lives nearby and often takes the dogs past the big sign. 'That neon, man. Incredible.'

Stewart nods. 'That's where the buzz starts.'

'Absolutely. It's just an amazing place. Hopefully it'll be there forever.'

We carry on up the path, heading for Deep Purple, and Carol, Bo and Randy go on their way. It has been a brief encounter of a very Glasgow, a very Barras, sort; one based on a pleasure understood and shared.

'All right, guys,' she calls over her shoulder. 'Mibbe see you in the Barrowlands!'

The Burryman

JOHN NICOL, A South Queensferry man living in Leith, returned to his home town yesterday to make final practical and psychological preparations for the lead role in Scotland's oddest ceremony. By half-past eight on Friday morning, in a back room of The Staghead, one of nine pubs he will visit over the next eleven hours, his transformation into the Burryman is almost complete.

Nicol is a well built thirty-five-year-old, six foot two in his socks, but disappearing fast behind a spiky veneer of 11,000 seed pods, or burrs, from the burdock plant. These are being stuck all over his body by friends and family who could not be more chuffed about the ordeal he is about to endure. 'We are really proud of John,' says his mother, Senga, who has arranged flowers all over his bowler hat. 'But I worry all day. It's a hard thing he's going to do.'

Her son is standing with his arms folded across his chest, scowling with concentration, his long hair tied back. Over his trousers and T-shirt he has pulled long-johns and a thermal vest to which the burrs are stuck. Next he puts on a full-face balaclava. 'Goodbye, honey,' says his girlfriend, Emma. It sounds like the sort of joke couples make, but she's in earnest. Once the hood goes on and those final burrs are applied, Nicol no longer feels like himself. He has become the Burryman, a creature which some believe has walked the streets of Queensferry on every second Friday in August for the last 900 years. According to Doc Rowe, the folklorist who directs the dressing process, the first written mention of the ceremony is in the writing of Sir Walter Scott. Rowe is, I'm told, 'the Yoda of this ritual' –

91

the man who makes sure it is all done right. 'This is my thirtieth year of coming here,' he says. 'I've known five Burrymans, I think.'

Whatever his provenance, the duties of the Burryman are these: walk around Queensferry all day, never sitting down, never eating, never lowering your outstretched arms and never refusing whisky. In addition to the pubs, people come out on the street in front of their homes and offer a dram, holding the straw to the Burryman's lips. Often, these straws are green in acknowledgment of Nicol's love for Hibs. It is considered a great honour to have a drink with the Burryman and his two supporters, George Topping and Steven Cannon, who – tricked out in tartan trews – are responsible for helping him get around safely. This duty is compromised by the fact they match him drink for drink, but the lads do a grand job for all that. Nicol himself prefers 'a nice gin and tonic', but, out of respect for tradition, sticks with the whisky. The only clue to his increasing intoxication is the pinking of his eyes, just visible within the dark holes of his mask.

He has been Burryman for eleven years and – according to his mother – is minded to try for the record of twenty-seven. When he was first approached about becoming Burryman, the head of the selection committee asked him: 'Are you aware of the dangers? Are you fit? Are you able to take on board some whisky? Have you got some sensitivity to the tradition? And are you mental?' To all these, he answered yes.

At a quarter to nine by the Jubilee Clock, a lion rampant flag having been tied around his waist, Nicol is led from The Staghead. He is heralded by twelve-year-old Cameron Forrester who clangs a bell and sings, 'Hip hip hooray! It's the Burryman's day!' This anthem is taken up by many adults and children as we walk along High Street, stopping traffic, and up a steep hill. Red and yellow bunting is strung across the street, and there is a frolicsome air about the occasion, but something a little eerie too. The Burryman is a rather frightening figure; he looks like a malevolent cactus impersonating a Morris dancer, and it is little wonder that some boys and girls, seeing him pass, cower behind their mothers' legs. Just a few miles south-east, the Edinburgh Festival is in full swing, but nothing on offer there has the authentic strangeness and wonder of this.

Nicol grasps a floral staff in each fist; George and Steven each take one of his arms, holding them out from the sides of his body, and keep their eyes peeled for potholes. Already, Nicol is 'melting' inside the heavy costume. Itchy too. The burrs saw into his flesh as he walks. The pain, heat, whisky, lack of food and air, the restricted vision and movement – it's an intoxicating mix. You can black out if you're not careful.

'That's the frightening aspect,' he says. 'If you are over-confident about this, it will kick your arse. You need to be careful and respectful. That's why I take the week off work beforehand. It lets me rest and get into the right head space.'

Today, the problem is heavy rain, which makes it easier for the spikes to penetrate Nicol's clothes. But it's not raining hard enough to stop the wasps from buzzing round his head, attracted to the flowers. One year, a wasp crawled in an eye hole and stung him. He tries hard not to think about the fact that the burrs are teeming with insects – earwigs, millipedes, lots of little flies. 'You are a magnet for lots of horrible things,' he explains. 'But I don't think the Burryman should be moaning about anything. The Burryman should just take it.'

At 9 a.m. we make the first stop. This is at the house once occupied by the late James Milne, former provost of the town. He used to offer the first dram, and now his granddaughter Donna travels from Belfast each year to stand outside the home and give the Burryman a drink. This commitment is indicative of how seriously Queensferry takes the ceremony. The Burryman is part of the town's soul and collective memory. His passage through the streets is a celebration, but there's something elegiac about it too. We stop, for instance, outside a house on Stewart Terrace, where whisky has been left on a doorstep beneath a dishtowel.

'Drink to Harry on the train,' Steven Cannon instructs Nicol.

'Harry Docherty was a good Ferry lad,' Nicol explains to me. He died suddenly on the train back home from Edinburgh and was found on arrival in Dundee. Docherty used to love the Burryman visiting for a dram and so his widow, Mary, carries on the tradition.

The Burryman seems particularly meaningful for the very young, who regard him as a magical figure, and the very old, for whom he is a reminder of their own magic youth. Wee girls wearing angel wings or dalmatian-spot raincoats go up to Nicol and get burrs for luck. At 9.25 a.m., seventy-nine-year-old Betty Archibald offers the third whisky of the day. She's delighted to see Nicol. Her own father, Sam Corson, was Burryman just after the war. 'He did it just the one year,' she says.'They brought him hame in a wheelbarrow, he was that drunk.'

Inevitably, there are those for whom the ritual means nothing. A mystified workman laying a new road says: 'We're in Wicker Man country, I nearly shat myself when he came round the corner', and it is left to Nicol's father to explain the Burryman is supposed to bring good fortune. The idea is that evil sticks to the burrs and he thus cleanses the burgh, like some metaphysical nit comb. For forty-six-year-old Rick Compton, visiting from Florida, the pleasure he takes in this tradition is more basic: 'In Orlando, we got seven dwarves, fairy princesses, Mickey, Minnie and Goofy. But we don't have any Burlymen.'

Round and round the town we go – beneath the bunting, beneath the rainclouds, beneath the Forth Road Bridge.

At half-past eleven, Nicol nips behind some bushes in the Ferry Glen for the only toilet break he allows himself during the ritual. This necessitates being cut out of his costume and then sewn back up. There would be no disgrace in The Burryman wetting himself, he says, but he just can't bring himself to do it. 'He had a pee over there last year,' says Doc Rowe, that inexhaustible chronicler, pointing to a nearby spot.

At lunchtime we stop at Nicol's parents' house, where there is a gazebo in the garden for a party. Emma is there. Nicol sticks his tongue out through his mask of burrs, and she leans up to touch it with hers. A Burryman snog and it's on to the pubs. The Hawes, the Anchor, the Two Bridges, the Boat House, the Ferry Tap. Every entrance is greeted by applause. 'Is that, like, jaggy?' asks one young barman. Yes, it, like, is. The burrs are digging into the skin of his face. 'I take comfort,' Nicol says, 'from the fact that there's some sort of symbolism in my pain.' Too right. As the afternoon wears on, as the Burryman stoats slowly along the cobbles, the ritual no longer feels like a joyful pageant; it's more like the self-flagellating procession of a penitent, and the unceasing clanging of the bell takes on a woozy, hallucinatory air.

At 6 p.m., after drinking the last whisky of the day, his twentieth, in just two sooks, Nicol staggers to the back room of The Staghead and, seated in the middle of the dance floor, is cut from his burry prison. It is, he says, a feeling of being reborn. His hair is tousled, his clothes sweat-soaked, and he has blood all over his back. But it's the ecstasy on his face as his boots are removed that will stay with me.

'Oh!' he slurs. 'It's worth it just for that, eh?'

Balnakeil

GO NORTH. Follow that magnetic arrow six hours out of the Central Belt, far from the crowd of maddies, and carry on until you almost run out of land; then, at Durness, take a left, crest the brow of a rise, and you're there – Balnakeil Craft Village, the most north-westerly community in Britain, laid out below you in all its turreted whitewashed strangeness. This is what you have come to see.

'As you come over the top coast road,' says Anita Wilson, one of around forty residents, recalling the first time she ever saw her future home, 'there's nothing, nothing, nothing, nothing, nothing, *nothing*. It was November, and although it was beautiful there was still nothing there. Then you come round and you hit Ceannabeinne beach and Durness and Balnakeil, and it either really appeals to you, or you think, "I'll never come here again in my life." Well, I just kept coming back. I'd always been around artists and musicians, and I didn't have a nine-to-five attitude, so it just seemed like an awesome sort of place. It's a more natural way of being.'

Balnakeil Craft Village is fifty years old this year ... probably. None who live there would quite swear to the anniversary, though neither would they deny it entirely. Out on the frayed edge of mainland Britain is a place where notions of time have become tattered. No one seems able to remember the exact date of anything. Changing seasons, tides, the bloom of the wild poppies, the boom of the bombing exercises at Cape Wrath which take place each February and September – these are the temporal markers that count around here.

The 'village' is like no village you will have ever seen; a cluster of around thirty bunker-like concrete buildings, single-storey, flat-roofed, each with a large rectangular water-tower pointing accusingly at an overcast sky. Some are decorated with fishing buoys, artfully hung, and bright murals of flowers and sunbursts, but there is no denying the utilitarian shape of the homes themselves. They are blunt, brutalist, built in 1954 by the Ministry of Defence to house and cater for the staff of a planned military radar station which was being constructed on the nearby prom-ontory, Faraid Head. These were barracks, mess rooms, a medical bay, a canteen. Then something happened. Local legend has it that the Russians shaved a couple of minutes off the time it would take for a nuclear missile to travel to the UK, meaning that any early warnings from Sutherland would not be quite early enough. The station became obsolete, and in the late 1950s, the buildings at Balnakeil were abandoned to the locals and the elements. Windows and fittings were broken, birds nested, and the salty wind scoured each breeze-block shell.

'Oh, it was an eyesore,' says Hugh Powell, an eighty-four-year-old sculptor who lives, with his wife Molly, in the old manse next to the village. 'It was getting smashed up and people were stealing the lead. Nobody knew what to do with it.'

Powell, in 1963, was head of industrial design at Leeds College of Art. At Easter, he drove up to Sutherland for the first time, in a Volkswagen caravanette, carrying a load of drainpipes for a friend's septic tank. While he was unload-ing these at the side of Loch Laxford, a little boat pulled up alongside, containing within it two worthies from Suther-land County Council. They were on their way to Balnakeil to discuss what could be done to prevent it from falling into further ruin. Powell, who knew that many of his students would love to work in a place like this, suggested that it be converted into a community for artists and crafts-people.

And that was that. Powell bought the manse; the money was used by the council to purchase the rest of the buildings from the MoD, and adverts were placed in the newspapers calling for tenants. Rent was set at £5 a year, for which you got your freezing concrete bunker, without electricity or running water, and found yourself living in what is, arguably, the most wondrous landscape in the whole of these isles. This was known as The Far North Project. It drew dreamers, wild-schemers, the unorthodox and the idealistic. The first person to move in was Hector Riddell, a silversmith from Turriff, followed in short order by a worm-farmer.

'When we first came there were just three or four others and the buildings were totally vandalised,' recalls Lotte Glob, a Danish artist who now lives nearby in a croft overlooking Loch Eriboll. She and her husband, Dave Illingworth, were among the early settlers. 'We came on July 24th 1968, at three in the morning, with two babies, a dog, a small electric kiln, a potter's wheel, a ton of clay and five pounds in our pocket. There was a huge military exercise going on, with helicopters flying overhead. We had a lot of choice of buildings because so many were empty. We chose the old hospital. Windows were broken, doors were broken, the toilet was ripped out and you could look straight into the sewer. There was no power. All the copper pipe was pulled out. We found one room with a door and a window where we settled down with the kids. They were two-and-a-half and six months old. We didn't have electrics for three months and I had to wash nappies in the stream. It was tough, but I was only twenty-four. So.'

You've got to love that 'so'. It speaks to a certain devil-may-care, last-roll-of-the-fluffy-dice attitude among those who came to Balnakeil then, and to an extent among those who still come today. It takes just ten minutes to walk around the village, which is picturesque in a rough, bohemian sort of way. Early in the day, you see more cats than people. A line of bright washing is strung between two drainpipes, a wagtail perches on a rusty mangle, the wind howls like God blowing across the neck of a bottle.

It is the height of summer yet the weather is poor. The oystercatchers have the beach to themselves. A woman hanging out clothes explains that up here every item, even unto the humblest sock, requires several pegs to hold it in place. Most of the craft village is, these days, residential, with interior decor ranging from chintzy suburban to shabby freak-pad. You never quite know whether you are walking into the set of *Abigail's Party* or *Withnail and I*. There are, however, still a number of businesses here, among them a bakery, a busy boatyard and the most remote bookshop in mainland Britain. You can buy chocolates, paintings and crafty knick-knacks from the people who made them by hand. You can get your trumpet fixed. There is even a masonic lodge, with carved square and compasses on the door, in the old helicopter fuel store; odd, one might think, but then where better for freemasons to practise their craft than in a craft village?

Arguably, though, the most precious commodity in Balnakeil are the people themselves. You get all sorts and then some, and then some more.

Philipp Tanzer, who is thirty-five, has moved from Dresden to become the village's newest resident. He plans to open a hairdressing salon and massage parlour. A one-time holder of the title German Mr Leather, he has had notable success as an actor in gay pornographic films. His *annus mirabilis*, 2009, saw him win best duo sex-scene, best three-way sex scene and best actor at the Grabby Awards. He performs under the name Logan McCree, a homage to his love for Scotland, his love for the comic-book character Wolverine and his love for God (McCree being derived from the Gaelic for 'son of the King'). His body is covered in tattoos, including the Archangel Michael on his chest.

He has been coming to Scotland on holiday for many

years, wild camping with a friend from his time in the military. 'I feel at home here,' he says. 'It just feels very familiar.'

He has built his home and business premises on his own, mostly. Although it looks striking now, with a wolfskin on one wall and stuffed birds of prey glaring down from various perches, it has been a struggle. For the first week of construction he slept in the car, then – during a storm – built a shed and subsequently slept in there with his dog, Ares, a husky-shepherd cross. 'Then a hurricane blew off parts of my roof and it rained for weeks. There is still a lot of humidity in my house and my floor is warped.'

He remains without electricity and water, lost fifteen kilos during the build, and seems exhausted. Yet he is determined to finish what he has started. He has had what sounds like a turbulent life, one of those people with too much past, his mother having been murdered when he was sixteen, and it must be hoped that he is able to find peace and a future in Balnakeil. Certainly, the locals seem untroubled by the way he has earned a living. 'Oh, the porn star?' says John Morrison, the ferryman, when asked about Tanzer. 'Aye, he's good craic.'

Morrison, in his sixties, is the only Sutherland native living in the village, this being a place which tends to attract its recruits from among city-dwellers keen to leave the rat-race far, far behind. No one calls him Mr Morrison, much less John. He is known as Carbreck after the old cottage where he was brought up and which his late mother is reputed to haunt – in company with a spectral wildcat.

Carbreck has been the ferryman for many a year, taking folk back and forth across the Kyle of Durness, a crossing of only a few minutes, though tricky with treacherous sandbanks, which gives access to the wilderness of Cape Wrath. He has bright blue eyes and a weatherbeaten face full of character and mischief. He keeps a bottle of twenty-year-old Macallan under the seat of his boat against the hope that one fine night he might catch a decent fish and feel the need to toast his success with an equally decent whisky. Between May and September, the tourist season, he makes eight to ten crossings each day, seven days a week, there being, as he puts it, 'No God in Durness in the summertime.' He has raised his family in the craft village and has been, in his time, a lorry driver, a ghillie and a stalker of deer. He is also much in demand as an accordionist. Yet ferryman seems to have been his calling, just as his father's vocation was shepherd – the last shepherd on Cape Wrath. 'Thirty years, aye,' says Carbreck, 'and I've never regretted it at all.'

It takes a certain sort of person to make a go of things here. Not everyone can thole Ultima Thule. There was a documentary made about the craft village in 1974, one of those now unintentionally hilarious BBC jobs in which a sub-Alan Whicker in turtleneck and moustache headed north to marvel urbanely at the hippy kids who were, in every sense, totally far out. 'You know,' he says at the start, peering over the steering wheel of his Land Rover at the snowy single-track, 'this might be the loneliest road in Europe ... If you started at the toe of Italy and drove right up to the north-west of the Common Market, this is where you'd end, at a place called Durness, and there's nothing between you and the Arctic then but miles and miles of sea.'

Of the villagers interviewed in the documentary, only one remains resident. Liz Harvey, almost four decades on, is still recognisable as the rather melancholy young woman with a curtain of hair who had moved from London. Today, she smokes a hand-rolled fag at her work-bench, which is covered in obscure leather-working tools, as she recalls what brought her here. It was the late 1960s and she was managing to find some work making clothes for Carnaby Street, but it wasn't easy to earn a living as a craftsperson then. So she and her husband were looking for a new start.

'Pete was much more adventurous than me,' she says. 'I have to be dragged along. But we made an appointment and came up and were interviewed by a local councillor. Pete brought his big transistor radio to see if we could get a decent signal for Radio 3 and John Peel. If we hadn't, we wouldn't have stayed.' But they did.

The marriage ended in the mid-1970s and Liz left Balnakeil for a year, returning to her family in Oxford, but for reasons that she finds, at this distance, difficult to explain, she came back and made her life here. It was something to do with space and time to think. The aloneness seemed necessary. So now she lives with the radio and roll-ups, at 125 feet above sea level, with purple geraniums around the door.

Summer brings tourists and income to Balnakeil (Durness receives in excess of 20,000 visitors annually) but the dying year brings slow time, darkness, the cold and sometimes loneliness. 'In the winter, very often, people meet for coffee on Sunday mornings because it increases the conversation level for the week,' says Anita Wilson of Cast Off Crafts, whose constant companion is her spaniel, Wee Shuggy. 'You might go for a couple of weeks without talking to anybody.' It isn't silent, though. The south-westerly wind makes window panes sing and bulge.

Interpersonal relationships, in such circumstances, can become intense. 'People don't hide behind façades in a setting like this,' says Undine Downie, known as Charlie, a German woman who has lived in the village since 1988. 'People feel free to open up and say what's happening in their lives. People share their emotions more freely and feel safe to do that.

'It goes beyond borrowing a cup of sugar. I think it is because it is so remote that we are so intimate. It's got the downside that you don't have a great deal of private life. If you want a private life, move into the city or become an arsehole that nobody will talk to. Those are the options.'

The fiftieth anniversary, according to some, is a pivotal moment for Balnakeil. There are about half the number of craft businesses there were during the late 1970s, most residents are middle-aged to elderly, and there are no children living there now. A looming demographic crisis? It is difficult for newcomers to set up home in the village; the Thatcherite right-to-buy scheme meant that the buildings passed into private ownership. They have, in many cases, increased in value enormously and come up for sale only rarely. You could not now arrive in the middle of the night with a fiver and a ton of clay and start to build a new life.

There is much talk now of fundraising and development plans and consultancy firms; of finding a way to make Balnakeil more attractive to visitors, and affordable for artists and crafts people who may wish to make it their home.

'This is a crunch point where the craft village will either pick itself up and grow, or lose its identity and become just a collection of buildings that are holiday homes, places that people live, and one or two remaining businesses,' says Kevin Arrowsmith of the Durness Development Group. 'I would hate to see it all fall apart.'

Indeed. This area of Sutherland has a troubled history of occupation and land ownership. In the 1840s, crofters were evicted from a number of local townships as part of the Clearances, to make way for sheep. Recently, the Scottish Government backed a community buy-out of land around the lighthouse at Cape Wrath. It is possible to see the story of the craft village in this socio-political context and against the backdrop of a longer human history of people who value these wild places and choose to live their lives amid such emptiness. For the military, Balnakeil was a front line in the Cold War; for the people who live here now it remains frontier territory, a place of essentials and extremes.

'There is the land and the sky,' says Liz Harvey, 'and you are sort of between the two.'

The Circus

BACKSTAGE AT ZIPPO'S, seventy-six-year-old Norman Barrett, unblushingly billed as 'the world's greatest ring-master', is waiting to make his entrance. He stands, head bowed, behind red velvet, the spotlight passing through a gap between the curtains, painting a silver stripe down the front of his body from top hat to shoes, and intensifying the already considerable twinkle in his bright blue eyes. He punches a white-gloved fist into a white-gloved palm, psyching himself up, and, as the curtains open, steps into the familiar glare and roar, a perfect grin transforming features which a moment ago were serious, perhaps even steely. 'My lords, ladies and gentlemen,' he bellows, 'welcome to the circus!'

It shouldn't exist any more, the old-fashioned circus. Health and safety legislation, political correctness, and the ever increasing sophistication of children should, in theory, have done for the big top and its motley denizens. The fact that circuses continue to tour Scotland and still seem able to pull considerable crowds is a cause for cheer. It shows that we haven't grown so jaded that we can't be thrilled and delighted by the ingenuity and pluck which these performers demonstrate twice daily during the season.

There is nothing quite like the circus. It is the complete sensory experience. The audience, packed closely together in our banked plastic seats, feels snug in the dusky humidity, yet alert to everything from flames reflected in a fire-eater's eyes to the chessboard design combed into a stallion's glossy rump. There is a gaudy, bawdy beauty to all of this. I could spend the whole show looking away from the ring, entranced instead by the shadow of the rising trapeze artist as it spreads like a dark stain across the canvas roof.

The arrival of the circus is part of the texture of summer. Riggers raise that tent in just a few hours. Somehow, the public never see it happen. It seems to spring up overnight like a great hallucinogenic mushroom. Zippo's big top is a creamy white with Saltires and lions rampant fluttering from the poles. The air, as one approaches, smells of cut grass and sawdust and diesel and popcorn and horse muck. Inside, before the show, the ring is sunk in undersea gloom. The performers – or 'artistes' as they are known with typical circus emphasis on genteel formality – are, a few hours before showtime, still relaxing in the huge wagons in which they travel. These are real homes, complete with all mod cons, satellite dishes propped up on bricks and pointing skywards.

Grooms, bent like Pissarro peasants, stagger beneath bales of straw through the mud towards the stables. There are many people who loathe the whole idea of animals in the circus, but my own impression is that the horses look well because they are looked after well, rather like the working animals one sees on decently run farms. There are, indeed, a number of Weegie glamazons sitting in the audience who would pay good money for a beauty regime even approximate to that of these pampered palominos.

In addition to fifteen artistes, Zippo's travels with riggers, mechanics, electricians and carpenters, adding up to about forty people on the road together for ten months of the year. The travelling circus is often likened to a family, and within it there are actual family groups – husbands and wives, parents and children and siblings. It is a close, sultry atmosphere in which romances and enmities, like hothouse flowers, blossom with greater speed than they would in the more temperate outside world. 'Oh, yes,' says one artiste, rolling his eyes. 'People are falling in and out of love all the time.'

Andrea and Emil, the Delbosq Clowns, became engaged earlier in the tour, Emil going down on one knee in the ring – a circus tradition – and asking for Andrea's hand in front of the cheering crowd. They have, in fact, been together a couple for years and have a three-year-old son, who snoozes in a pushchair backstage while his parents administer comic beatings to each other in the ring. 'It's not easy because we're on tour all the time,' says Emil. 'But I think about it this way – my grandmother went on the road with eight kids and we've only got one.'

'At the moment,' Andrea adds, pointedly.

Meeting the artistes is fascinating; an exotic lot, Pollyannas and polyglots. Ask a question in French and you'll get a cheerful answer in Spanish, Romanian or Italian. 'We speak circus', is how one puts it.

The Ukraine, a country in which the circus is nationalised, is well represented at Zippo's. Roman Stefanyuk, a forty-three-year-old Ukrainian clown who can do remarkable things on a trampoline, used to be a gymnast and was trained during the great Soviet era of state-sponsored sport. In his home country, he says, circus artistes receive pensions and benefits. Clowns in Britain have nothing to fall back on.

Still, performing in a circus seems more like an inherited obligation than a job one might choose to do. In the hours I spend hanging around backstage, I meet only one 'josser' – the slang word for a circus worker who was not born into it. This is Kane Safronoskas, an eighteen-year-old from Swindon who, as ringboy, is charged with taking props in and out of the ring. It is his great ambition to become a clown. 'My mum didn't want me to join the circus,' he says, 'but she knew she couldn't stand in the way of my dreams.'

The artistes, by contrast, all seem to come from circus dynasties. They are the third generation in their family; the fifth, the seventh, the eleventh. This great-great-aunt, a trapeze artist, performed for Queen Victoria; that great-grandfather, a unicyclist, for Nicholas II. The sense of history and swirling DNA is more dizzying than anything in the ring.

Norman Barrett the ringmaster is a relative newcomer, if one can say so about a septuagenarian who has been in the business since 1948. His father was a farmer with a taste for training animals; George Barrett first joined a circus and then bought his own. Norman grew up in show business. He started out in his early teens with a goat and dog act – 'the goats jumped through hoops and the dogs jumped over the goats' – and then spent some time as a rather poor clown before his potential as a ringmaster was recognised in the late 1950s. He is very much in favour of elegance, gets his scarlet tail-coats made by Geno, an old Italian tailor in Preston, and believes that the most important tool in the ringmaster's kit is a decent shoehorn, the better to ensure quick backstage changes from wellies to dress shoes. 'The best shoehorns,' he confides, 'are from Ikea.'

Barrett has, since 1962, performed a bird act. Since before The Beatles he has had budgies. They pull a toy car, fire a little cannon, climb a tower and unfurl a Saltire. It is quite splendid. The ringmaster uses eight birds in his act – Willie, Manfred, Jonti, Albert, Percy, Morris, Fred and Albert – but travels with fourteen. 'It's like a football team,' he says. 'The performance is only as good as the reserves.' When one bird dies, a new bird inherits the old name, which keeps things simple. There must have been a great many Freds and Alberts over the years.

Budgies have a reasonable lifespan – the ringmaster has a nine-year-old veteran in his act – but they are also extremely sensitive and have been known to pass away from fright during thunderstorms. With the blithe air of one whose own money was not involved, Barrett tells the story of a man in Birmingham who paid £2,000 for a budgie which could say twenty-eight phrases – only for it to die the following day. Its last words? 'I told you I was ill.'

During Zippo's 5 p.m. performance, I go behind the scenes to watch the entrances and exits. It is a cramped and busy space, wet grass covered in sawdust, but somehow no one ever gets in anyone else's way. A Shetland pony called Baz breaks wind gently. The Delbosq Clowns slurp Coke and roll cigarettes. Gabriel Carmonna, a graduate of the National Academy of Tango in Buenos Aires, sprays water on his long black hair so that it will not catch fire as he swings burning bolas round his head with his teeth.

To the audience each routine looks effortless, but the artistes are dripping sweat when they return behind the curtain. The grand finale is the Globe of Death – three Brazilian motorcyclists looping-the-loop within a small steel cage at approximately fifty miles per hour while Paula, wife of the lead biker, stands inside, wearing a feather headdress and a fixed grin. Paula finds this terrifying, but trusts the riders, and thus far has sustained greater injuries from her other circus job – operating the candyfloss machine. Nevertheless, the moments before the act are tangibly anxious. The Brazilians huddle to pray before mounting their golden Yamahas, and Paula crosses herself behind the curtain. When, a few minutes later, the four return unhurt, the sense of relief is even more palpable than the earlier anxiety.

One can understand why the artistes say they find this way of life addictive – the adrenalin buzz must quickly become a physiological need. Nevertheless, it is astonishing to think that they will all be doing this again in a couple of hours, then tomorrow and tomorrow and tomorrow.

'Circus will never die,' says Emil Delbosq with an air of proud defiance in no way undermined by his red nose. 'This is our job, our passion, and we give it our all.'

on, cold beers. 'You pit yourself against your friends to see who can lift the heavier stone. The heavier it is, the better I like it.' He shrugged hairy shoulders; pressed a plug of Icelandic tobacco up a nostril. 'It's just what we do. We throw big rocks. It's in our genes, I guess.'

More than sixty Highland Games take place in Scotland each year between May and September. Cash prizes are on offer for those winning the different heavy athletics disciplines. The money isn't huge but it adds up. A high-performing 'heavy' could walk away from a middle-range games with £500 cash in his sporran, and if he is able to travel to two or more each week during the summer, he can earn a decent whack. At Inveraray, home of the World Caber Championships, there is £400 for the winner of that event alone. There are expenses, of course, notably fuel for vehicles and those cavernous, ravenous bodies – 'You eat more than you win,' says one Scottish competitor – but, especially for those athletes who come from eastern Europe and the Baltic states, the Scottish games represent an opportunity to boost their incomes considerably.

The Wenta brothers, Sebastian and Lukas, are regular winners on the scene – iron bros, made in Poland from girders. They come from the town of Tczew. Sebastian still lives there, working as a house builder, but Lukas moved to East Kilbride eighteen months ago and has found work as a mechanic. Lukas is the younger and smaller, aged thirty-five, and relatively puny at a mere six foot six and 120 kilos. Sebastian, known as Wentyl, has four years and an inch on his brother, and weighs 155 kilos; his neck is almost two feet around, as are his biceps. But those are mere statistics. What they don't give you is the look of the man: an extraordinary genetic splice of Eric Cantona and Popeye's nemesis Bluto; the crucifix gleaming between his pecs is a golden statue in an alcove above the flying buttress of his belly. Wentyl is more gothic architecture than flesh, a soaring cathedral of meat and muscle. His nickname on the scene – 'housewife's choice' – comes larded in irony.

'Why Highland Games?' he says in broken English. 'For me, very good events. How many will I go to this year? I think twenty. My best – twenty-nine – two years ago. Scotland is good place.'

Sebastian, I ask, have you always been so big?

'*Tak*,' he replies. 'Yes.'

There are fourteen athletes taking part at Inveraray, only six of whom are Scottish. The international contingent comprises the Wentas, Heisi, an American, an Irishman, a Swiss, and a German with *Schottland* written across his T-shirt. England is represented by Scott Rider, a shot putter who has escaped for the day from the athletes' village of the Commonwealth Games in order to attempt a defence of his caber world title. The Scots, inspired perhaps by the cosmopolitan air, are keen to show off their foreign language skills: 'The weather today,' muses Stuart Anderson from Lochearnhead, 'is fuckin' scorchio.'

Six homegrown athletes out of fourteen is considered a decent ratio these days. You go to some games and there isn't a single Scot. Heavies do not receive the funding given to Scots competing in mainstream athletics – discus, shot putt etc – and there is concern that without future support, the talent gap between us and the rest of the world will widen until, as the Highland games historian David Webster has written, 'Scotland's wonderful heavies may be in danger of becoming an extinct species'.

Despite this prospect of national embarrassment, there's no noticeable tension at Inveraray, which is one of the few games to offer a separate tier of prize money for native competitors in order to make it worthwhile for Scots to show up; indeed, a fist-bumpingly fraternal air of friendly rivalry seems to characterise the heavy athletics scene. 'We welcome anybody,' says Stephen King, Inveraray's 'local heavy', a title with a happier resonance than it would have in, say, Govan. 'We'll throw against anybody. We'll take them on and beat them.'

Listen a little closer, though; talk to people off the record, and you do get to hear suspicion and resentment given sour voice. 'You are aware that most of the foreign athletes are junkies?' says one Scottish competitor on the phone. 'They've got arses like pin cushions. They don't care about tradition. They don't have any morals. They just want the prize money and they'll win at any cost.'

The Scottish Highland Games Association has worked with UK Anti-Doping to carry out random tests for a range of banned substances including anabolic steroids and growth hormones. There have been fifty or so tests carried out since 2009, and only one athlete, an American, has tested positive. He was banned for two years.

The World Highland Games Heavy Events Championships, which is not SHGA-affiliated, also operates a random testing policy. 'I have not ever taken any steroids or any performance-enhancing drugs,' says Daniel McKim, the thirty-two-year-old from Kansas City who is the current US and previous world champion. 'I hate to see it come in and be a part of our sport, but it is.'

Is doping widespread in Highland Games?

'Not like in strongman or power-lifting, but it is and it's growing, I feel.'

McKim is a fascinating character. Six foot five and 300 pounds (above which weight he snores horribly, much to his wife Natalie's displeasure) he looks like an all-American Hulk – blond-haired, bright-eyed and totally, totally pumped – driven by rapture rather than rage.

The son of a preacher man, raised in Maryville, a small Missouri farming town, he is a devout Christian and father to five boys. He holds Bible study classes before Sunday Games, inviting his 'brothers in bulk' to pray, and identifies with Behemoth, the awesome and mysterious creature described in the Book of Job: 'Behold now, his strength in his loins and his power in the muscles of his belly. He bends his tail like a cedar; the sinews of his thighs are knit together. His bones are tubes of bronze; his limbs are like bars of iron.'

McKim competes at the Highland Games for the glory of God; the divine, he feels, is revealed through his strength. 'When I turn the caber,' he says. 'I want people to see and understand Him, not me.'

The world championships move around the globe. McKim won his 2013 world title in Dana Point, California. This year the venue is the slightly less sun-kissed Pittencrieff Park, Dunfermline. Unlike most Scottish Games, the championships are invitation-only, and so today's field of ten, including two Scots, represent some of the world's strongest men. For those who have flown here from across the Atlantic, the grumbling of Iceland's Bardarbunga volcano is a concern. If it erupts, their return flights may be cancelled, leading to the one thing these toughs truly fear – angry wives.

It is no accident that the world championships are taking place here, in a beautiful park overlooked by Dunfermline Abbey, the last resting place of Malcolm Canmore. As the historian David Webster, dazzling today in full Highland dress, explains in his running commentary, the eleventh-century King of Scotland held what can be regarded as a progenitor of the modern Games in the year 1040. The real flowering of Games took place during the nineteenth century, however, their popularity boosted greatly by the patronage of Queen Victoria.

Webster, an Aberdonian, is an important figure in the development of Games overseas. He attended his first Games in 1937. On his first visit to the Braemar Gathering he had no interest in the presence of King George VI, being captivated instead by strongman royalty – the sculpted specimens of Scottish manhood busy with stones and caber. Webster has been organising Games since the early 1950s and is the founder of these championships. He is a Zelig-like figure, internationally ubiquitous in his blue Balmoral bunnet. Just back from one Games in Ontario, he is about to fly to another – in San Francisco.

For several years Webster was chief judge of the strongest man competition at Arnold Schwarzenegger's sports festival in Ohio. Arnie and he are pals from way back. 'I've known him since he was nineteen,' says Webster. 'He was a body-builder and I was a judge at Mr Universe in London. He's always pulling my leg about my age. He says I was a wine waiter at the Last Supper.'

Since the nineteenth century, when ex-pats formed Scottish societies in America, Canada, Australia and New Zealand, our native heavies have crossed the oceans to compete. The best known was Donald Dinnie from Aboyne, a globetrotting Victorian superstar, all waxed moustache and constant kilt; despite his huge earnings, millions in today's money, he refused to spend any of it on trousers.

The promotion of Highland Games overseas accelerated during the 1960s, '70s and '80s as Webster took groups of heavies on tours of America, Canada, Scandinavia and Japan. Also important during the same period was Douglas Edmunds, a heavy athlete, well-connected, who has promoted the sport and culture worldwide. Edmunds is a giant of the Games, literally and figuratively, twice world caber champion. The World Highland Games Heavy Events Championships are staged by Edmunds and his family, organised from their home in Carmunnock, a sort of ranch for heavies in which, at any given moment, one can stop by and find Russia's strongest man singing Leadbelly songs in the front garden.

Edmunds is known on the scene as The Godfather and, as he is rather unwell at the moment, spends his time at Dunfermline seated at the side of the field, a Don Corleone-ish presence, black-clad and crag-faced, receiving tribute from the international athletes who approach for respectful handshakes and the chance of a few words.

'I've been involved in the Highland Games since I was seventeen and I'm now seventy,' he says. 'I've been involved in more Highland Games, either as organiser or as an athlete, than anybody else in history. One of the things I've always tried to do is bring the Games into prominence. It annoys the hell out of me that the Scottish Government and others don't recognise their economic and cultural importance. Everybody and their granny's wee society seems to get funding, but not the Games. There's this idea that they are always going to be there, but they are not. The Games are in decline, and without foreign athletes they'd be in big trouble.'

Edmunds believes that as well as creating an exotic, crowd-friendly spectacle, the international heavies raise the standard, forcing domestic athletes to train hard if they are to have a hope of winning. He is strongly opposed to the system of having two tiers of prizes – one exclusively for the Scots. 'To me, that's just looking after your own midden-heap. It's a pathetic attempt to keep your wee pot of money to yourself, and not in the interests of the Games at all.'

The foreigners certainly bring character. Look at Burger Lambrechts, the South African shot putter, a former Commonwealth Games gold medallist now enjoying an Indian summer as a heavy. Six foot six, built from bricks, in his spare time he likes to write poetry and hunt wildebeest. On arrival at Glasgow Airport, asked to state his business, he peered down at the customs officers from beneath the brim of his leather bush hat and declared: 'I am here to learn to be a tosser.' The officials, unamused, spent a long time questioning him. Thus, a lesson was learned – in Scotland we like our burgers properly grilled.

Alan Hebert, a fifty-seven-year-old Californian with a bandana and Abe Lincoln beard, isn't in it for the money or glory. 'I'm not here to win,' he said in Inveraray. 'I'm here to be here.' Visiting Scotland for the first time, he was keen to see the lands of his ancestors, and to fit competing around hiking with his wife. An IT guy at Stanford University, he has swapped Silicon Valley for testosterone glen and is having the time of his life. He's what you might call 'a lad o' pairts' – an accomplished sailor and clarinetist, he plays in a klezmer band and makes his own kilts. He doesn't care that he's the oldest guy on the field – 'If I stop, I'll die. So I ain't stopping.' He's moved by the idea that the rocks and weights he is throwing in Scotland have been graced by the skin and sweat of the great heavies of the past.

'If you're a thrower, this is heaven,' he said. 'A lot of these tough Scottish guys probably wouldn't say this, but it's spiritual. It's simple and it's spiritual and it's good for your head.'

There is a certain grim irony in the fact that Games in North America and elsewhere draw huge crowds – tens of thousands in some cases – while the Scottish originals are often precarious; run by volunteers, short of cash, only ever a couple of wet summers away from oblivion. Yet a Highland Games on a sunny day can be a wondrous thing: the skirl and birl of pipes and dancers; the picnic rugs, the Scottie dugs; and most of all the true spirit of athleticism. It is too easily forgotten, amid all the tartan hoo-ha, that for the heavies these events are a serious business. 'We're here to compete. We're not here to entertain the fuckin' tourists,' Stephen King said in Inveraray. He is forty-five, has been throwing for thirty years, and set two world records in the light and heavy hammers; yet, as he says, he has never once appeared on the sports pages of his local paper. He wants respect – for himself, for his peers, for the tradition of his sport. He finds the kitschy focus of the media maddening. 'It is not my sporting ambition,' he said, 'to get my picture printed on a tea towel.'

Given this lack of appreciation, it's understandable that the present dominance of foreign athletes might stick in a few craws. Yet to outsiders, the personalities of some of these heavies are hard to resist.

Take Matt Vincent. A thirty-one-year-old from Baton Rouge, Louisiana, he is six feet tall, 270 pounds, and has thighs so large they make Chris Hoy's look like Kate Moss's. These serve to distract somewhat from his feet, which is a shame as he has DIRTY SOUTH tattooed across his toes; the nails painted robin's egg blue and decorated with dainty golden anchors. Vincent has worked as a bouncer in a strip club, a tour manager for a rock band, and is now a sales rep in the oil industry. He describes himself as 'equal parts asshole, clown, hipster and vagabond'. His voice is all bluegrass and mint juleps when he says: 'I enjoy gettin' pissed every now and then and causin' a little trouble. You gotta live, too.'

He likes to travel, smoke good cigars, eat foie gras when he can find it. He wears sunglasses and a baseball cap while casually throwing a fifty-six-pound weight over a bar sixteen feet above his head. He listens to heavy metal on headphones to drown out the Dunfermline District Pipe Band. His socks are pink, his humour black. If he were a fictional character, he says, it'd be Patrick Bateman from *American Psycho*. He quotes Nietzsche and Henry Rollins. He trains long and hard, motivated by idealism and self-loathing, and it is hard to imagine anyone more distant from the clichéd porridge-packet image of a heavy; yet this is the guy who this year, right there in Dunfermline, wins the world championship. The best Highland Games athlete in the world is a freakadelic Hercules with bourbon breath and a molasses drawl. And why not?

'Winning in Scotland feels fuckin' great,' he says afterwards, already packing his flight case. 'Now it's back to the States. Volcano permitting.'

117

The Bass Rock

THE BASS ROCK, by half-past seven, is still a few miles distant, but already filling the skipper's window, a dark and frosted hump rising from the leaden water as if some leviathan were surfacing for air.

I had left Glasgow at a little before five in the morning, the only car on the road; the eyes of startled foxes shone green as traffic lights. It would have been possible to take the lunchtime sailing instead, but I had wanted that feeling of travelling beyond the quiet dark city, from the centre to the edge, towards the noise and wildness and whiteness of the Bass. Already, as the *Fisher Lassie* ploughs through the waves, Dunbar harbour feels very far behind.

'Just look at that,' says Gordon Easingwood, the skipper, nodding towards the island. 'Would you no' say that's awesome?' Being a sixty-three-year-old lobsterman and not a daft teenage boy, Easingwood is using the word 'awesome' in its older, truer meaning of something weird, almost dreadful, provoking reverential fear and wonder. And he's quite right. The Bass Rock is awesome. Robert Louis Stevenson, in *Catriona*, called it 'an unco place by night, unco by day' and noted its unsettling sounds, worse on calm evenings, when the haunting noise of water in the tunnel that runs through the crag jangles the nerves of anyone attempting to sleep.

The Bass Rock is a huge lump of volcanic clinkstone, 350 feet high, red with iron in places and in others a serrated grey. At its base, where it meets the Firth of Forth, it bristles with limpets and is slick with kelp. From the air, or from the battlements of Tantallon Castle, it looks like an iceberg, but this glacial appearance is an illusion. As the *Fisher Lassie* nears the island, it becomes apparent that what seemed a cloak of ice or snow is in fact thousands of birds – to be specific, gannets or *Morus bassanus*.

Around 150,000 gannets call the Bass Rock home; it's the largest concentration of the species on any single island in the world. Though St Kilda has slightly more, the gannets there are spread across the archipelago. Scotland, as a whole, has 60 per cent of the world's gannet population. The birds live and breed on the Bass Rock between February and October, arriving from warmer climes around Valentine's Day with sweet loving on their minds.

We put in at the East Landing, one of two relatively safe places, depending on wind and tide, where it is possible to get onto the island. There are twelve of us on board the small lobster boat, not counting the two crew, mostly amateur wildlife photographers.

As soon as the first passenger steps on the gunnel, a gannet flings itself on to the deck with a loud bang. This is quite alarming. They are Britain's largest seabird, with a six-foot wingspan and a wicked bill. They are panicky and can be aggressive; not long ago, a man had an eye pecked out when he tried to rescue an injured gannet on a beach in South Wales. Eric Gray, one of the *Fisher Lassie* crew, grabs the gannet, holding its bill closed, and heaves it overboard. He's left bleeding from one hand. 'Don't worry about your fingers,' the skipper tells him. 'They'll grow back.'

'You should have distracted it with something,' says Maggie Sheddan, the guide on these tours run by North Berwick's Scottish Seabird Centre.

'If I'd had a hammer,' Eric replies wryly, 'I could have distracted it with that.'

Clubbing gannets, as Eric hints, is the way to kill them. You can't really wring their necks; they have tough muscles there, designed to withstand the impact of hitting the water at up to sixty miles per hour as they dive for fish. The guga-hunters from the northern community of Ness on Lewis club the gannet chicks – or gugas – they catch each year during their annual trip to the small island of Sula Sgeir. Some 2,000 gugas are taken and eaten. The hunt is licensed by the Scottish Government on the grounds of its cultural significance. On the Bass Rock, as elsewhere, gannets are a protected species.

Standing on the deck of the *Fisher Lassie*, feeling the swell, it is astonishing to look up at the rock. It is like being inside one of those photographs of ticker-tape parades in New York. In this case, the skyscrapers are the sharp and vertiginous cliffs on every tiny ledge of which sits a bird. The air is thick with gannets wheeling and gliding, approximately cruciform in silhouette. There are so many of them in the air that it is a miracle they do not collide. As they come in to land, their wings form a V and there is something of the avenging angel about their appearance – ghostly, noble and without mercy.

We step onto the Bass, climb steep stone steps and walk through the ruins of the old prison. This was, during the late seventeenth century, a sort of Scottish Alcatraz. Covenanting preachers were imprisoned here. Their diet included herring and mackerel regurgitated by gannets. The island also includes the remnants of a garrison and a tiny church.

St Baldred's Chapel is a stone shell with gannets perched on every arch and in the gap where the keystone should be. It is thought to have been built in the sixteenth century on the site where the saint, who died 900 years earlier, in 606, had his hermit's cell. In 1961, the chapel became home to Dr Bryan Nelson, the world's foremost expert on gannets, who spent three years living on the Bass Rock with his wife June. They erected a wooden hut, twelve feet by eight, inside the chapel walls, and spent a jolly and productive time studying the birds and developing a taste for herring gull eggs, eaten with chips. Now seventy-nine and living in Galloway, he recalls: 'It was a very restricted life and the weather was often severe, but the experience was peculiarly satisfying because you were cut off from all the distractions of everyday life and you could concentrate entirely on your work. You become tremendously attached to a romantic, wild place like that.'

He and June shared the Bass at that time with three lighthouse-keepers, but since the coming of automation in 1988, the lighthouse, which was built in 1902 by the Stevenson family, has lain empty. Inside, it smells of rot. A rust-crusted tobacco tin full of tacks sits alone on a shelf. A window sill is covered in feathers. There is a very strong sense, everywhere on the Bass Rock, that this is no longer a place for humans. The birds have taken over almost entirely. The ruinous fortifications add to the idea that this is a surrendered territory.

'Just seven years ago, I could walk all the way round the chapel and up that path,' says Maggie. 'I remember saying to the Seabird Centre, "You've got to land regularly or you're going to lose the path." It's really become a no-go area.'

Everywhere you look, there are gannets. They have annexed every single spare patch of ground. The Bass Rock has been described as 'a seabird city' and that's exactly how it feels – a great thronging wen of the sort Hogarth would recognise, full of drama and violence and sex and death.

Visiting is an entire sensory experience. The Bass Rock stinks so strongly of ammonia from the guano that you can almost taste it. Fishermen are said to be able to navigate in the fog by the smell. Then there is the noise. The massed gannets utter a sort of mesmeric, pulsing croak, which makes perfect sense of their Shetlandic name, crockak.

Lower down the rock, perched on the crooked chimney

pots of an old cottage, a brassy gang of herring gulls try to keep their spirits up with a defiant seaside shriek, but they are like travelling support at a football match, their noise drowned out by the home fans.

Although the gannets protect their nests and gugas very aggressively, pecking at each other and at visitors, it is possible to get surprisingly close, actually within arm's length, if you move slowly and calmly. The most striking feature, up close, are the birds' eyes, which are surrounded by a light blue rim, recalling the pale water round a Hebridean island.

After three hours on the Bass it is time to return. Gordon and Eric have been away hauling up their lobster pots, and the *Fisher Lassie* is full of their catch. The skipper knows these waters incredibly well. He's fished them since leaving school in 1963. He knows all the rocks and treacherous shallows by their local names – Satan's Bush, The Beggar's Cup, Wallace's Head. Yet he never tires of the Bass Rock or its gannets. 'Look at that one banking,' he says, admiringly. 'It's like Concorde.'

As the skipper steers the boat back to Dunbar, Eric throws whiting and flatfish into the water. This creates a sensation among the gannets; they fold up their wings and dive at great speed into the waves, visible beneath the surface, pale green and fizzing. The Hockney splashes of their ingress have barely subsided when they are up and out again, swallowing the fish.

It is extraordinary to think that by November this will all be over. Most of the gannets will have fled their craggy city in search of winter sun, and the Bass Rock will become – as Stevenson might have put it – unco quiet once more. For the moment, though, out there in all that freezing, killing vastness, it remains awesomely alive.

The Riverman

THIS IS A story of blood and water. Blood inherited and spilled. Water loved and feared. It is the story of a man called George Parsonage, a city called Glasgow, and the river which passes – like a soul, like a scythe – through the lives of both.

George Parsonage is the chief officer of the Glasgow Humane Society, an organisation that since 1790 has been dedicated to saving the lives of those who fall, either by accident or with grim intent, into waterways in and around the city. He is stocky, strong, quick in his movements. He favours orange boiler suits and stout work boots, softening the leather of each new pair by immersing them – baptising them – in the Clyde. He has a rolling way of walking, as if dry land is a dubious surface. He has white hair and brown eyes; his large hands are rough with years of work, burned by rope and ice, scarred by the jutting, cutting bones of a body recovered from Govan wharf. On Tuesday, he will turn seventy. He was involved in his first rescue in 1958, assisting his father who did this job before him, and has saved about 1,500 people since then, his most recent last month.

There must be thousands of children alive now who owe their existence to the fact that a member of the Parsonage family, long ago, was deft and determined enough to pluck their grandparent or great-grandparent from the merciless Clyde, deferring death for a while.

'Rescue is a privilege, isn't it?' Parsonage says. 'It's not everybody in this world who gets the chance to help someone.'

123

He lives with his wife Stephanie and two teenage sons on Glasgow Green, in a house on the northern bank, just up from the beautiful blue and gold suspension bridge and his own boatyard. He was born here on 15th October 1943, six years after the house was built. He was one of four children – two sisters and an elder brother. His father Benjamin, known as Bennie, was chief officer from 1932 until his death in 1979, although he made his first rescue as a teenager in 1919. To call this a family business does not go far enough; it was more like being raised in a faith. The words GLASGOW HUMANE SOCIETY are carved in ecclesiastical-looking block capitals above the lintel of his home.

In the study, in the evening, Parsonage writes up the minutes of each day's work. He has minutes going back to the eighteenth century, and it is his desire to produce a complete history of the society's endeavours. It will be, he hopes, a message to the future about safety on the river, a way of continuing his work when he is gone. He wants to open a museum by the house. The history of the Humane Society is, he feels, a social history of Glasgow; it reveals things about the life and mood of the city, its pastimes and its pain: people attempt to kill themselves in greater numbers during times of war and economic depression; in high spirits, through booze or simple bravado, they attempt to go swimming and die.

Reading through the accounts of drownings and the recoveries of bodies is to glimpse citizens at moments of crisis to which, regardless of the archaic language, any of us could relate; 'desponding state of mind' is a common reason given for suicide, while deaths are often caused by being 'the worse of liquor'. People throw themselves from bridges and river banks because they are 'labouring under mental derangement' or 'brain fever' or have been 'disappointed' by a 'sweetheart'. They drown 'while trying to sail a toy boat' (1897), 'while attempting to drown a cat near to Polmadie ferry' (1897), or while 'slightly unhinged by bad news from abroad' (1892). These people were weavers, carters, lamplighters, sweeps, prostitutes, hawkers, bare-knuckle boxers, and children who would never know the world of work.

There are thousands upon thousands of these stories, these brutal statistics, yet sometimes you come across one that stands out, that has a sort of dreadful poetry in it. In the early spring of 1958, a four-year-old from Maryhill fell into the canal and was lost; another boy, the only witness, went home and told his mother what had happened to his pal. 'Jackie,' he said, 'has gone away with the swans.'

Such accounts can make the Clyde appear accursed or even actively malevolent. Certainly, it is dangerous – deep, steep-sided and very cold. Yet George Parsonage feels no loathing; indeed, he takes joy in the Clyde, and needs little persuasion to leave his study and take to the water. 'I'm away down to the boats,' he shouts up the stairs to Stephanie. 'I'll be out on the river.'

* * *

It is a mild afternoon in early September 2013, but it could be 1938 or 1963 or 1979 as a man called Parsonage is searching for a body in the Clyde. The police had come to the door just before lunchtime and asked George if he could help look for a young man who had been missing for almost a week. So, here he is, a few miles upriver from the Green, his restless eyes scanning the river and its banks.

Although rescues are the dramatic, newsworthy aspects of the society's work, these searches have, over the years, been much more common. Parsonage, like his father before him, is skilled in the use of grappling irons – a heavy four-pronged steel hook lowered to the river bed by two ropes and used to drag for murder weapons, stolen goods and corpses. 'It's actually quite a science,' he says. Parsonage can tell from long experience whether he has touched wood or metal; the feel of flesh, sensed along the rope, is unmistakable. 'The body begins to rise with gentleness, an uncanny lightness,' he has written in an unpublished essay on what he calls the ancient art of grappling, 'and the rope user has to be very quick and gentle in raising the body to the surface. It is like lifting a balloon. If you stop lifting, the balloon will float off and away, so with a body.'

It is a matter of honour for Parsonage that his grappling irons do not leave marks on the bodies. Indeed, his knowledge of the horrors that being too long in the water can inflict is one reason he has always done his best to recover victims of drowning as quickly as possible. He prefers to spare family members the sights with which he is familiar, even if that means long hours out in the freezing dark.

Yet, in truth, searches and rescues are, these days, just a tiny fraction of his work. In 2005, the then Strathclyde Police took the responsibility for rescue away from the Humane Society and gave it to the fire service; the police themselves now recover bodies. It was a bureaucratic decision that felt like the passing of an age; the end of a certain sort of civic heroism. Parsonage sometimes finds himself in the right place at the right time, and the emergency services still, on occasion, seek his help. But the days of being the go-to guy in each life-or-death situation are over. Without police funding, the Humane Society struggles for money, and Parsonage himself no longer takes a wage. He works, now, out of a sense of vocation and, one suspects, forward momentum; like a great ship decommissioned even as it slides down the slipway.

But he is busy. Make no mistake. The Humane Society receives a grant from Glasgow City Council, and has a key role in promoting safety on the river. This is the focus now – preventing people from falling into the water in the first place, or at least making it easier for them to be saved, through the adequate provision of quayside ladders and the like. Parsonage maintains about 300 lifebelts along the banks of the river, retrieving the twenty or thirty each day that are thrown into the water by eejits and drunks. He was responsible for introducing a GPS system which means the location of people in the water can be identified readily when 999 is dialled. He continues to argue for fencing and bridges to be made more safe, making it harder for people to fall or jump, and has had some notable success. 'Glasgow's way ahead of any other city,' he insists. 'Goodness knows how many lives we've saved.'

Nevertheless, as someone who has, since childhood, been conditioned to respond to emergencies, he does find the present situation difficult. 'Every time I hear sirens, or see blue lights downriver, or see the helicopter hovering over the river, my heart misses a beat and the adrenalin starts running. You wonder, "What's going on?" It's very hard to keep out of it. You want to be part of it. There's the public expectation, too. The public could be told a hundred times that I'm no longer on call, but as long as I'm here they will expect me to answer the call. And in this section of the river, we do answer the call.'

When I visited Parsonage one bright Tuesday morning, he was still buzzing from having carried out a rescue on the Sunday night; a boat had crashed into the gates of the tidal weir near his home, and its occupant had been thrown into the water. On some level, he needs this. It's not that he's a thrill-seeker; he is, rather, a man who takes pleasure in performing the function at which he excels, and which he regards as a vocation.

'God gave me the ability to be a good rower,' he says. 'I used to win an awful lot of races. But I didn't realise until later on in life that the greatest races I was winning was when I was rowing to get someone out the water. That ability, that boatmanship, is there for a purpose. Maybe I'm reading things into it that aren't there. But it's nice to think that way.'

Retirement, therefore, is not an option. 'There's a future for the society, and I'm here fighting for it. As long as I've got enough strength to keep going.'

* * *

Each squeak of the rowlocks, each creak and splash of the oars takes us a little further upstream, a little further into the past. Parsonage is rowing, the memories flowing: 'Oh, wonderful river. So much has happened in it.' He nods over to the northern bank. 'I found a woman there. She was face down and her shoes were sticking out. We had to get picks and shovels to dig her free. Terrible that I know every inch of the river, and an accident in every inch. I've been here too long, eh? Too long.'

Bennie Parsonage loved the river, and – fanciful as this sounds – it seemed to love him. On the day of his funeral, the rain was so heavy that the grave flooded and he was lowered into water; the following day, the gates of the tidal weir jammed open and the Clyde dropped until, as Parsonage recalls, 'it was hardly a stream in the middle', as if it did not want to continue without the man who had for so long stood sentinel over it.

Parsonage had been working as an art teacher while devoting his evenings and weekends to assisting his father, but on the day of the old man's death – 1st October 1979 – he did not hesitate to take over the role. 'The love of the river was greater than anything else.' He made a search for a missing woman that very afternoon. Was it, though, a burden he took up entirely willingly? 'Don't know. I had no choice. We had nothing. My mother was in a wheelchair, my sister was at home looking after my mother. There was no house to go to if I had chucked the job. And that very afternoon, when the phone went and somebody needed help, I just did it. That was it. Sucked straight in. I don't think my father ever wanted me to be here. But I don't know. I can't say that.'

It wasn't a job, it was a calling, and you gave yourself to it. There was no possibility of going on holiday, or out for a meal, or even to put on a pot of soup. You had to be available to run for the boat. Parsonage is glad his sons cannot and will not inherit that life, although he was proud to have his eldest at his side during the recent rescue at the tidal weir. Bennie Parsonage was more than a father to George, he was a hero. He was a wee man, five foot one, and he came from Bridgeton. He had a deep religious faith but was only in church once in his life, and that at his own funeral. He was modest and taciturn. Once, asked by a young newspaper reporter whether people often drowned in the Clyde, he gave a five-word reply that was a masterclass in dry wit: 'Naw, son. Just the once.' George, by contrast, is able and willing to tell the story of the Humane Society, to carry that cargo of memory and love.

We pass under bridges. St Andrew's, King's, Polmadie, Dalmarnock. The banks are overgrown and choked. There are apples and pears, rasps and brambles; giant hogweed lends a sinister fairyland air. Parsonage photographs trees falling into the water; he'll see these are cleared. He points out the piles of an old wooden bridge, poking like rotten teeth just above the surface. He knows what hazards lie in the Clyde's murk – the deep holes, the sandbanks, the dumped combine harvester that has lacerated canoes. Everything suggests a story. Here's a length of pipe at the spot where, in 1971, he dived twenty feet below the water to rescue a mother and her five-year-old son. Here's the bridge where neds almost killed him by dropping a concrete block on his head. Parsonage loves opera, Puccini is his favourite, and it is tempting to imagine a soundtrack playing as he rows, perhaps the aria 'O Mio Babbino Caro', Oh my beloved father. It would, if nothing else, take one's mind off the sewage works stink.

In his boatyard, we talk over tea. Outside, his colony of rescue geese chatter and rasp. These birds are music lovers and have enjoyed many bands performing on Glasgow Green over the years; the only act they found unbearable was Marilyn Manson, preferring to head upriver to Rutherglen for the duration of his performance. George laughs as he tells this story, playing the entertaining host, but there's a part of him that isn't in the room at all. He has positioned his chair so he can keep an eye on the river, making sure that if any of the rowers overturn he will be able to act swiftly. He is an amiable man full of anecdotes, but that brain is forever calculating worst-case scenarios and plans of action.

I ask about his attitude to the river. Can he define how he feels about the Clyde? 'It's a love/hate relationship. The river can be a wonderful friend, but a cruel, cruel master. You're fighting against it, and thinking all the time of what it can do to you. You've got to give it the greatest respect.'

In some ways, Parsonage is the last of the true rivermen. Read through the Humane Society records and you're struck by how many vessels and people were on the river at one time. No longer. It is a tradition in the Parsonage family to see in the new year on the Clyde. George and his father would drift downriver in one of their boats and listen to the bells in the Trongate steeple; then, on the stroke of midnight, Bennie would sound his klaxon. It is something George continues, at Hogmanay, with his eldest son, Ben – blood on the water, thinking of the past, looking to the future.

'Once, all the ships on the river would reply,' he says. 'But now, sometimes, there isn't a single answer coming back.'

The Wall of Death

EIGHTEEN FEET UP, his body parallel to the wicked wooden floor, flashing by on a motorcycle of pensionable age, Ken Fox rides the Wall of Death with the insouciance of a man born to it – which he was. The noise in this great bright wooden barrel is extraordinary: the roar of the throttle, the sudden gunshot as the engine backfires. It's too loud to hear the punters speak, but Fox has learned over the years to lip-read certain phrases, which he is pleased to observe as he blurs past. 'Fuck me!' they say. 'He's mad!'

The Ken Fox Troupe, in Edinburgh for the Scottish Motorcycle Show at Ingliston, are the last Wall of Death riders in Britain, survivors of a fairground trade that not all have survived. It is a family affair. Ken is the boss and the daddy. The travelling showman is of indeterminate age and will not give it. Though he is losing his hair and gaining some white in his beard, and though he has his share of scars, he remains lithe and boyish; one suspects frequent rub-downs with motor-oil. He has been riding the Wall of Death getting on for forty years, and long ago introduced his sons – Luke, twenty-six, and Alex, eighteen – into the act. Alex's girlfriend, Abby, is a recent addition to the troupe; they became a couple last year after she saw the act in Pickering, and now she rides, beaming with joy, on his handlebars. 'It feels,' she says, 'like Christmas has come early, like taking off in a plane.'

Ken's wife, Julie, is also part of the troupe. A former dental assistant, she saw Ken ride one day, twenty-eight years ago, and that was that – her days of drills and molars were over. They married in a registry office and had a blessing inside the Wall of Death – which they consider to have been their proper wedding as it is, for the Fox troupe, a sacred space.

These days Julie drives one of the lorries that transport the wall, works in the paybox, and makes the tea. But what is it like to see her husband and sons put their lives at risk night after night? 'I feel proud,' she smiles. 'Especially when all three of them are on the wall together and the crowd are mesmerised and everyone's cheering. I think, "Oh, that's my boys up there." They started learning when they were about eleven, and I was very nervous. My heart was pounding. But the way they've been brought up, they've loved motorbikes since they were toddlers.'

How, though, does she cope with the inevitable accidents? 'Most of the time I'm outside selling tickets, and you can hear the bikes going around; all of a sudden there's a crash then deadly silence, and you think, "*Ohhh, God*". It's a horrible feeling, but if they haven't hurt themselves badly they always try and get back on and continue the act, and the crowd cheers like mad.' She laughs. 'I go in after to mop up the blood.'

Ken Fox's Wall of Death is eighteen feet high and has a circumference of eighty-eight feet. It weighs twenty tons and is made from knot-free Oregon pine. The wall is painted blue and red outside. The floor is red and yellow. The waterproof roof is yellow and blue. There is something of the medieval war tent about it.

The crowds look down from above and are fragranced by a rising incense of engine fumes. The point is to thrill the audience, not to scare them. The riders begin by circling the floor, then up on to a ramp, and finally they are riding perpendicular to the wall, arms outstretched, rising and dipping, sometimes high enough to leave tyre marks at the very top, prompting squeals from the crowd. For superstitious reasons, they only ever travel in an anti-clockwise direction. They get so close you could reach out and touch them, make some sort of brief physical connection with that speeding miracle of guts and grace and centrifugal force.

'We look like ballerinas on the wall,' says Ken. 'But it takes a lot of effort, a lot of mental and physical concentration. You can feel the G-force. We're pulling about three Gs. On a hot day you can feel very faint and start to black out.'

They don't wear helmets or safety gear, as – apparently – this would make it harder to steer and to see. But the third reason is pure showbiz. 'The men want to look heroic and the women want to look gorgeous.' And just how fast are they going? 'A mile a minute and a thrill a second.' He laughs. 'It's about forty-five miles per hour.'

The first Wall of Death is thought to have come to Britain from South Africa in 1928. Soon after, a company called Silodromes began building walls and hiring them – and trained riders – out to showmen. There were more than fifty walls in Britain during the 1930s, the peak era, but after the war they began, gradually, to lose popularity. There were, as you might expect, some tremendous characters among the riders; forces of nature like Tornado Smith, Cyclone Jack, Hurricane Pete, and not forgetting Armless Alf – who somehow managed to work as a Wall of Death rider, and during the off-season a mechanic, despite having been born without upper limbs.

Old photographs of fairgrounds show walls sited next to rifle ranges and freak shows ('See Inside! The Lady with a Pig's Face!') and emblazoned with the skulls and crossbones which the Fox Troupe still favour today. The old riders are all of a type – tough and strong and Brylcreemed within an inch of their lives; they favour leather jackets and jodhpurs; one man has a bear balanced on his handlebars. Ken Fox, out of respect for the history of his profession, has painted on the front of the wall a list of riders who are no longer living. It is something of a rogues' gallery and he points to each name with glee. 'He was a gangster. He was a ladykiller. He was always drunk. Harry Holland, he got bit by a tiger, or was it a lion? She broke her neck. She murdered her boyfriend. Tornado Smith was tight-fisted; he used to take a knife into the gents so he didn't have to spend the penny; and he once paid a twenty-pound fine with a wheelbarrow full of farthings.'

'I think,' says Luke, 'the Wall of Death sends people slightly nuts.'

The bike Luke rides dates from 1921 and used to belong to Tornado Smith. The Fox troupe bikes are beautiful machines, Indian Scouts, red and gleaming, with leather saddles from which tassels fly as they speed along. Despite their age, they are in great nick, and when they crash are easily fixed with a crowbar and sledgehammer. Safety is a priority, but falls are inevitable.

Ken, for his part, has come off the bike around twenty times. 'I've broke me wrist, taken chunks out me eyes, me shoulders, bruised me arse, damaged me ego, broke women's hearts, but I've always bounced well, always been a good bouncer. My grandad, he had seventy-two stitches putting his face back on. He was the first man to put a go-kart on the wall. He got the go-kart on the Monday, put it in the show on Tuesday, and it put him in the hospital on the Wednesday.' Fox is the third generation of his family to ride the Wall of Death. He was taught by his father and uncle. How his grandfather, Walter, learned to ride is lost in the mists of time. It is thought that he had started in 1931, but by the time Ken was a boy collecting tickets from the punters, Walter had quit riding and taken to spieling, pulling the crowds with his patter, his skin brown and leathery from years of Skegness sun.

These days, the Fox family are based in Ely, Cambridgeshire, where they have their winter quarters and their yard, but they are on the road for ten months of the year, performing on approximately 120 days. Fairgrounds are no longer the main part of their business; they prefer to appear at music festivals, including Glastonbury and T in the Park.

Trying to work it out is probably a fool's errand, but it would seem that Ken Fox travels about 4,500 miles each year inside the Wall of Death, which comes in at about 180,000 miles during his working life so far. That's seven times around the Earth, and looking at it like that seems fitting somehow. There's something eternal about the wall, about the endless roaring circles, about all that history and mystery and anecdote crammed within this wooden orb.

'Let me take you inside,' says Ken, keen to finally explain his passion. He leads the way through a door in the side, and suddenly there we are, standing in the centre, looking up at the wall, our voices echoing slightly as we speak. 'You hear that?' he asks. 'It's like going into a church. The Wall of Death, for us, is almost religious. This is a special place, a special life, and I'm going to carry on doing it as long as I am able.'

Ramadan

IN THE HUMID basement of a shabby tenement at just before half-past three in the morning, as drunks stoat the damp pavements outside, Radio Ramadhan is broadcasting the call to prayer. Recorded in Mecca, high in some minaret, the call goes out, sad somehow and sonorous, proclaiming the greatness of Allah across the drizzly city, carrying into the homes of Glasgow's Muslims a cooling whisper – just audible in the background – of the distant desert wind.

It is time to stop eating. It is time to stop drinking. It is time to stop smoking and to stop having sex. The plates of rice and daal and mango in the radio studio will now go unfinished. 'We'll see you on the other side,' says the young DJ Muneeb Gill. The twenty-seventh day of Ramadan has begun.

Ramadan is the ninth and holiest month in the Islamic calendar. It is believed to be the time during which the word of Allah was first revealed to the Prophet Muhammad. During the period of daylight, the intake of all food and fluids is forbidden, though exemptions are granted to the sick and to women who are pregnant, breastfeeding or menstruating. The pre-dawn meal before each fast is called Sehri; the meal after dark which breaks each fast is Iftar.

The Islamic calendar is lunar; each month begins with the appearance of the moon. The traditional method of deciding when Ramadan begins, therefore, is for it to be sighted either by the naked eye or by telescope. However, dreich weather and the glare of street lights means that the moon is not always visible in Scotland's cities. In these circumstances, the imams from the various city mosques

136

will confer, negotiate and sometimes openly argue, taking into consideration whether the moon has been sighted from various Muslim countries, deciding eventually by majority vote.

It is felt to be important that the imams reach an agreement on when Ramadan starts and ends, otherwise it can lead to tension within families, with, say, one brother observing the fast while another continues to eat, and the holiday of Eid al-Fitr – sometimes described as a Muslim Christmas – being celebrated on different days by different family members.

The Glasgow mosques are, this year, unified on the matter; in Edinburgh, however, there is division – a couple of mosques began Ramadan a day later than the rest. Even in Glasgow, though, home to around three-quarters of Scotland's estimated 60,000 Muslims, the situation is not clear cut; the Al-Furqan mosque in the west end has timetabled the fast to begin up to around forty-five minutes later than the main mosques in the city centre and Southside. In the wee small hours, Radio Ramadhan broadcasts the timetables of each, so its listeners know when to stop eating regardless of which mosque they attend.

Because of its long summer daylight, Scotland is, at the moment, one of the most difficult countries in the world in which to observe Ramadan, which begins around ten to eleven days earlier each year.

'When Ramadan was in winter, everything was cushty,' explains the Glaswegian imam and leading Islamic scholar Amer Jamil. 'It was only a ten-hour fast; just like having a late lunch. But now that it's summer and the days are longer, the fast is a lot harder. You are starting at around three in the morning and finishing around ten at night.'

Muslims living in those areas of Scandinavia where there is no real darkness at all during summer are sometimes given a special dispensation to follow the Ramadan timetables of either Saudi Arabia or the nearest Muslim

137

country – Morocco. Scotland, however, is not quite far north enough to be granted such special treatment. Therefore Scottish Muslims must starve themselves for that bit longer. It is typical to lose half a stone during Ramadan. The fast will remain tough here for the next eight years or more as Ramadan gradually moves back into spring.

Many Scottish Muslims, if they are able, take holidays from work during Ramadan, but this is not possible for everyone, and working can be difficult when you feel tired, thirsty and weak. One Muslim police officer tells me that the worst he ever felt was when he had to carry protesters away from the Faslane nuclear submarine base on a baking hot day while wearing full riot gear.

Naveed, a thirty-five-year-old shopkeeper in Bellshill, says that observing the fast while running a business is exhausting. He can't afford to take time off. 'I'm self-employed, I've got people who rely on me, and customers come in expecting the same service as always. But getting up in the morning is really tough.' Naveed arrives home from prayers at the mosque between midnight and one. He tries to stay awake for the next couple of hours so that he can eat something filling shortly before the fast begins. He rises at 7.15 a.m., which means he's getting by on four hours of sleep every night. He keeps a sleeping bag in the shop but there never seems to be a moment to nap.

For those Muslims working in the restaurant trade, surrounded at all times by forbidden food, Ramadan can be even harder. 'Oh, my God, it's horrible, man,' says twenty-seven-year-old Abdul Ali, whose family run the Kismot in Edinburgh, home of the infamous Kismot Killer, a curry so hot that diners have been known to leave by ambulance. 'I'm in the kitchen, cooking away, and we're counting down the minutes and seconds until Iftar. Then we go for it, mate, we go straight for the kill. Whatever we see to eat, buddy, we're in there.'

Lifelong Muslims will, typically, have been observing

Ramadan since puberty and the annual fast is, therefore, part of the routine and texture of each year. It may not be easy, but they are used to it. For newcomers to the faith, however, it can be a challenge.

Alana Blockley, a twenty-year-old student and waitress from Bridgeton, is a recent convert. Two years ago she was supposed to go to Tenerife on holiday, but the volcanic ash clouds meant her flight was cancelled so she went to Fuerteventura instead. It was an important twist of fate, for there she met her future husband, a Muslim from Morocco. Impressed by his character and the strength he took from his faith, she found herself drawn to Islam, an attraction that deepened into belief. Now wearing hijab, despite the attention that a white woman in a headscarf inevitably attracts – 'I wouldn't walk about in my area wearing it, I have to be in the car, I don't feel safe ... someone would definitely come up and batter me' – she finds it a relief to not have to fret about either her personal appearance or leering men.

This is Alana's first Ramadan. She thought she wouldn't even last one day. 'I had no faith in myself. I love my food too much.' But the weeks have flown in and she is already looking forward to next year. 'I do feel as if I've been brought closer to Allah.'

Rahillah from Glasgow, a thirty-one-year-old mum to two young boys, explains that Ramadan is an opportunity for 'self-purification' and attempting to become a better person. Muslims are supposed to not argue during the month. 'I'm finding it very hard trying not to shout at the kids when they make a mess, to keep calm,' she says. 'But there are times when you get cranky, especially when you are hungry; cooking meals, cleaning nappies – it's an ongoing thing as a mother. But my dealings with the kids and my mother-in-law who I live with, that is also a part of worship, not just the five prayers I do during the day.'

In the Glasgow Central Mosque, as the shadows outside

lengthen and the golden crescent on the minaret glows in the twilight, around 400 people – men, women and children – have come to pray and end their fast. Another hundred men are spending the last ten days and nights of Ramadan in the mosque, secluded from the world, lost in prayer and the dim green light. The atmosphere is at once festive and solemn.

Food, paid for by donations, is provided to whoever cares to attend. The voices tell their own story – Urdu, Weegie, Punjabi, Pashto, Arabic, Kurdish, Farsi, Igbo. Here is Glasgow's immigrant population in all its polyglot pomp. Many of these people are asylum seekers, fleeing poverty and violence, here to take advantage of a free meal and to eat Iftar communally as they are used to doing in their native lands.

The kitchen is the domain of Dilshad, a highly respected greybeard who runs a takeaway when he isn't volunteering as head chef; every evening during Ramadan, Dilshad and his team take thirty-five kilos of rice, five lambs, seventy chickens and innumerable samosas and naans, and produce a feast that is literally divine. He also does a nice line in gulab jaman – milk powder rolled into doughy balls then deep-fried and dipped in syrup – which I hear described fondly as 'heart attack material' and which seems to be a sort of Islamic version of the infamous battered Mars Bar.

Sitting in long lines on the floor, kneeling or cross-legged, the Muslims wait for the call to prayer, which comes at precisely two minutes to nine, and then bend to break their fast, first with a few dates as Muhammad did. Despite the parched throats, despite the empty stomachs, there is no sense of relief. This is a ritual.

'So that was the twenty-seventh day of Ramadan,' someone says to me, rubbing his belly through his silken tunic and washing down a gulab jaman with a gulp of Irn-Bru. 'As-salamu Alaikum – Peace be with you.'

The Drag Queen Ball

With two hours to go until the start of the annual drag queen ball, Thom Glow, a rangy twenty-three-year-old with a passing resemblance to a young Tom Cruise, sits on a towel on the floor of a friend's bedroom in Springburn, wearing nothing but Calvin Klein trunks and Celine Dion's signature scent. He is trying to apply eyeliner, but a headstrong chihuahua, Doris, keeps coming into the room and distracting him from his preparations. On the bed lies a leather corset. Midnight will be drawing near before he puts it on.

When in drag, Thom goes by the name Vanity von Glow. Originally from Dunfermline, he now lives down south, but has come to Glasgow to perform at the ball. 'I really want to look thin tonight,' he says. 'I don't want people to say, "Oh, she went to London and she put the pounds on." But me and Lady Munter went for a KFC today, so ...' He sighs and sips his vodka and Irn-Bru, casts a critical eye at his psoriasis. 'It makes my legs look corned-beefy, which is kind of annoying when you want them to look like Nicole Scherzinger's.'

Tonight is the third annual drag ball, sometimes known as the Vogue or All-Stars ball, hosted by bi-monthly gay club night Menergy. The drag queen who can most impress the judges with their look, moves and attitude on the catwalk will be crowned the scene's best. 'People really bring it,' says Thom. 'You see young people, maybe eighteen, who have worked hard on their image and make-up. But you can't just look good on the runway. You've somehow got to go up there and project personality. It's all very camp.'

141

There are no curtains in the flat. Across the road, an old granny smoking out a tenement window gets a right eyeful. Another drag queen, Candi Latte, keeps popping in from the living room with updates from *The X-Factor*. The chihuahua, by this time, is covered in glitter. Thom calls himself Scotland's top female impersonator and is certainly convincing in a showgirlish sequined mini-dress, imperial blue cape and crown of golden stars. If he weren't about seven feet tall in heels, one might be taken in. His style icons are Kate Middleton, Liz Hurley and Sarah Palin. He has never heard of Stanley Baxter. 'Right,' he says, fluttering his lashes (£25 a pair) in the mirror. 'Let's go.'

Down the stairs and out to the car. We drive into town, Vanity in front, Candi in the back. Candi's real name is Ross. He's in his twenties. Quite often, he says, straight guys will try to pick up drag queens, mistaking them for very glamorous, sexy women. 'I was walking down the strip in Zante once,' Ross recalls. 'I didn't even have my tits in, and this British guy asked me back to his hotel. Then he clocked my hairy chest.'

The ball is at Forbidden, a lapdancing club on Maxwell Street by the Clyde. Working the door is James Faulkner, the well-kent milliner, wearing a golden robe and a gigantic headdress of pheasant feathers. 'C'mere, sweetheart,' he says to Lady Munter, who runs Menergy. 'I need to do a mum on you.' Gently, he wipes smuts of bright pink lipstick from the corners of his friend's mouth.

Downstairs in the show bar, Lana Del Rey's 'Video Games' is playing at high volume. Drag queens sip cocktails, pout into camera phones and sniff each other's scent. 'What do you smell of? Tom Ford's Tuscan Leather? Oh, you rich bitch!' The scene is extraordinary, a great mishmash of looks – glossy glamazons and *hommes fatales*, some channelling Nicki Minaj, others Morticia Addams. A brace of buff waiters in bow-ties and briefs. A hipster in fishnets and a Frank Zappa beard.

John Maclean, an eighteen-year-old make-up artist from Stornoway, has a face white as paper and long hair black as ink; his lips are red as a royal seal. 'I'm not a drag artist,' he says. 'I'm like this every day of my life. I do not recognise gender identity or sexual identity. I am a couture work of art.'

Drag culture is, as one of the queens puts it, 'a rabbit warren' of complexity and nuance. For some, wearing make-up and women's clothing is a key part of their identity. For others it is simply a laugh at the weekend. Some try to pass as female, arranging foam padding beneath their clothes to affect an hourglass figure. Others say that looking and acting like a drag queen – vampish, trampish, vicious, delicious – is an end in itself. The whole thing is a great perfumed pageant of drama, glamour, high camp and low comedy. Vanity stands astride the catwalk, head tilted back, one arm aloft, singing Divine's 'You Think You're A Man'. Next month she plays the Mecca Bingo in Aberdeen.

'It's people like this who make the world go round,' says Tina Warren, who runs the burlesque night Club Noir and is one of tonight's judges. 'They are putting Glasgow on the drag map. I just love their bravery and passion.'

Scotland has dozens of drag queens. Even their names are a treat. Bella Houston, Barbra La Bush, Cybil Partnership, Harmony LeBeau. Often, the drag queens invent interconnecting back stories; Candi Latte was supposedly the mistress of Vanity von Glow's late husband. This is a subculture which, in its glam way, is every bit as geeky as Dungeons and Dragons. Cosmetics brands, for instance, are fetishised, none more so than Illamasqua, adored for its ability to cover stubble. 'A girl wouldn't wear this,' one queen says of her Illamasqua foundation. 'This stuff is heavy duty. It's make-up for the alter ego.'

Upstairs, in the foyer, as lapdancers totter to and fro, Jacqueline Demure is a vision in burgundy. Away from the nightclubs, he is a mid-forties Glaswegian man called Jack who owns a beauty salon. Tonight, she is somewhere between Aphrodite and Beyoncé; she made her dress herself and customised her size nine stilettos with pink crystals. 'I was in a ten-year relationship and together we ran a gay guesthouse in Italy,' Jacqueline says. 'But it was an abusive relationship, so I walked out and came back to Glasgow with nothing. One day I got asked to help my friend out doing the drag show at Delmonica's, and it all snowballed from there. It's given me my confidence back again. I'm enjoying life and have stopped making excuses for who I am.'

Ryanaaa Chanice looks like Louise Brooks: flapper headband and sleek black bob. 'When I'm a boy, I can be shy,' Ryanaaa says. 'But when I do drag, each layer of make-up paints over more insecurities. If I walked out into the street the now and someone said, "That's disgusting", I'd be like, "Fuck you. You're disgusting because you're so narrow-minded." When you go out in drag, you get noticed because you're fabulous. It's fun to walk into a club and get that shocked reaction of "Is that a guy or is that a girl?" But I don't feel like I'm a woman trapped in a man's body. I feel like I'm me.'

Barbara Fritzl, during the day a twenty-five-year-old barman called Bobby, is wearing a scarlet and black body-con dress, a leather dog collar with a diamanté padlock, a red wig bought on Amazon, and her flatmate's strappy shoes. 'I grind the heel away on all of mine, so I keep stealing his.' TK Maxx is favoured by drag queens as it stocks plenty of discount heels in sizes larger than those usually bought by women. Barbara says it takes about an hour to get ready, most of which is spent shaving. 'It's about being bigger than the ordinary, and apart from anything else, boys' clothes are rubbish. You get to throw a little glitter on and have huge mad hair. So why wouldn't you?'

On stage, Lady Munter is inviting all the 'fierce ruling

divas' to come forward and be judged. The walk is about to begin. This is the part of the ball in which the drag queens vamp and vogue along the catwalk, towards the stripper pole at the end, hoping to impress the judges with their style and strut.

The inspiration is the New York ball scene of the 1980s, as recorded for posterity in the documentary *Paris is Burning*. To the music of Peaches, Scissor Sisters and RuPaul, the drag queens give it laldy. One, in a silk kimono, black veil and bobbed red wig, throws herself onto the flashing catwalk and grinds along with such vigour that the plastic pelvic bone she is wearing as a choker falls to the floor. In the end, though, it's Jacqueline Demure who wins. 'I was bricking it,' she says, demurely.

Outside, at about 2 a.m., drag queens are smoking in the smirr, smirking through the smoke. '*Danke schön*! *Danke schön*!' says Lady Munter, cadging a fag and light. Munter, otherwise known as David, is an extraordinary creation. A towering inferno of red hair, matching sequined dress, and silicone breasts of Rabelaisian proportions. 'Do you like them?' she asks. 'J-cups from boobsforqueens.com. They cost six, seven hundred quid. It's about dedication to your art, girls.'

Munter pauses to cram someone else's chips into her mouth, smudging her lippy, then decides to abandon the interview altogether.

'Sorry,' she says, stoating off in silver ankle boots, heading for the ladies. 'I really need to pee.'

The Eagle's Bairn

MAURICE HENDERSON IS a fiddler on Fetlar (population sixty-nine), a beautiful island in the Shetland archipelago 150 or so miles north of the Scottish mainland, and has spent his life bringing the old music and tales of his native land to a new global audience.

Yet he would not have existed at all had his great-great-great-great-great-great-grandfather not saved his great-great-great-great-great-great-grandmother from the nest of a hungry eagle, high on sea cliffs a few miles from what is now the Henderson family croft house.

'It was my grand-uncle who told me I was descended from the eagle's bairn,' the forty-year-old says. 'It's a story handed down by folk on the isle for generations.'

This is how it goes. One late summer's day in 1690 on the island of Unst, a white-tailed eagle – a bird with an eight-foot wingspan also known as the sea eagle – swooped down to the fields where the Anderson family were gathering barley, and picked up in its scimitar talons their infant daughter Mary, who had been lying sleeping in a woollen shawl.

The bird set off across the water to its eyrie on the neighbouring island of Fetlar, three miles south. Mary's father William and fellow crofters set off in pursuit, crossing the water in an old leaky boat, straining to see the black dot in the sky. Landing on Fetlar, they made for the cliffs and, arriving above the spot where the bird was known to nest, let down a rope 400 feet above the water.

A local boy, Robert Nicolson, being light and used to climbing, volunteered to descend to the nest. There he found Mary asleep and unharmed, the thick shawl having protected her from hungry beaks. He gathered her to him, climbed back up the rope and handed her to her grateful father.

Some years later, Nicolson had business on Unst and took a notion to visit the Anderson croft to pay his respects to Mary. He found her grown into a pretty young woman. 'It was love at first sight,' says Maurice Henderson, 'or, as they say, second sight.' The two married and raised a family. Their descendants – the bairns of the eagle's bairn – still live on the islands and are proud of their ancestry.

The sea eagle has not been so fortunate in its genealogy. The last in the UK was killed in Shetland in 1918. The female bird had lived for years without a mate and was said to be an albino, the end of her line, a ghost even before she was shot dead.

This story illustrates the complex and often uneasy relationship between humans and sea eagles, a relationship that led to their dying out in Britain almost a hundred years ago and to their re-introduction from Norway in the 1970s. As that grim centenary approaches, it is thought that the milestone of there being a hundred breeding pairs is about to be reached. We killed them and then we brought them back to life.

'The sea eagle was brought to extinction through man's persecution, so it seemed only right that we should do something to bring it back,' says the naturalist and author John Love. 'Righting a wrong that had been done to it in the past.'

Love, now sixty-eight, was hired by the former Nature Conservancy Council in 1975 to manage the reintroduction programme. Over the next decade he made several journeys to Norway, where sea eagles are relatively abundant, to choose chicks in their nests and accompany them back – in RAF Nimrods – to Scotland. The first bird, Loki, was released on the Hebridean island of Rum on 26th

September 1975. Love remembers the moment vividly, its historic weight. 'I got the same buzz every time I released one into the world,' he says.

The sea eagle is Britain's biggest bird of prey. Its relationship with the people of these isles goes back to ancient times; they may even have been sacred to us. When the 'Tomb of the Eagles', a Stone Age burial mound, was excavated in Orkney in 1976, it was found to contain talons and skulls of sea eagles, mingled with the bones of prehistoric humans.

Pictish symbol stones and the Book of Kells show the great hooked beak. Anglo-Saxon poetry describes sea eagles feasting on the flesh of slain warriors. Gaelic poetry calls it *Iolaire sùil na grèine* – the eagle with the sunlit eye. Those golden eyes, which now scan some of Scotland's wildest landscape, once looked down over the whole of the British Isles.

Farmers, gamekeepers and sportsmen hastened the demise of the sea eagle. Estate owners regarded them as vermin preying on valuable sheep and game birds, and offered bounties for eggs and severed heads. By 1800 there were none left in England. A proposal five years ago to reintroduce them in East Anglia failed in the face of local opposition.

The last bird in the UK, that albino in Shetland, was photographed a few years before its death. Blurred and grainy, it is the only picture taken of a true native British sea eagle and there is something guilt-inducing and wraith-like about it; a phantom accusing its killers.

Although initial reintroductions took place on Rum in 1975, ten years passed before breeding succeeded and a chick hatched – the first 'Gaelic-speaking sea eagle', as Love puts it, to be born in Scotland for decades. This happened on Mull, a large island south of Rum, to which the birds had spread. On the thirtieth anniversary, Dave Sexton, a Royal Society for the Protection of Birds officer who witnessed the hatching, leads the way down a rough track and points across a loch to the site of the nest where new birds are raising young. 'This is where it all began,' he says. 'This wood should be a national monument.'

Sexton is fifty-four. Originally from Bromley, Kent, he had first come to Mull in 1978 on a school trip. He moved here in 1984, a new recruit with the RSPB, despatched to Scotland 'on a secret mission' to find, watch and protect sea eagle nests.

The fateful summer of 1985 was one of the wettest and most miserable he had ever experienced. He and his RSPB colleague Mike Madders had been supplied with an ancient leaky tent, and they would work twenty-four-hour shifts, monitoring the comings and goings of eagles from a nest they had identified as promising. It was cold, damp and boring. 'What the hell am I doing?' was a not uncommon thought. 'You are like an expectant father,' Sexton recalls, 'waiting for some sign that the egg has hatched.'

But 4th May 1985 dawned warm and sunny, an omen perhaps. At about five in the morning, Mike Madders was watching the nest through his telescope from the other side of the loch; Sexton was on a ridge above the nest, his view slightly obscured by the oak leaves which were beginning to come through. 'Then,' he recalls, 'my walkie-talkie started crackling away, and Mike's words to me were, "I think we're both daddies." We had sat through wind and rain for about five weeks, and suddenly we had chicks. I just remember sitting back and thinking, "This is the beginning." It was an amazing privilege to have been part of that.'

How did it feel – in that moment? 'Huge, huge relief. And great delight for the birds that they were now parents for the first time in their lives.'

There were two chicks. After six weeks, one died in the nest. Suddenly, there was panic: 'This *cannot* fail at this stage.'

Sea eagles don't fledge until they are twelve weeks old. One evening in July 1985 – 'A momentous and hugely emotional moment' – the chick took off from the nest and flew above the oak wood. But this triumph was short-lived; it ditched in the loch. Sexton and Madders thought it was going to drown. 'I felt utterly sick.' They thought about swimming out to rescue it, but by the time they reached the shoreline it was nowhere to be seen. It was getting dark, there was nothing to be done but wait for the next day. 'We didn't tell the bosses that we might have just lost the first chick in seventy years. It was the worst night I can ever remember.'

The next day, at first light, they returned to the loch. Madders, eye to his telescope, spotted the bird on the shoreline, standing on a boulder. 'The relief of knowing that chick was alive was overwhelming,' Sexton recalls. 'Mike said, "I've got it! I've got it! It's alive!" I think I cried at that moment with the stress and strain of it all. I remember falling back into the heather.'

Sexton's memories and emotions around this are bound up with what later happened to his friend. In August 2009, Madders and his seven-year-old son Daniel died when their kayak overturned on Loch Maree, near Ullapool. There is a painful irony in the fact that the man who had been terrified that an eagle's chick should drown would, years later, lose his own life and that of his child in the waters of a loch. 'It was a great loss,' says Sexton. 'He was a grand colleague, friend and a very experienced eagle man. It was very comforting to have someone like that alongside.'

The white-tailed eagles are, Sexton says, Madders' legacy. The two men followed that chick through the Mull summer, into autumn, and by the end of the year it had gone, departed for who-knows-where. These days it would have been fitted with satellite tags, but back then it didn't even have identifiers on its wings. Did it survive the winter? Did it go on to have chicks of its own? 'He could still be out there now,' says Sexton. 'We'll never know, but we can dream.'

Sea eagles are protected under the Wildlife and Country-side Act, with a maximum penalty of six months' imprisonment and/or fines of up to £5,000. The Mull birds have been targeted by egg thieves in the past and now irresponsible wildlife photographers who get too close; some nests are protected by security cameras and razor wire. There are twenty nests on Mull, the exact locations of which are kept hush-hush.

These are valuable birds from both an environmental and economic perspective. Mull is marketed as 'Eagle Island' and it is estimated that the birds attract up to £5 million of tourism a year. Even on a wet day the open deck of the Mull Charters boat is busy with visitors wowing at the sea eagles swooping down to take fish from Loch na Keal.

'Is that not the most spectacular thing you've ever seen?' asks Martin Keivers, the boat's skipper. Perhaps, but 'spectacular' is not the right word. 'Awesome' is better. 'Dreadful' would be better still. A sea eagle in silhouette, circling a hundred feet above, has a heavy, oppressive, almost hostile presence that brings to mind a bomber aircraft. You can all but hear the engine of the Junkers.

The trick is to balance the magnetic pull these birds exert on tourists with the need to keep them safe. An informal network of islanders observes the nests and reports any suspicious characters to the police. Mary van Heerden, known as 'Eagle Mary', is sixty-nine and moved to Mull from Zimbabwe ten years ago, feeling forced out of the country amid growing security fears. She had been the victim of an armed robbery that left her traumatised.

She started running a B&B on Mull, but suffered periods of depression until, one day in 2007, Sexton asked her to keep an eye on a pair of eagles about to nest. She has watched them ever since, enjoying the sound of the wind in their wings as they fly overhead. 'After two or three hours, I come back feeling all is right with the world,' she says. 'It has been a wonderful therapy. I pride myself that I've never taken antidepressants. I've never had counselling. These eagles are better.'

Not everyone regards them so positively. Many farmers on Mull would happily see them die out once more. Sheep farming is an important part of the island's culture and economy; lamb is part of the sea eagle diet. Between those two facts lies anger and conflict.

'It's an escalating problem,' says fifty-five-year-old Lachlan MacLean, the third generation of his family to farm on Mull. 'It's having a huge impact.'

MacLean farms 10,000 acres and keeps 2,500 ewes. It was on his land, in 1985, that the first sea eagle hatched. But he takes no pride in this. That beak poking free from the egg was, for him, the beginning of a disaster. He says there are now four nests on the farm, four on the periphery and a number of non-nesting juveniles. 'We're surrounded.' Besieged.

Putting a number on the livestock he loses to sea eagles is difficult, he admits, but says the losses are significant. A lamb sells for about £60 and females are worth more than that in subsidy. A new scheme offers financial support to farmers who have nests on their land.

But MacLean says he is still losing money. 'It's very emotive, it's folk's livelihoods.' He appreciates the boost the birds give to the island economy, and is by no means calling for extermination, but would like numbers to be somehow controlled, or for compensation to be paid by the Scottish Government. There is a feeling among farmers that these birds have been imposed on them and – although no sea eagle on Mull has been shot since reintroduction – a sense of envy of great-grandfathers who were not prevented by law from taking action.

There are thought to be about fifty or so sea eagles on Mull, although there are also populations across the

Hebrides, down the west coast and on the other side of the country in Fife. It is likely that this month, or next, the hundredth breeding pair will be confirmed. 'That feels like an important milestone,' says Sexton. And the future? 'I would say that two hundred and fifty pairs in Scotland over the next twenty, thirty years is a reasonable target.'

This will be music to the ears of conservationists and tourist businesses, but for MacLean it sounds a discordant note. 'These birds were extinct for a reason,' he says, 'and they are now creating the same problem that was here in years gone by.'

Back on Shetland, Maurice Henderson is walking along the cliffs, high above the hungry sea. We have been to the old ruined croft where the bird is said to have lifted the bairn and we are now on Fetlar, looking for the site of the nest. Henderson is a member of the folk group Fiddlers' Bid and keen on the folklore of these islands, but this is the first time he has made this pilgrimage, following the flight of the eagle. It is an auspicious moment.

The local press is reporting the arrival of sea eagles on Orkney, to the south, so it's only a matter of time before they are back on Shetland, the scene of their extinction becoming a cradle of their resurrection.

He stands near the edge, looking down on the crag where he believes the nest must have been. Strange to think if that boy long ago hadn't had the courage to climb down a rope and rescue a baby, their descendant would not now be taking pictures. That's if you believe the legend. Henderson does and is grateful. 'I would have missed out on a lot of fiddle tunes,' he laughs.

That sea eagle almost cost him his life. We have cost the eagles theirs. Now humans and birds must learn to live together. It is, as Sexton puts it, 'an uneasy peace' at times, but one, surely, that is worth trying to keep.

* * *

153

Postscript: On 28th May 2015, just twenty-three days after I visited the site on Mull where the first chick fledged, it was confirmed by the RSPB that the hundredth breeding pair was nesting on Hoy, one of the Orkney islands, a short flight from the Tomb of the Eagles with its ancient skulls and talons.

Almost exactly one month later, Lachlan MacLean died suddenly, aged fifty-five, on his farm on Mull. A hugely respected and well liked Muileach, his funeral at Salen Church was attended by hundreds. He was buried at Pennygown Cemetery, notable for its ruined chapel and medieval grave slabs – a suitable resting place for a man of this land.

In Praise of Small Towns

ARBROATH, FIRST THING on a sunny working day, presents to the world a fresh face and the smell of fresh fish being gently smoked while the church bells chime over the Kirk Square.

Old Bill Spink, a town worthy, is already hard at work in his shop down a close off Market Gate, as he has been for most of his seventy-nine years. He wears a tweed bunnet and wellies, an outfit he might have come out of the womb wearing, as he ties gleaming haddock by their tails to a charred-black stake. Smoke drifts from a turret above his shop, passes over the Brothock burn, from which Arbroath takes its name, and out to sea. Spink was born and bred in this town and remembers the thriving fishing industry. His grandmother sold fish round the countryside from a creel on her back, his mother used a barrow. He himself spent time on the waves. 'Now,' he says, 'there's just one fishing boat left here. That's all away.'

That's all away. This is the refrain I hear as I travel around the towns of Angus. Visit Arbroath, Kirriemuir or Brechin and you will find that these places are beautiful in their understated way – all gables and steeples and old red stone. Yet you will also find a sense of loss, even grief. There has been a growing feeling over the past few years that all is not well with Scotland's towns, an air of stagnation and sterility. We see the vacant stores. We see the stoating drunks and the young folk without work. We see the morning queues for methadone at quiet, quaint high street chemists. There is, then, a feeling that Something

155

Must Be Done, or, to be precise, that something must be done but without spending any money.

'Towns are the backbone of the community in Scotland,' says Ross Martin, head of the think tank Scotland's Towns Partnership. 'We shape our towns, but they shape us as well. They make us who we are. They shape our values and our character.'

A foreign visitor walking along the main shopping street in Arbroath might be forgiven for thinking that the chain store To Let is doing rather well. There's a run of vacant premises and plenty others which, going by the lack of custom, would appear to be on a shoogly peg. One young woman, Stacey Black, mother of four children, welcomes the recent arrival of giants such as Asda and B&Q – 'I used to have to go into Dundee for a tin of paint' – but local shopkeepers are less keen.

'Arbroath has seen better days,' admits Ian Beattie, a local barber, 'but I believe it's a sleeping giant.'

Beattie is proud of the town and has photographs of its historic monuments on the walls of his salon. Since 1973, he has been cutting the hair of Arbroath – 'I'd like to see it in a heap' – and believes that locals, sometimes known as Red Lichties, are 'fine resilient people'. Angus's largest town, with a population of around 22,000, is still a fairly traditional place, he believes. There are some old fishing families from the 'fit o' the toon', the area around the harbour, who still refuse to mix with 'the toonsters' – everyone else – and would kick up hell if their daughter wanted to marry a toonster lad. 'It takes you a long time, if you weren't born in Arbroath, to get your citizenship,' says Beattie.

Travelling around Angus, from Arbroath to Brechin, one is struck by the architecture, the way that dark closes and pends give way to long beautiful streets. This, I think, has something in common with the folk themselves. They can be reticent at first, their charms shut away, yet spend a bit of time and they begin to open up. Down a pend next to the court, I meet three middle-aged ladies who have stopped for a blether. Arbroath, they feel, has no luck. Forfar and Montrose are blessed by comparison. There is a sense of something thwarted about Arbroath. 'It sounds daft,' acknowledges Annie-Marie Slater, but she feels the local bingo is an example of this. Only here, she explains, do you have to share the £5 prize if more than one player shouts house at once. 'Do they think folk in Arbroath are daft? Ach, it just scunners you.'

One can understand why people feel anxious or even depressed about their towns. But, of course, towns are about more than just shops. There is a particular spirit in Scottish towns – a mix of kookiness, couthiness, drollness, sentimentality and pride – which is absent from villages and cities. Somehow, it needs a town to flourish.

Perth's ambition, lately realised, to become a city has always seemed to me wrongheaded. Perth is a town. A grand old town. It is the size of a town and it feels like a town as you walk around within it. The idea that the granting of city status represents a restoration of Perth's 'ancient dignity', as the council has it, is a joke. There is nothing undignified about being a town. On the contrary, many Scottish towns, including that other pompous over-reacher Stirling, have a douce grace that would be the envy of many a city.

Leaving Arbroath, I drive inland, past golden fields full of gulls, to the bustling town of Forfar. It feels very different from Arbroath – busier and more prosperous, right at the heart of farming country. There are problems with drugs and poverty here, you're told, but what you think is – well, there must be money in tatties yet. The streets are full of well-fed farmers and ladies who lunch. 'We're just ordinary hard-workin' fowk,' says Elizabeth, a woman in her fifties. 'Friendly, too. You've got to stay in Carnoustie seven year afore the fowk'll say hello to you.'

If anything, Forfarians are desperately keen to know

157

your business. 'As soon as you come into Forfar, you'll be asked where you are from and where your parents are from,' says Ian Whyte, landlord of The Plough, a pub better known as The Ploo.

'When I go to Kirrie,' says one of his regulars, an Englishman, raising his head from a plate of steak pie, 'and they hear my accent, they don't even ask. They hit first.'

Forfar's great rivalry is not between people from different areas of town, but between those who eat the bridies from McLaren's and those who prefer those baked by Saddler's. Like the Old Firm, both bakers are great Victorian institutions with one favouring a green colour scheme, the other red, white and blue. The preference in bridie is passed from father to son, mother to daughter, family loyalty intensifying with each new generation. Forfarians, however, are united in their belief that pies made in Arbroath are inedible, though the fish suppers – they admit, grudgingly – are all right.

The spirit of small town Scotland is alive and well in Forfar. I can say this with confidence having met Martin Gray, groundskeeper and kit man with Forfar Athletic, the second division team known as The Loons. Gray is in his forties and has had a hard time of it lately. First the grass at Station Park was replaced by artificial turf and then, just three weeks ago, his beloved collie cross, Giggsy, was put down by the vet. 'Heartbreaking,' he says. 'You lose the pitch and you lose your fuckin' dug.'

Giggsy, named after Manchester United's Ryan Giggs, despite being a bitch ('My pal, his dad's cat was called Larsson,' Gray shrugs) was a familiar sight around Forfar, forever running beside her master's push-bike. She was a public figure, really, at fifteen an old worthy in her own right. She was given special dispensation to enter The Ploo and many local shops which would normally be forbidden to animals, even including Jarvis Brothers – 'the Harrods of Forfar'.

Gray has a tattoo of Giggsy on his right forearm, has buried her within the grounds of Station Park, and is raising funds to pay for a memorial bench for his dog. He has been touched by the hundreds of pounds which have already been donated by fans at matches and in the pub. The Loons' recent 4–0 victory over Stenhousemuir was dedicated to Giggsy. Martin shakes his head with emotion when considering all this. 'Aye,' he says, 'and she used to love a bridie.'

It's all there, isn't it? Humour and pathos, comradeship and compassion, generosity of purse and spirit. The soul of a town and its folk.

A clock is striking five as I leave Angus, throwing the steeple's long shadow on the emptying streets. The way forward for Forfar and Arbroath, Kirriemuir and Brechin, and all such places is, of course, uncertain. Nobody wants to see shops close and money vanish, but it seems to me that towns which have such people as Martin Gray and Bill Spinks in them have reason to be proud and to face the future with a fair degree of fortitude.

The Scottish Resistance

THE TUNNOCK'S CHOCOLATE factory rises above Uddingston, a small town seven miles south-east of Glasgow, with the authority of a cathedral – a cathedral of snacks – the giant Caramel Wafer on its front glowing red and gold in the cold Lanarkshire night.

This place, in truth rather kitschy, lacks the haunted solemnity of Culloden moor, and the date 14th January 2016 – unlike Bannockburn 1314 – is not etched on the undaunted heart of every Scottish school child and sports fan. But it was here and then that an unlikely battle in the war for Scotland's soul was fought. A group calling itself the Scottish Resistance – the so-called 'shock troops' of Scottish nationalism – staged a protest against the decision by the company to rebrand its best known product as 'the Great British Tea Cake' in adverts on the London underground. This marketing decision made Tunnock's, in the eyes of the Resistance, 'a bunch of traitors and collaborators', so they turned up outside the factory with a microphone, an amplifier and a home-made sign featuring the Scottish lion rampant, which they claimed had been removed from packaging.

'We are the Scottish Resistance!' shouted the group's sixty-year-old founder, James Scott. This *cri de coeur* did not impress a small group of hecklers, among them Rita Calder, a sixty-eight-year-old from nearby Blantyre, who staged a counter-protest by stuffing a Tea Cake into her mouth, chewing it slowly and with great pleasure in front of the Resistance. 'That lot are a shower and an embarrassment to Scotland,' she says later. A committed Unionist, she had been upset when the large Saltire hanging on the front of her garage was defaced with graffiti including 'Death to the Union' and 'We love you, Nicola'. The flag, she feels, belongs to everyone in Scotland, and has been 'hijacked' by the independence cause. 'So my humph was up,' and she decided to take out that anger on the nationalist group making all the headlines. 'I'm not a confrontational person,' she says, 'but the attack on Tunnock's was one step too far.'

The deeds of that day were not recorded on parchment or vellum, but rather Buzzfeed and Twitter, and it was the moment when the Scottish Resistance became known – and mocked – beyond Scotland. Yet, in the face of scorn, they refuse to give up the fight. Numpties, zoomers, eejits – these are the names that bounce off their thick skins. Those sympathetic to their cause and tactics call them patriots. Others view them with amusement. Their actions have a tendency to turn into comedies of errors. A recent ritual public burning of a David Cameron speech was delayed when the lighter went missing. A few years ago, a leading member of the group attempted to occupy a bank in Glasgow, only to find that the branch had closed. Little wonder that J. K. Rowling tweeted 'The Scottish Resistance are comedy geniuses', and claimed to be buying their T-shirts as joke presents for Union-supporting journalists.

'They are laughing at us, but it doesn't bother us,' says fifty-four-year-old Sean Clerkin, a prominent Resistance member. 'They know how serious we are. They're afraid of us.'

Wait – Rowling is scared of the Scottish Resistance? 'Yes, absolutely ... Afraid of groups like us getting Scottish independence and redistributing income from rich to poor, so that J. K. Rowling is no longer the rich woman that she currently is ... The millions that she's got in her bank account should be redistributed to the poor, to the working class. She's afraid of what we stand for.'

So who are the Scottish Resistance and what do they stand for? James Scott formed the pro-independence, anti-austerity group in January 2014. He claims they have 7,500 members, but this figure is based on Facebook likes; there are a hundred or so card-carrying members, and only a handful who turn up to events. Nevertheless, their profile and impact is out of all proportion to their numbers. They have a knack for stunts that make the papers, such as their attempt, in December, to have the prime minister arrested for war crimes.

Meanwhile, the Scottish Conservative leader, Ruth Davidson, credits Clerkin with changing the course of history. During the run-up to the 2011 Holyrood election, Clerkin and other protesters pursued the then Scottish Labour leader Iain Gray into a Glasgow sandwich shop; Gray's perceived reluctance to discuss Labour's policies, Davidson argues, proved so damaging to his public image that it allowed the SNP to form a majority government, leading in turn to the independence referendum and all the political turbulence that has followed. The public, she said, 'saw Iain Gray run into a Subway and thought he was a diddy and said: "That man shouldnae be First Minister."'

Known for his forceful heckling of politicians, Clerkin insists that he does not get a buzz out of confrontation. Political leaders have grown too used to living in protective bubbles, he says, and it's his mission to prick them.

Even Nicola Sturgeon, a saint in the eyes of many SNP supporters, is considered a sinner by those most zealous nationalists frustrated that she isn't calling a second referendum quickly enough. 'I don't believe she wants an independent Scotland,' Clerkin says. 'I think she's just in it for the power.'

What about Clerkin's own motivations? It is often suggested that he is simply an attention-seeker and narcissist. In Edinburgh earlier this month, around a hundred independence supporters gathered outside the Court of

Session in support of IndyCamp, a bivouac of caravans and tents assembled next to the Scottish Parliament, which the authorities were trying to have removed. The atmosphere was upbeat, but some IndyCampers, noticing Clerkin and Scott, turned hostile. 'Don't you know you're undermining the cause?' shouted a woman with red hair. A young, bearded man snarled at Clerkin: 'It's all about Sean, isn't it?'

That's a question worth asking. So, is it? 'I reject that completely,' says Clerkin. 'I've never been interested in attention-seeking, or money, or going up the grubby pole.'

When yelling through his megaphone, Clerkin can sound like a Glaswegian Dalek. He has been accused of being a fanatic with nothing in his life but protest. Not so, he insists. He lives with his elderly parents in a bungalow in Barrhead, helps to look after them, and works in a call centre. He is father to an eighteen-year-old daughter. He sings the songs of Bob Dylan in the shower. 'I have a girl-friend as well. I'm not a robot. I'm a human being.'

How seriously should we take the Scottish Resistance? They have a public profile somewhere between two Monty Python sketches – the Spanish Inquisition ('Nobody expects …') and the People's Front of Judea. Yet, while many will disapprove of their tactics, it might also be true to say that they do reflect a not insignificant sector of Scottish society who feel frustrated, thwarted, bewildered, paranoid and even scared following the no vote. Arguably, they reflect the emotions, most of all, of the so-called 'missing mil-lion' – those people from poor communities who had never voted before the referendum, and who are now scunnered in the extreme that their X for independence didn't count for much.

This all exists amid a broader context of widespread and growing disenchantment with UK institutions. The recent Scottish Social Attitudes survey shows that less than a quarter of Scots believe the Westminster Government acts in their best interests. Less than half feel the BBC represents Scotland adequately.

'All that Indyref emotion had to go somewhere,' says Peter Geoghegan, author of *The People's Referendum: Why Scotland Will Never Be the Same Again*. 'Traditionally, politics has changed very slowly here, but we went through this incredibly intense political moment and we're not out the other side yet. It can be difficult for people to find a mooring in that. Anger, alienation, rejection and fear is what you can end up with. So to just see the Scottish Resistance as comical and silly misses the sociological significance, and doesn't take account of where this has come from.'

On a cold, wet Sunday last month, the Scottish Resistance came together within the portico of Glasgow's Gallery of Modern Art to remember one of their fallen. There were twenty or so people gathered, but one face was missing. Philip Malloy had taken his own life, at the age of twenty-seven, a year before. Resistance members and relations held blown-up photos. In one, taken at a rally in George Square, Malloy was dressed as a Roman legionary, with a Saltire slung over a shoulder. 'Phil was my right-hand man in the Scottish Resistance,' said Scott. 'I tell you something, I've never met a more patriotic Scot ... One Phil Malloy is worth two million bloody Unionists.'

Music played through a small amp: songs from *Les Misérables*; Andy Stewart's 'A Scottish Soldier'. Someone lifted a can of Buckfast heavenwards. A neon artwork glowed above their heads, bright slogans of ironic patriotism displayed above the doors of the gallery: We ♥ Bonnie Prince Charlie; We ♥ Alcohol; We ♥ Failure. Phil Malloy's father, also Philip, a solid-looking man with silver hair, remembered his boy: 'He grew up with me telling him all about Scottish history. I told him about the Highland Clearances and all the bad times, the tyranny we went through for hundreds of years by the English ... He'd say: "Da, why are we no' independent?"' Malloy said that those who had voted no at the referendum were cowards. 'I know my son wasnae one. James called him a Scottish foot-soldier. Well, to me he was a general, and I loved him very much.'

Afterwards, over a drink, Malloy explained that his son had got himself into trouble before becoming enthused about Scottish nationalism. He had a history of prison, once for assault. Joining the Resistance marked a positive change. He found a sense of purpose and loved speaking at rallies. 'It meant an awful lot to him,' he said. 'He told me what they were trying to achieve, and it was the first time I had seen a determination in him.'

Then life began to get on top of him. He lost his job as a barman, had his benefits sanctioned, and became homeless – all this on top of the no vote in the referendum, which he took hard. It was, his father says, one of the things that led him into darkness. He was in the Clyde for five weeks before police divers found him.

On 24th March 2016 – the day Scotland would have become independent had the vote gone the other way – James Scott awoke at home in Rutherglen to the knowledge that his country was not yet free, but determined to play his part in freeing it before long. The Scottish Resistance have been campaigning for a second referendum to be held in 2017 although Scott, personally, favours some sort of unilateral declaration of independence.

'To me it's just another day,' he says, over coffee. 'They were never going to allow Scotland to get independence.' He believes the referendum was rigged, and not only that, but fixed so that 45 per cent of the electorate appeared to vote Yes in order to associate the movement with the doomed Jacobite rebellion of 1745. 'That number's in the fuckin' Scottish psyche,' he says. Such conspiracy theories are not uncommon in the outer reaches of the independence movement; belief that the referendum was 'stolen' is widespread and perhaps, in its way, consoling.

Scott works as a self-employed financial consultant. In protest against their previous opposition to independence, he boycotts Tunnock's, B&Q and Asda, and would boycott the BBC too, if he had his way. 'The wife sticks it on for *EastEnders*, but I keep turning it over.' His activism has required personal sacrifice. 'There is a wee bit of a rift between me and my daughter. She's a police officer and she wants me to stop protesting.' He joined the SNP in 1973 and was a member until last year, having been suspended for his part in protesting at a Labour rally in Glasgow during the general election.

The Scottish Resistance is regarded negatively by the leadership of the SNP. 'If you want to win a referendum, you can't afford to put any people off unnecessarily,' says one senior party insider. 'The polls indicate that a huge number of people who voted no would potentially vote yes in a future referendum. If there's an element among independence supporters who are putting across an unattractive image, then that raises a wholly unnecessary barrier.

'Even the name is unappealing. Who are they resisting? Surely not the 55 per cent who voted no, because they are the people we need to try really hard to persuade to vote yes next time.'

The name has history and resonance. It calls to mind the Wars of Independence, when Wallace and Bruce wrote their names in English blood. More recently, Scottish Resistance was a phrase associated with a particular school of thought that developed within the SNP in the early 1980s: that future success would be built upon working-class support. In a 1982 pamphlet, Alex Salmond – then still a young firebrand – quoted with approval a motion passed by the SNP party conference 'that a real Scottish resistance and defence of jobs demands direct action up to and including political strikes and civil disobedience on a mass scale'. In a letter to the *Glasgow Herald* that same year, he reiterated the point: 'Given the impotence of their present political representatives, working people are starting to mount their own "Scottish Resistance".'

This wasn't just talk. At the SNP party conference in 1981 a resolution was passed in favour of a civil disobedience campaign aimed at opposing the Conservative deindustrialisation of Scotland, and a few months later Jim Sillars and five other members of the party's left-leaning 79 Group acted upon it, breaking into and occupying Edinburgh's old Royal High School building. Sillars, now a well-liked elder statesman of the independence movement, sees no relation between his actions then and those of the present Scottish Resistance. 'Over the years in Scotland there have been similar groups with romantic titles who could not burst a paper bag,' he says. 'Totally irrelevant.'

Scott, no doubt, is well aware of the resonances of the name. He is a keen student of history. A much less well-known aspect of Scottish Resistance activity is the guided walks they offer to places of historical interest. The idea is that the Scots need to be 're-educated' about their own history so they no longer regard it from a pro-Union perspective.

He finishes his coffee and leads the way across the street to Rutherglen's Old Parish Church, where, in 1305, William Wallace was betrayed to English forces. 'I got married here in 1979,' says Scott. 'On the Wednesday, there was the rehearsal. I went into the church and there were all these Union flags. So I says to the minister, "See when I come in here on Saturday, I want all these removed." I did not want to get married in a church, associated with Wallace, where they were flying that flag.'

He glares up at the red, white and blue flying from the town hall. For years he has been trying to persuade the council to raise a Saltire instead. He won't give up, though, on the flag, or anything. His seriousness of purpose insulates him against mockery. Look at David Icke, he says –

people used to laugh at him. 'We will just keep protesting until things happen. No one ever thought the Berlin Wall would come down.'

What happens, though, if Scotland does, eventually, become independent? What will Scott and the Scottish Resistance do with their lives then?

'Well,' he says, 'there's Tibet ...'

A Car-Boot Sale

GEORGE THOMSON GRINS, shrugs and spreads his hands, palms outwards, silver earring flashing in the bright morning sun. 'I've got OCD,' he confesses. 'Obsessive Car-Boot Disorder.'

Every Sunday without fail, the sixty-three-year-old plasterer, out of work at present, gets up early – often in darkness – and drives from Drumchapel to Blochairn, a district in the north-east of Glasgow, to attend Scotland's largest car-boot sale. He is not alone. The sale attracts around 400 traders and anything up to 20,000 punters keen on a bargain. More specifically, George is usually in the company of his fiancée Cathie and their pal Marina. Cathie, when I meet her, has just bought some glue – for carpet tiles, she insists, not for sniffing. Marina has her eyes on a nice scarf which she hopes to secure for a pound. Marina was in the huff through the week, George explains, because he and Cathie went to the car-boot sale at Polmadie and she couldn't make it along. 'If she doesn't get to the car-boot with us, she gets depressed. She gets withdrawal symptoms.'

George, so far today, has bought a chip pan and a thick tartan shawl, the latter item which he and Cathie hope to sell at a significant profit on their forthcoming holiday in Ukraine. Wearing a swish cravat, George looks a bit of a dandy. 'You can dress yourself to the nines in here for next to nothing. Designer stuff, too.' He has a wardrobe full of car-boot clothes he has never had a chance to wear. 'I hardly ever go up the toon now,' he says. 'I'd be no' weel if I spent twenty pounds on a shirt.' He buys so much at the car-boot sale that he has to bring a van. And he bought the van here too.

The Blochairn car-boot sale is a weekly ritual within the city. It's some place. Massive. It takes place on the site of the fruit and veg wholesale market which runs through the week. There are pre-booked pitches available in the market halls, many of which are used by professional traders, and mention must be made at this point of the fish man, his stand resplendent with lion rampant and Saltire, who goes by the splendid name of Watty Boak. Casual pitches outside and in can be secured by those willing to turn up early and queue, and these tend to be used by those clearing out cupboards and lofts, keen to make a bob or two. Demand is high. Would-be traders are queuing, sometimes, from 8 p.m. on the Saturday evening. It is possible to get on the site by midnight and, though the sale does not begin officially until 6 a.m., it is common for informal trading to begin hours earlier, bargain-hunters examining merchandise by the light of miners' helmets while sellers wrestle trestles out of their boots.

At 6.30 a.m. the market is already busy. It's a beautiful morning but very cold; pale, golden light like chilled champagne. Many traders are keeping warm in the traditional Scottish way with a tartan rug and twenty fags. The air is clear and free of fog, but nevertheless certain traders are already hawking their wares – 'Therr three perra knickers furra pound! Gaun furra thong!' – in voices which could, if employed by the coastguard, warn shipping away from the Clyde coast.

You see some sights at the car-boot sale: a lanky goth, all cheekbones and piercings, clutching a giant teddy the exact same shade of blue as his nail polish; a toddler pushing an old petrol mower through the crowds; a Falstaffian Hell's Angel type, belly jutting through his leather jacket, long grey beard half-obscuring his gold Harley-Davidson necklace, a skull and crossbones bandana keeping off the cold.

This last is Frank Starrs, sixty-eight in years, in height about five feet and change, who comes to Blochairn from 5.30 a.m. every Sunday 'for a wee nosy aboot'. He is a taxi driver and used to haggling, which comes in handy here. Often, he's looking for bits for his bike, but when I bump into him he is rifling through packets of biscuits – 'dookers for tea' – using hands so bright with golden rings it is a wonder he does not spend his days being pecked by magpies. Frank's wife says he buys a load of rubbish, but he wouldn't stop coming here for the world. It's his routine. Later, this car-boot Sisyphus laden with bling and Bourbons will go to Polmadie and then on to the sale at Lanark.

Car-boots are booming. The economic crash is to their advantage. People who can't afford to shop on the high street, or who consider paying full retail price a mug's game, are drawn here by free entry and the prospect of a bargain. Shopkeepers who can no longer afford to pay rent on their shops set up stalls instead. Not everyone who comes here is poor – some pay for goods with bulging wallets, but there are also those who keep their eyes on the ground, scanning for dropped coins.

Britons spend millions every year at car-boot sales, much of it doled out a pound or fifty pence at a time. There are thousands of sales across the UK, transforming car parks and red blaze football pitches into islands of possibility in which treasure may be found buried deep beneath a pile of scratched Glen Daly LPs. Well, so goes the secret hope in everyone's heart. The truth is that genuine precious antiques and undiscovered Caravaggios seem pretty thin on the ground at Blochairn. A ratty fox-fur is more likely. Scuffed brogues, old *Vogue*s; strimmers, zimmers; greasy throttles, ships in bottles. You can buy it all here – furniture, electronics, great rusting lengths of chain. I would say everything but the kitchen sink, but there's a few of those as well. On one occasion a man in a van tried to set up an ersatz sex shop, but the market officials chased him. He was attempting to flog – if that is the word – a blow-up doll for £459. 'At a car-boot!' folk say, more offended by the indecency of the price than the object itself.

Second-hand clothes are big at Blochairn. 'They're ma wife's troosers, but she left me,' an apple-cheeked trader tells a middle-aged woman. 'Check the pockets, there might be money in them.' The woman tries on a hat. 'Aye, that looks nice on you,' the trader says. 'The wife husnae worn that since she got rid of her nits.'

Some of these guys have the patter. Big Gerry is selling boxes of crisps and sweets out of the back of a van. 'It's all for charity,' he barks. 'William Hill, Coral, Ladbrokes.'

There are traders whose sales technique is more than merely functional, reaching instead the level of street poetry. Take, for example, Stevie Broon, a butcher-auctioneer operating from a trailer with a big hatch in the side. 'Look at the scales, guys, buy with your eyes,' he tells the crowd. 'That's the equivalent of sixty-five pounds-worth of gammon there and I'm doing it for twenty pounds. Gammon, gammon, gammon. Lovely jubbly. Twenty quid the lot.'

He spots a customer, an enormously fat man with a walking stick. 'You want chicken legs?' the butcher asks. 'Chicken wings?' The man puts a hand to his chest and scoops up a moob. 'Naw,' he says. 'Chicken tits.'

By about half-ten, the car-boot sale is peaking. It is due to finish at three, but by then most people have drifted away to the Barras and elsewhere. The air smells of chips and curry sauce. A septuagenarian on a mobility scooter has somehow crammed a big spare wheel between his knees and the steering column. Young Nigerians lift used tellies into the back of a flat-bed truck. A man in a bunnet consults a 1958 map of Weston-super-Mare.

Sitting with a cuppa, two putters sticking out of her red shopper, fifty-six-year-old Mary Chambers from

172

Castlemilk explains that she comes here every Sunday despite bad knees and a walk-in cupboard with no remaining room in which to walk. 'I met that Anita Manning here once,' she says. 'I had just rubbed Ralgex on my knees before we shook hands. She must have wondered what the smell was.' The attraction of the sale, according to Mary, is anticipation. You never know what you are going to find.

Then there is the pleasure of haggling, far from beloved by all sellers but esteemed by regular customers as an important part of car-boot culture.

'Much is this jaiket?' a punter asks.

'A fiver,' says the trader.

'Ach,' says the punter, screwing up his face. 'Can you no come doon a bit?'

The trader squats on his hunkers. 'Still a fiver,' he says.

Above Orkney

IT IS 16TH April 2012, exactly 897 years since the martyrdom of Magnus, Orkney's patron saint, and the puffins, as if in acknowledgement of the anniversary, have chosen this day to return to their sea stack off Westray after months in the North Atlantic. Meanwhile, Captain Stuart Linklater, a senior pilot with Loganair, lifts the nose of the small plane known as the *Islander* from the runway at Kirkwall and plunges once more into his own natural environment – the cool blue air above these green islands. 'Isn't it beautiful?' he says. And it is.

Linklater is one of three pilots who, between them, fly several times daily from Kirkwall Airport, its name written in sharp steel runes above the main entrance, to the North Isles, the remote and sometimes sparsely populated islands beyond the Orkney mainland. The archipelago is spread wide in every direction. While the islands of the south are linked to the mainland by causeway and regular crossing, the North Isles are isolated. There may be just one ferry each week, sailings to Kirkwall can take almost three hours, and in winter – when the swell of the sea is more than any pier can handle – the furthest islands can go three weeks without a boat being able to land. In such circumstances, the plane, as Neil Rendall, a farmer on Papa Westray, puts it, means 'the difference between daylight and darkness'.

These flights are lifeline services without which it would be difficult for the North Isles to sustain their populations. The plane carries teachers to schools, commuters to and from Kirkwall, and, on freight flights, food and booze to whomever has had the foresight – and the drouth – to place

174

an order. Loganair's inter-island service began in 1967, but there had already been flights between the islands from 1932, pioneered by Captain Ernest Fresson, whose Highland Airways was funded in part through a deal that saw *The Scotsman* newspaper being delivered to Orkney a day ahead of rival titles. Those flights ended with the outbreak of war, but some North Isles elders still remember Fresson and his little biplane – a visiting angel with beret and pipe.

Flying between the islands is a remarkable experience. These are short journeys. The longest, Kirkwall to Stronsay, takes twenty-five minutes, and the briefest, between Westray and Papa Westray, just two. This last is the world's shortest scheduled flight; passengers making the hop for the first time are given a certificate and a whisky miniature, the latter being a welcome restorative following exposure to gales howling across the tiny island known to locals as Papay, a blotted punctuation mark between ocean and sea.

The *Islander* is a versatile eight-seater with two propellers. If cross-winds rule out the runway, it can land in fields, where the wee black and white plane looks quite at home taxiing among oystercatchers. Those seated at the front are closer to the pilot than they would be to the driver in a black cab. 'It can feel like driving a bus,' says Linklater. 'You get to know the passengers and their foibles; the ones who are going to have difficulty fastening their seatbelts. You have a chat and get the news.'

Linklater is fifty-eight and known as 'the Orcadian George Clooney' on account of both a slight physical resemblance (it's the hair; maybe the eyes) and a certain wry affability. He has been flying the *Islander* for twenty-three years and has made around 60,000 take-offs and landings – 'so I'm just about getting used to it'. He has never had any interest in flying the big jets internationally; he is happiest in the skies above Orkney, serving the community to which he belongs. As the great majority of his passengers are regulars, the pilot's safety demonstration appears to consist of little more than advising against opening a window in flight as 'it'll get very draughty'. One of the great joys of these flights is in avoiding unbending security measures that assume everyone is a potential terrorist and therefore deserving of interrogation. Captain Linklater, however, is not afraid to pose tough questions when need be. 'So,' he asks one passenger while walking out to the plane, 'how's the lambing going?'

It is a bright afternoon when we take off for Sanday. As the plane climbs, its cruciform shadow races across green fields then out over the water. The sea is pale blue by the coast, darkening as it deepens. *Islander* pilots fly by sight rather than relying on electronic navigational equipment, keeping below the level of the clouds, sometimes as low as 350 feet. The landscape, at this height, never becomes abstract. It is, rather, miniaturised: turbines are toy windmills; fish farms are hoopla. This, then, is the ideal air service for voyeurs and gossips – types in which, one is told, Orkney abounds. 'You can see the washing on people's lines,' says Linklater. 'You can see the silage being cut, the different crops growing and when they're starting to harvest. You get a feel for the season and the change in the light. It doesn't feel like you are flying above the country, it feels like you are flying through it. You're still part of it. There's a sense, too, that you're flying through history.'

The pilot notes, as he flies, points of interest below. Balfour Castle on Egilsay, where Robert Louis Stevenson stayed and which is said to have inspired parts of *Kidnapped*. Carrick House on Eday, where you can still see the stains of blood spilled during the capture of a notorious pirate. The small island of Gairsay, once home, says Linklater, to 'the last real Viking', Sveinn Asleifarson, whose plunderings with axe and fire are chronicled in the *Orkneyinga Saga*.

Orkney, with its many ancient homes and bones and

stones, is a place where temporal barriers seem porous, in which past and present coexist, and from an aerial perspective the sense of collapsed history is even more acute. It is easy to imagine that pirate, Viking and writer are still down there somewhere; that life goes on at Skara Brae and POWs observe an eternal mass in the Italian Chapel.

From the cockpit, Sanday appears first as a dark hump on the horizon, a surfacing whale. One of the larger North Isles, with a population of around 600, it is known for its beaches, great white arcs, a coastline strung with crescent moons. The descent feels fast. The gritty track of the landing strip runs out amid daisies and dandelions. The plane halts, a door opens and a wooden box is shoved down as a makeshift step. Jim Lennie, the airfield manager, offers a hand. He is a retired farmer, big and strong at seventy-one, with a handshake that could choke a heifer. 'Bonny day,' he declares, brooking no argument. Jim has looked after the Sanday airfield since 1967. His wife Mary is one of the firefighters. His duties include making sure the runway is fit for purpose, meaning free of geese. How, precisely, does he do this? 'Shoot to kill,' he replies. 'Have them for tea. That maks them stay away mibbe.'

This is the ideal man to have in charge of an airfield. Heathrow could do worse. He is calm in a crisis and has a similar approach to life as he does to his whisky: 'Tak it as it comes.' He has a reputation as a wind-up merchant and an accomplished spinner of yarns. Kirsty Walter, a member of Loganair's cabin crew, sums him up fondly as 'a yap o' shite' – a description in which he glories, enjoying perhaps the way the phrase identifies him with other stalwart features of the Orkney landscape: the Point o' the Scurroes; the Knap of Howar; the Yap o' Shite.

Jim and Mary have been married since 1969 and have six children. They met while working the harvest together. It must be love, he says, because she came originally from an island – Shapinsay – that had electricity and mains water but nevertheless settled in Sanday, which had neither. In her time as airfield firefighter, Mary has never had to fight a fire. There was once a crash, however – over twenty years ago now. 'It was like it happened in slow motion,' Jim recalls. 'The plane came doon in the field and went right through two fences. The tail rudder was knocked off. Mary was in the bedroom with our twins – just peedie bairns. I just saw this plane coming straight at oor hoose. I could hardly move. Then it hit a bump and it turned and there were nobody hurt.' He pauses, relishing his punch-line. 'The folk in the plane were interviewed and said they saw very little difference fae a normal landing.'

The passengers on these inter-island flights are various. Itinerant teachers, farmers, hairdressers, health visitors, tourists, vets, hard-hatted workies out to fix the power cut on Papay. Passengers are allowed to take their dogs on the plane, so it's not unusual to see a wet nose peeping out from beneath the seat. One woman, alighting on gale-scoured North Ronaldsay, buttons her poodle tight inside her duffle coat lest it be gusted off to doggie Valhalla.

There are times when life at Loganair seems rather like *The High Life*, as scripted by George Mackay Brown. Jackie Delaney, station manager at Kirkwall Airport, moved to Orkney from England four years ago and is still getting to grips with the local dialect. Once, when she was quite new to the job, the phone rang and an elderly woman asked whether the 'toe wife' was on the flight to Eday. 'Who on earth is the toe wife?' Jackie whispered to her colleague in the office. 'That'll be the chiropodist,' Inga explained.

Anne Rendall, a banker with RBS, is the most frequent flyer. Based in Kirkwall, she is fifty-two and has been trav-elling to the North Isles, visiting a different island each day, offering cash withdrawals, deposits and other services, for almost half her life. 'I've been keeping a tally and that's over 9,000 flights now,' she says. Despite the unorthodox manner of her commute, there is something pleasantly old-fashioned about Rendall's way of doing business, harking back to the days when people actually had a relationship with their bank manager. The banker before her, the late Maisie Muir, did the job for twenty-two years, right from the start of the inter-island flights. Before Muir was Willie Groat, who went by boat. For Rendall, the plane is part of her routine. Rain and wind do not worry her. It takes a lightning storm to interfere with her calculations of interest.

The weather in Orkney rarely takes its ease. The *Islander* can fly in up to fifty knots of wind, which is getting on for sixty miles an hour. During a flight from Kirkwall to North Ronaldsay, the wind is blowing at forty-two knots, and the sea below billows and heaves. Spume froths into the geos of the jagged coast. Rain cascades along the cockpit window. It feels, in some ways, more like being on the waves than in the air. Indeed, Linklater's navigation methods are similar to those used by a seasoned skipper – he looks for landmarks and shifts course appropriately. Flying directly above the rusting wreck of the tanker *Juniata*, scuttled in Inganess Bay in 1939, reassures him when haar shrouds Kirkwall that the airport is dead ahead.

We begin our descent into North Ronaldsay, skimming in low over flat, dark rocks that seem to ascend like steps from the sea. This is the northernmost of the Orkney Islands. Impressive from the air is the thirteen mile encircling dyke that keeps the sheep on the shore, where they subsist entirely on seaweed. There are roughly 3,000 sheep and only around seventy people. The Victorian lighthouse, a gigantic barber's pole, has 176 steps, the same as the number of verses in the 119th Psalm. Religion, one can imagine, might be a comfort here. We are right out on the edge. Norway is due east. In 1916, when Bergen burned, the islanders saw the horizon glow red.

The plane is met, as it is three times each day, by

Helen Swanney, the airfield manager, a seventy-six-year-old shopkeeper in deep pink headscarf and Bible-black anorak. 'You won't meet anyone more North Ronaldsay than Helen,' says Billy Muir, the lighthouse keeper. 'She has lived here all her life.' Swanney has been manager for sixteen years, taking over following the death of her husband Ronnie, a crofter who had held the office since 1968. For her it is not just a job, it's a duty of care for the place that has always been home. She remembers the days of the horse-drawn plough. She has seen the coming of the car to her island, the coming of television and electricity. Her father-in-law, Ken, ran the airport during the Highland Airways years of the 1930s. The Swanneys are a landing-strip dynasty. Swanney describes herself as a 'gatekeeper' – and indeed she does seem a sort of presiding spirit of North Ron, a headscarfed idol before whom each traveller, alighting from the plane, ought to bow down and pay proper homage.

Still, it can be a cold, wet job. Does she ever think of retirement? 'Well, not yet,' she replies, softly. 'I enjoy this very much, and I'll do it as long as I can.'

We take off, before long, into ashen skies. The North Isles are spread beneath us. Sunshine, breaking through cloud here and there, slants down onto the water, creating islands of light, a radiant new archipelago scattered among the existing headlands and holms. This is Orkney much as it might have looked when observed by a raven released from its cage on board a longship. That was the great Viking trick: to carry half-starved birds. Freed, they would fly in the direction of land – and food – and the Norsemen, hungry for fresh conquest, would turn the rudder to follow. The *Islander*, therefore, gives a raven's-eye view of the North Isles, and they look as seductively verdant now as they must have done then.

Captain Linklater, for his part, counts it a privilege to be able to survey daily this landscape he loves. Soon, he will be unable to do so. Aviation rules mean that when he turns sixty he will no longer be allowed to fly a plane in which he is the only member of crew. 'I'm not looking forward to it one little bit,' he admits. He will be grounded, a caged raven. He could work out of Glasgow airport and fly larger aircraft with a co-pilot, but that would mean leaving behind the great sights to which he has grown accustomed: the Westray waterfalls blown upwards by the wind; pods of orcas in the North Ronaldsay Firth; the whole glorious, dolorous presence of the islands and the sea.

'This is my home,' he says. 'This is where I belong.'

Nihil Sine Labore

GLASGOW, 1973. A shipyard on the Clyde. It is the first day for a hundred or so apprentices, in clean boilersuits and stiff new boots, unfamiliar work clothes that make them feel like wee boys dressing up. They are gathered in the training shed; eyeing each other, expectant, taking short draws on nervous fags.

Suddenly, a man stands before them – a brawny, thrawn-faced shop steward of about sixty in a white hard hat. In silence, with great solemnity, he uses his oxyacetylene torch to heat a steel poker until it glows fierce orange, then applies the tip to his tongue. A hiss like a cornered snake prompts answering gasps from the apprentices. He glowers into the cowed hush and begins his usual commencement speech.

'Youse,' he says, 'are lucky bastards. The luckiest bastards in the whole of Glesga. The world's made up of water. And what does water need? Ships! So what will the world always need? Shipbuilders!' The frown fades and he grins at them, spreading his hands before him. 'Youse'll never be unemployed.'

They believed it then. The union men. The apprentices. The workers in the yards. A whole generation that regarded the shipyards as eternal. A job for life. For many lives. That word, Clydebuilt, was a sort of promise; a guarantee of longevity on every level. Now, four decades later, there are two shipyards left on the upper Clyde, where once there were almost forty. It is a trade that has brought work, identity and purpose to the area since the Victorian age, and Ministry of Defence contracts keep BAE's Govan and

Scotstoun yards going, but the future always seems to be in doubt. In what many regard as a symbolic act, the five dockside cranes which for years were an iconic part of the riverside skyline have been dismantled and removed.

'It makes me sad when things disappear,' says one Govanite over a cuppa in a café on the Govan Road. 'I love it here. Sometimes, when I walk around, I feel like I wasn't born, but grew up out of the ground.'

The city did much the same. Glasgow became industrialised with astonishing speed and on an astonishing scale. By 1914, the city was building one-third of Britain's locomotives and one-fifth of the world's ships. At the start of the nineteenth century the population was 77,000; by the 1920s it was over a million, with almost three-quarters of those employed in manufacturing. It's hard to imagine the city as it was then, when even the nicknames of the factories and furnaces, spoil heaps and lakes of wastewater had a kind of awesome poetic resonance – Tennant's Stalk, Dixon's Blazes, Jack's Mountain, the Stinky Ocean; the sorts of names one might expect to find on a medieval mappa mundi, hard by Here Be Dragons.

Even now, with around 30 per cent of Glaswegian households workless, and the hopes of the future seemingly hung on those shoogly pegs otherwise known as the retail and service sectors, the idea of the city as a place that makes things remains the most vivid aspect of its self-image. In its own imagination, if not in the ledger book, Glasgow remains industrial, a city of steel and fire, albeit tarnished and beginning to burn low.

Scotland's biggest city is a fankle of class, race and religion; poverty and wealth; beauty and horror; sorrow, joy, humility and pride. It seeps across the map like a Rorschach inkblot in which one might see no end of wonderful, terrible things. Glasgow is around thirteen miles from east to west, ten from north to south, and contains within it a seemingly inexhaustible seam of stories, laid down in strata from generation to generation, Glaswegian lore lying thick as ore. Glasgow, of course, has plenty of gifted novelists and poets, but the city's storytelling culture is essentially oral: close-singers, windae-hingers, pub philosophers and right gabs in black cabs. As William McIlvanney wrote in his novel *Laidlaw*: 'It's not a city, it's a twenty-four hour cabaret.'

Take, for example, the Fairfield Working Men's Club. Approached from Crossloan Road in Govan, on a wet Tuesday afternoon, it is unprepossessing – a squat brick building with its name painted in red across a dripping verandah. Walk inside, though, past the sign forbidding patrons from wearing of shellsuits or trackie bottoms on Friday and Saturday nights, and you enter another world. Two dozen couples are on the dance floor, circling and embracing, as a man on stage performs 'For The Good Times' (the Perry Como version, naturally) in a baritone redolent of lost love and lipstick traces. Glittery curtains sparkle in the disco lights, and the gentle movements of the elderly dancers throw shadows on a large black and white photograph, framed on one wall, of *HMS Hood* being launched, just up the road in Clydebank, almost a century before.

Fairfield WMC was founded in 1895 and functions, these days, as an important focus for the local community and as a great treasure house of anecdote. Go to the bar for your diluting orange at 25 pence a half-pint and you are as likely to come away with a life story. 'I met my wife in 1968 at the Majestic dance hall,' says a bequiffed septuagenarian with beer on his breath. 'She gave me four good sons and two daughters, and deceived me after thirty years.'

Most of the dancers here, Mr Majestic aside, are alumni of the Plaza ballroom, since demolished, and although these are men and women of pensionable age, some of them married and widowed more than once, they are still in touch with their inner teens, and have not forgotten who dumped or clicked with whom, or what it felt like to dance with a sweetheart and feel so much future ahead of you, unknown.

A tug at the sleeve. Here comes another tale. 'See that man there?' you're told, with a nod in the direction of a tall, rather infirm-looking man on the dancefloor, stooped over his wife, as they make a shuffling circuit to 'Blueberry Hill'. 'Polish. A survivor of Monte Cassino. He was pinned down under fire for two weeks. Then he was in a prisoner-of-war camp in Siberia. They had to eat rats and caterpillars. But Stalin swapped him for a British prisoner and he ended up getting sent here. He was a brickie. A right hard case in his day. Oh, aye, I've seen him split bricks on his knee. Now look at him. This is all he's got left. This and his wee wife. He's been so used to living with death, I don't blame him for loving the dancing.'

Everyone is dressed to the nines. Sparkly frocks. Jackets and ties. Check out Davie Barr with his Versace belt, Bling Crosby, eighty-three years old if you can believe that, snow-white hair and lithe as a boy. Aye, he says, he'll talk to me, but he must get his quota of dancing in first. He has no shortage of willing – nay, demanding – partners among the elegant ladies present, and draws a finger across his neck to indicate the fate that would befall him should he fail to be available for the expected number of rhumbas.

Between a tango and a slosh, Barr has a moment for a blether. He was born, he says, in 'Old Govan' and left school at fourteen in order to work at the Queen's Dock, where he and Billy Connolly's Uncle Huey, who is also at the dancing today, were office boys together.

There is a theory that the famous Glasgow humour – black and often absurd, as popularised by Connolly – emerged in large part from the docks, shipyards and steelworks, shaped by the rough, hard, dangerous work that went on in such places. Barr is happy to confirm this – 'All the patter of the day amongst the dockers, son' – and to illustrate his point by means of a small vignette.

'Right,' he says. 'I've been to a budgie's funeral. How did this happen? I had a mate called Dougie Pincock. Came from Partick. So I walks into the office this morning and Dougie's sitting there. "Morning Dougie!" Someone nudges me, says to shush. "Dougie's had a bereavement. Wee Joey died at half-past two this morning." This was his budgie. "Aw, Dougie," I says. "Ah'm awfy sorry to hear that." He tells me thanks, the funeral's at eleven o'clock, tea break. "We're burying him at sea." So I looks over, and he's got a shoebox and on top of it's a Union Jack. I kid you not. Inside: the budgie.'

Could you see the budgie?

'No, son. It wisnae an open casket.'

I nod at this, and Davie Barr continues.

'So, it comes to eleven o'clock, and we aw line up at the edge of the quay, and Dougie goes to shove the shoebox into the Clyde. Now, I'm a Rangers supporter, and the dockers were all different gangs, depending. Of course it's a funeral, so everyone takes their caps off. Then, all of a sudden, this man McNulty – a Celtic fanatic – shouts, "By the way, whit colour was the budgie?" Somebody tells him blue, of course. "That'll be fuckin' right!" he says, sticks his bunnet back on again, and walks away. But we didn't mind. Dougie came back in the afternoon with a bottle of whisky and half a dozen screw-tops and we had a wake.'

* * *

'See the yards?' says Skippy the welder. 'We don't just build ships. We build people as well.'

On the Govan Road in Glasgow there is a long brick wall the colour of scabbed blood, maybe ten feet high if you count the barbed wire coiled along the top. Follow this wall and you come to a three-storey red sandstone building, constructed in 1890 but lying empty and boarded-up for the last decade. The main entrance is secured by a steel door covered in graffiti scrawls, but there's no mistaking its grandeur even now: flanked by statues of a shipwright and an engineer; topped by a brace of mermaids and a bust of Neptune. This is the old Fairfield building, once the headquarters of the most prestigious shipbuilding business in the world. The impression from outside is of dereliction and decay, a sad relic of a proud past, but do not be fooled. Behind this building and behind the wall, men – and even some women these days – still build ships.

The BAE yards here and across the Clyde in Scotstoun are the last remaining shipyards in Glasgow, and as such represent a rich living history, the embodiment in brawn, sinew and technological know-how of a tradition that is a key part of west of Scotland identity. 'I was born to be here,' the workers will tell you. 'It's in my bloodstream.'

Glasgow's shipyards are part of the city's creation myth. As Eden and Canaan are to Christianity, so Govan and Scotstoun are to Glaswegianity. So much of the west of Scotland identity comes from the yards: the hard man, the big man, the tough wee man; the drinker, the grafter, the joker; the left-winger, the right moaner, the maker of things; kindness, too, and thrawnness, and the ability to thole. Thole not dole, that might be the motto of the shipyards: better to endure the punishing physicality and economic uncertainty of the job than suffer forced idleness. And that word 'ship', it's in so much of what the yards are about – comradeship, craftsmanship and sometimes hardship. The yards are not just a workplace, they are a repository of identity, a great flooded dock brimming with shared attitudes, values and history. Shared achievement, too.

'There's been a lot of tough times through the years and I've been here for thirty-two of them,' says Andrew Watson, a forty-eight-year-old welder known, inevitably, as Winker. 'We've seen guys come, guys go, but we're still here building ships. We're the best at whit we dae.'

The first shipyard in Glasgow was established in the early nineteenth century at Stobcross, on the north side of the river, where the Finnieston crane is now. Ships were built in wood and later iron. Steel came in around 1880. By 1913, more than 100,000 people were working in thirty-eight shipyards and ancillary industries strung along the river like black pearls; 'Clydebuilt' became a stamp of quality, recognised internationally. The word resonates even now, when Japan and South Korea have replaced the UK as the world's great shipbuilding centres, and has come to denote strength and integrity; when the great trade union leader Jimmy Reid died, Alex Salmond described him as Clydebuilt.

Even those of us who feel a devotion to this idea of Glasgow, whose hearts are small shrines to St Mungo, can sometimes have our faith tested by its darker side. Walk off the London train, a couple of cans to the good, on a Friday evening, and you feel it straight away: the buzz of the place, the reckless, feckless, up-for-it-ness of folk heading for the pubs. I like that feeling, but there's sorrow in it, too. A fifth of the world's ships; that feels like a fairy tale now, the city of 'Once upon a time ...' The dramatic statistics of our present age are those which illustrate the so-called 'Glasgow effect': that Glaswegians have a 30 per cent higher risk of dying before the age of sixty-five than residents of comparable deindustrialised cities in England; that you are 54 per cent more likely to die from alcohol-related causes if you live in Glasgow than if you live in Manchester or Liverpool.

Wrecked, steaming, hammered; all those industrial words for the havoc we visit upon ourselves. That creation myth – the Clyde made Glasgow and Glasgow made the Clyde – has become a destruction myth. This is an ice cube of a city, floating on drink, dwindling and sinking into it.

The bubble in the optic, the broken bottle by the kerb, the wine on the breath; it sometimes feels that these are Glasgow now, more than any shipyard. The bird, the tree, the fish and the bevvy.

Still, for all that, on a cold, grey February morning, BAE's Govan yard presents a grand spectacle – and a sense of hope. From twenty-three metres up, on top of the *Queen Elizabeth* aircraft carrier being built within a gigantic, hangar-like space, you can look out past the giant cranes and north across the Clyde to riverside ziggurats of luxury flats, the red-terraced tenements of Broomhill, and beyond the city to the snow-cloaked Kilpatrick Braes.

Shipbuilders work at all hours in all weathers. The great halls, known as sheds, where the ships are built, face onto the river and are open to the elements. This winter it got down to –15 Celsius, and there were sheets of ice in the water as thick as the steel in the yards. But the job went on. Welders working the night shift resembled silverback gorillas: the frost came down overnight and covered the backs of their overalls; bent over the hot torch, their fronts remained clear. 'Hard as nails, so we are,' says Stuart Gray, the supervisor of the fabrication shop. 'Does the cold bother you? Yes it does, but by Christ it makes you hard. I think the Clyde gives you a new immune system.'

It is at desolate moments like that when the well-known shipyard sense of humour comes into play. A belly laugh can warm you better than a cup of tea.

The fabrication shop, known as the fab shop, contains the panel line, known as the penal colony. The standard joke among the older workers, who have been here for decades, is: 'Ah'd huv been oot quicker fur murder.' The panel line is where ships begin. Here, plates of steel measuring twelve metres by two are welded together, using a large machine called the seamer, into enormous sections of deck and hull.

Inside the yards, the outside world fades and you become

immersed in the world of shipbuilding. It is a noisy world: the python hiss of the burning torch; the grinders which buzz like giant insects in giant jars and which throw great arcs of sparks. The ventilation system rumbles like thunder. Blue sheet lightning glimpsed through doorways indicates a welder at work, as does the strange smell of antiseptic which seems to accompany that process. Everyone is busy. The pride in craft is tangible.

It is easy to feel dwarfed in a shipyard. Everything is on a grand scale. Perhaps in order to stand out amid this vastness, many of the workers have vivid personalities. Take fifty-five-year-old Alex Stewart. 'What can I tell you?' he says. 'Everybody knows me as The Singing Plater.' He then goes on to show why, performing – to the tune of Kenneth McKellar's 'The Song of the Clyde' – one of his own compositions, which concludes: 'Oh, it fills you with pride to work on the Clyde/The name BAE Systems is known worldwide/And I'm proud to say, whoever you are/Our aircraft carriers are the best by far.' Wiping the dirt from his forehead, he goes back to work.

'This is such a big, cosmopolitan place with every type of person,' says Jamie Webster, the GMB union convenor. 'A lot of people on the shop floor are amazing. You might think they are just ordinary craftsmen, but some are very clever. You wonder why they work in the shipyard, but you realise they made that choice. There's a lot of folk who just like a simple working life. You get welders interested in photography or archaeology.

'I remember I met this auld labouring man. I never met anybody as articulate and intelligent in my life. He had a kaleidoscope of knowledge, but he was quite happy labouring. There's confusion about what ambition means. A lot of folk think it means you always go up the way in life, but I've learned that sometimes the ultimate ambition is just being happy. So you almost get a philosophical education just by being here.'

190

Nicknames are common among the workers. Winker, Skippy, The Singing Plater, Laser Dave. Formality is a no-no. Woe betide the incomer who addresses a worker as Mr or, worse, sir. 'Ma name's Wullie,' you'll be told. 'You're in a shipyard, noo.' The lingua franca is the kid-on put-down. Bad language is rife, but not when women are near. An old-fashioned chivalry persists in matters of that sort. Doors are held open for female members of staff. Not that there are many of those, at least not in the yards.

One young woman says that, of the seventy apprentices taken on at the same time as her, only three were female. Lyn Gordon, a twenty-three-year-old now in her second year as an apprentice fabricator, explains the appeal of the shipyards. 'Better than hairdressing,' she laughs. 'Nah, I prefer a bit of hands-on work, up to my eyeballs in dirt and grease. Just what every other lassie wants really.' Growing up in Greenock, she was enchanted by the sight of ships and takes great pleasure and pride in the fact that she now builds them. 'It's all about heritage, isn't it? It all leads back. That I'm still working in a surviving shipyard in the Clyde is quite a big deal. To be able to say I'm part of it is pretty good. You get to gloat a wee bit.'

Despite the fact that shipbuilding in Scotland has been in decline for years, this sense of tradition seems attractive to young people. Alan Morris is a twenty-four-year-old design engineer working on the early stages of the Type 26 global combat ship. An ambitious young professional, he speaks the language of high-spec engineering and complex computer-modelling, but does not lack appreciation of the roots of his industry. 'Shipbuilding has been the lifeblood of the city,' he says. 'My grandfather was a sheet-metal worker on the ships. My great-grandfather was a riveter. A lot of people seem to think shipbuilding is dead, but it is still alive on the Clyde.'

Morris works in the Scotstoun yard, where work is continuing on the remaining three Type 45 destroyers which

BAE has built for the Royal Navy. To spend time on board one of these ships – the *HMS Dragon* – is to understand that modern shipbuilding is about much more than shaping steel. *Dragon* has been fitted with a complex weapons system. 'This is you in the combat zone; this is the ops room,' says Brian Carson, the combat system manager, who began here as an apprentice electrician at the age of sixteen and is now forty-eight. He points out the various features of the ship's operations room – a long, low, dim space with a new-car smell – including the 'soft-kill' area from which decoys are launched in order to 'seduce' hostile missiles away from *Dragon*. The ship's radar towers rise from the deck like a pagoda and a minaret. From near the top of the main mast sprout a number of conical structures, known as Madonna's tits, which are also part of the radar system.

Even the most committed technophobe and pacifist would find it difficult not to be impressed by this cutting-edge killing machine. These shipyards have long been at the forefront of naval technology. In 1861, Robert Napier's Govan yard built the *Black Prince*, one of the early iron-clad battleships. It was Napier who gave a start to John Elder, the genius inventor of the compound engine, who established the business in Govan now owned by BAE.

Over the years, the yard has changed hands many times. Shipbuilding firms tend to have genealogies which rival the Old Testament for complexity. Elder's begat Fairfield's begat UCS begat Kvaerner begat Marconi begat BAE. Sometimes the old names persist. BAE's Scotstoun yard is still known throughout Glasgow as Yarrow's; Govan as Fairfield's. There is a tremendous sense within the shipyards of the past breaking the surface of the present. This is formalised in the apprenticeship schemes in which the experienced workers pass on their skills to youngsters, having themselves been taught by the skilled craftsmen of their own day, and so on back to the birth of the industry. Thus an apprentice using a burner to cut steel today could trace a line back to a shipbuilder sawing wood at the Clyde's first shipyard, Scott's of Greenock, in the early eighteenth century. It is the industrial equivalent of the army's so-called golden thread.

BAE's present project is the construction of two aircraft carriers, the *Queen Elizabeth* and the *Prince of Wales*. Each will weigh 65,000 tonnes when complete. Standing at the foot of the partially built carrier, you have to crane your neck to see the top. It does not look like a ship; more like a skyscraper in embryo. The word 'aft' has been painted onto the appropriate side of the hull, and it is gratifying to note that some joker has prefixed the letter 'd'.

That says it all about the Clyde shipyards. Billions of pounds of investment, an engineering project on a hitherto unknown scale, and some subversive, daundering by with a pot of emulsion, takes a notion to write 'daft' right across it. That's your Govan right there.

* * *

'Never mind Scotland being independent,' says Tommy McMahon, 'Govan should be independent from Glasgow. The Luftwaffe couldn't damage Govan more than the Glasgow Council has. But we remember our proud history. I was born and bred here, and wherever I go in the world I tell people I'm a Govanite, no' a Glaswegian.'

Tommy is sixty-four, a retired sawmill worker, barrel-chested beneath a bright-yellow vest, Che Guevara tattooed on one strong round shoulder. He has a handlebar moustache, which appears to have been forged from gleaming steel, and he seems to embody the burgh motto, engraved in cast-iron on the nearby Victorian drinking fountain at Govan Cross – Nihil Sine Labore, nothing without work.

Govan has been inhabited since the Stone Age. It is the earliest known Christian site in the region. For 1,500 years, this has been a place of pilgrimage. On a bright Friday morning, starlings sing in the kirkyard rowans of Govan Old Parish Church. There are only a dozen or so folk in for morning prayers, but there is no doubting their faith as they worship in a small side chapel beside the ninth-century sandstone sarcophagus thought to have held the body of St Constantine. No doubting their belief, either, when – over tea and buttered pancakes – they discuss their home. You're not a proper Govanite unless you've been in Elder Park pond, they say. You can be baptised in the church, but the pond is the true Govan baptism.

'People tend not to be bland about Govan,' says the minister Moyna McGlynn. 'They are passionate about this place. When I think of Govan and Partick, I think of the old Glasgow, and in many ways think of them as untouched by the modern aspirations of the city. People here still see themselves as separate. That psychology may have been compounded by the decades of isolation when this was a no-go area – housing being pulled down, shops closed – but I think it was there anyway.'

Govan has energy. There are many parts of the city which are far richer, but which feel poorer in spirit. On the pavement outside an old-fashioned pub, a street party is starting up: kids with balloons; kids with ice poles; young men reeking of wacky-baccy; a merry seventy-two-year-old who introduces herself as Mad Betty Diamond, daughter of the stage comedienne Wee McGregor, and who is reputed to know more dirty jokes than anyone else in Govan. Next door is a salon which, of late, has found a new line of business providing waxes to pensioners.

'Lorraine,' says one hairdresser to the other, 'tell him about the wee woman of ninety that was waxed last week. She went skipping out the door, very near, she was that chuffed with herself.'

'Oh, aye,' says Lorraine. 'Better than the doctor. The OAPs come in for a blether and stay for a wax. They go to that shop' – she points across the street – 'get four scones for a pound and they'll sit aw day.'

Seated on a bench outside the studios of the Sunny Govan radio is Brian McQuade, known as Sir Brian, a director and presenter with the community station. Sir Brian is a great Govan character. His gaunt, craggy features and long brown hair bring to mind a more desiccated Ronnie Wood; it is, as he says, the kind of face you get when you don't eat properly and you drink too much. He has kindly eyes.

Sir Brian is fifty-seven, a staunch Govanite, tremendous autodidact and former alcoholic – pretty much in that order. He grew up in the Moorpark scheme, better known as the Wine Alley, an infamous slum. He was wild. 'Before I was ten, I robbed mair trains than Jesse James.'

The Wine Alley backed onto a railway goods yard and he'd lift coal from the halted freight, selling it on cheap at half a crown a bag. He broke into warehouses and shops, in the small hours of the morning, pulling away the crumbling old stone and stealing fags or whatever he could find. 'Eventually, I got charged with 147 burglaries.'

At thirteen, he was sent to an approved school, a kind of borstal, and for six months worked there as the librarian. Hardly any of the other boys could read so he had the place to himself, devoting his time to the discovery of leather-bound classics – Shakespeare, Dickens et al. Out on parole, he got a job in the cleansing department, lifting the bins from back-court middens. 'It was a dirty hard job but it was educational because people throw oot thousands of books.'

Among the ash and dirt, the broken glass and dead cats, he found a copy of *The Odyssey*, so beginning a love affair with antiquity. He taught himself Latin – 'enough to get by' – and ancient Greek. The world of Tacitus and Plato seemed solid and certain, 'like the Kingston Bridge'; the rest of his life perhaps less so. He went abroad and begged on the streets of Rome and Naples. He struggled with drink. He slept rough. One morning he woke up and decided to make a change. He studied for qualifications and eventually took two degrees at Glasgow University – in Classical Civilisation and History of Art. Sir Brian's is a tale of redemption and so it is perhaps unsurprising that he sees a similar arc in Govan's own story.

'Govan is like a phoenix from the ashes,' he says. 'I saw the tenements destroyed and the place a bomb zone. But they've built hundreds of new hooses alang the lines of the auld streets. The place is buzzing. It's just like being back in the auld Govan again, full of people and life.'

Charles Dickens wrote *A Tale of Two Cities* about London and Paris. Were he living now, he could write a book of that title and set it entirely in Glasgow. It is a city full of tension between rich and poor, construction and demolition, old and new, even – one could argue – good and evil. You can call it a concrete jungle or a dear green place, and you can pray that its future is as glorious as its past, but the one certainty is that this place is brimming with stories. Shop stewards licking red hot pokers. Classicists in Wine Alley. Budgies buried at sea. Glasgow has them all.

A Grouse Shoot

'THIS,' SAYS IAIN BROWN, head gamekeeper on the Burnfoot estate in Stirlingshire, 'is the last grouse moor in Central Scotland.'

He points his stick at the purple heather which grows in beautiful profusion on the 12,000-acre estate. 'That's our rainforest, that stuff there, man.'

It is 13th August, the day after 'The Glorious Twelfth', when the grouse season began. It runs until 10th December, a four-month window in which keepers on Britain's moors are kept busy driving the small brown birds towards shooters who may have paid £1,500 each for the pleasure of attempting to kill them. And it is a pleasure. A privilege, too. That's how the shooters – or 'guns' as they are known – describe it.

'I've not shot grouse for so long, I'm desperate to do it,' says one patrician-looking clan chief. After he bags his first of the day, he is delighted. 'Thank you very much,' he says to the keeper who hands him the limp and bloody bird. 'You don't know how satisfying that was.'

It costs a lot to shoot on a grouse moor, but a great deal more to run it – an average of £150,000 each year. So although some estates in the north of England run as commercial businesses, in Scotland, where grouse are fewer, it's more about landowners maintaining a cherished tradition.

'There's not many places are viable as grouse moors,' says Iain Brown. 'In Yorkshire, yes, but in Scotland we're just hanging on. This place of ours runs at a massive deficit. If it wasn't for the love and the passion for grouse shooting, this would all be covered with sheep or forest.'

Brown is an interesting man. Patriot, Burnsian and advocate for the countryside, he is forty-three years old, stocky, with silver hair and beard, dressed in tweed breeks and waistcoat. Keepers from different estates can be distinguished by the pattern of their tweeds. 'It's like the clan system,' he explains. Standing out on the moor, his right foot raised on a hillock of heather, his spaniel at his side, one arm holding aloft a red flag, he resembles a Socialist Realist portrait come to life.

As well he might. Brown seems to take 'A Man's A Man for A' That' as his personal creed, and is not one to tug his forelock in the presence of the upper classes who come to shoot. For him, Lord James Percy is 'Jim'. The Duke of Bedford, meanwhile, is 'Big Andy'. Don't go getting the impression that he's some sort of class warrior, though. Mostly, he's just obsessed with grouse.

He estimates that there are between 1,500 and 1,800 grouse on the moor, of which he says he can recognise many by sight, and he works long hours to ensure that they remain healthy and fruitful right up to the point where they are shot. It is, he grins, a paradox. He admires and respects grouse, and yet plans for and welcomes their death.

Grouse are entirely wild birds which eat heather and nest in it. They cannot be bred. Keepers try to increase their numbers by burning the heather in spring to promote new vigorous growth ('No bloom, no boom'), putting down medicated grit which staves off parasitic threadworms, and by slaughtering large numbers of predators such as foxes, stoats, weasels and crows.

The birds are baffling, though. Brown talks about 'the mystique of grouse'. Sometimes you do all you can to grow the population and it dwindles. Sometimes, like this year, the young grouse survive what everyone thought would be a killing winter.

Trying to get to the bottom of all this is partly what makes grouse such a fixation. Brown is the sort who has to be ordered to take a holiday, and he admits quite readily and regretfully that he spent little time with his two sons in their early years, leaving his wife Yvonne to do all the work. 'I've almost lost my family over a head of grouse,' he says, 'and there's many an estate owner has spent their child's inheritance and gone through divorces over grouse. It just consumes you.'

I was keen to understand this passion for myself, so had arranged to spend the day at Burnfoot. It's a beautiful area with an extraordinary view that includes both the Wallace Monument and the Forth Bridge. There is a wind farm on part of the estate, the turbines rising lighthouse-like from the moor. Hunting dogs continually vanish and resurface as they bound through the deep heather, bringing to mind dolphins breaching waves. Pollen rises like spray.

This isn't my first time on a grouse moor. For a few weeks before starting university, I worked as a beater on an estate in the Highlands.

Beaters are the infantry of a grouse shoot. They walk in a long, long line towards the guns, trying to scare the grouse up from the heather by cracking 'flags' – often plastic animal-feed bags attached to wooden poles. The movement of the line is monitored and controlled by the head keeper using a radio and phone, and signals are given by blasts on a horn.

I remember walking around ten miles each day over rough and wet Highland terrain. You had to keep up. Stragglers were not tolerated. One particular keeper, a leering sadist in a deerstalker, had an especially effective method of motivating tired beaters – reaching down and grabbing you by the most tender parts.

Burnfoot isn't at all like that, but the work is still exhausting. As Brown puts it, 'Grouse beating's like S&M in tweed.'

But it has its consolations. You get paid, for one thing. Not much, though. Forty quid for a day's work. Few, if any, of today's thirty beaters are in it for the money. Some are keepers from other estates who have agreed to lend a hand. Others have full-time jobs (there are loads of firemen and polis, for some reason) but spend their holidays working on the moor. A number simply relish the chance to give their dogs an opportunity to find and retrieve downed birds.

There is a festive, sunshiney air. Beer and spirits are offered at lunchtime. 'Would you like a wee G&T?' asks Gary Boyd, fifty-three, a broad-shouldered retired fireman from Grangemouth. He's working as a 'picker-up' and has blood on his shirt-cuffs. It's a real skill, noticing and remembering where the grouse fell. Picker-up is a job you earn after a long beating apprenticeship. Boyd has been at this for thirty years.

The guns lunch separately from the keepers and beaters. They are eating in a deep-green corrugated iron bothy. Walk in and you are hit with a hot smell of meat, wine and bonhomie.

There are ten guns shooting today – a well-to-do vision in tweed, gaiters and flat caps, cartridge belts sometimes slung below bellies. They are an interesting lot – farmers, businessmen, a couple of wealthy Americans who have flown here specially from Connecticut and are having the time of their lives. There's also Charlie Thorburn, from Perthshire, who was once a market trader but now breeds and trains hunting dogs. His clients include a Russian oligarch and a postman in Dundee.

Why is Thorburn here today? 'Because I was invited,' he says. 'It's not necessarily about having money. I have some pretty wealthy friends in London who have been shooting all their lives and have never been on a driven grouse shoot. You basically have to know someone who owns a moor.'

That someone is Nick Harvey-Miller. Having made a lot of money in the drinks industry, he became a co-owner of Burnfoot in 1990. A thick-set fifty-six-year-old in a green tank-top, his hair worn longish, never far from a lit fag, he is good company and dryly ungenteel. 'Don't shoot them up the arse,' is his sage advice to his guests.

In fact, Harvey-Miller is a serious champion of grouse moors, arguing that they are economically important (a new report estimates shooting generates over £20 million each year for the Scottish economy) and that a properly managed estate promotes biodiversity. He is proud of his birds – 'One Scottish grouse is worth three English grouse any time of the week' – and seems pretty chuffed at his own extravagance.

'The heather moorlands in Scotland would disappear unless you had idiots like us who were willing to pump money into them,' he beams. 'Yet we're doing all this for perhaps eight days' shooting each year. There is an element of madness about it.'

After lunch, I spend some time by the butts – the wooden screens over which the guns shoot. It's deafeningly loud and the smell of gunpowder fills the air. The grouse fly with a staccato whirr, travelling at up to sixty miles per hour and following the contours of the ground. They are considered the most difficult game birds to shoot.Those that are hit glide towards the ground with locked wings.

By 5 p.m., the guns have bagged 141 birds. Traditionally, each shooter is given two to take home. The rest belong to the estate and are sold to a game dealer for prices varying between £5 and £12 per brace, depending on supply and demand.

For Brown, another day is over, but even as he drinks a valedictory lager, he's already thinking ahead. What will tomorrow bring? There's a lot of worry in his job, even though he loves it. Earlier, someone had asked him if he was feeling happy.

'When was the last time you saw a happy grouse-keeper?' he replied. 'You know when I'll be happy? The 10th of December, when it's finished.'

201

You'll Never Walk Alone

FROM THE KOP; from the Jungle; from the heart, the throat, the lungs it comes. 'You'll Never Walk Alone', the greatest anthem in European football, half a century old.

This year is the fiftieth anniversary of 'You'll Never Walk Alone' being sung by supporters of Liverpool Football Club; it was adopted later by fans of Celtic, whose love for it, they'll tell you, goes just as deep.

The song began its life in another seaboard city, New York, as part of the 1945 Broadway production of Rodgers and Hammerstein's *Carousel*, but it has shifted shape and meaning in the years since, going from show tune to pop hit to terrace anthem to its current incarnation as a sort of secular hymn, an unchained threnody containing both grief and joy.

'It's got this history and resonance,' says the Liverpudlian songwriter Pete Wylie. 'It's almost a folk song. It's part of the community and the people.'

On a mild autumn day on Anfield Road, the words 'You'll Never Walk Alone' gleam in gold block capitals above the stadium gates. The song's message of optimism and common purpose feels, in truth, a little ironic when you walk the streets of forsaken terraced houses, each door and window shuttered in steel, which surround the football ground.

Here, too, hard by the gates, is the marble tribute to the Hillsborough dead, those ninety-six carved names; candles and scarves piled reverently on the pavement. 'You'll Never Walk Alone' is written here again and again and again, as a kind of last promise.

'When the disaster happened it made the song more poignant,' says Margaret Aspinall of the Hillsborough Family Support Group. Her son, James, died in Sheffield that day in 1989, aged just eighteen. 'It's the fans and especially the survivors of that day trying to let the families know they stand by us. We've never walked alone.

'It's so moving to us. It's like our prayer. It belongs to the families now. It's ours. I'm sorry, Gerry, but it belongs to the ninety-six.'

'Gerry' is Gerry Marsden, leader of Gerry and the Pacemakers, whose stately Scouse take on the song reached number one in October 1963. This is the version played before every home game by George Sephton, now in his forty-third season as the DJ at Anfield, who always makes sure he has three copies to hand – failure to air the song being unthinkable.

There is some debate as to whether the popularity of 'You'll Never Walk Alone' among Liverpool fans stems from or predates the Gerry Marsden cover. Most regard the former as gospel but there are plenty of believers in apocrypha. One stubborn theory, articulated by the novelist David Peace in his epic novel *Red or Dead*, suggests that the song was first sung at Hillsborough on 27th April 1963, following defeat to Leicester City in an FA Cup semi-final.

'For me, "You'll Never Walk Alone" represents Liverpool Football Club and, specifically, the Liverpool Football Club which Bill Shankly helped build and create,' Peace explains. 'In the words of the song and the way it is sung by the supporters, it signifies collective and communal endurance and struggle, through adversity and hardship, towards success and victory.'

There is a pleasing harmony in the fact that 'You'll Never Walk Alone''s fiftieth anniversary coincides with the centenary of Shankly's birth. An Ayrshire man, a former miner, he took over as manager of Liverpool close to Christmas in 1959 and over the next fifteen imperial years took the team from second division strugglers to the dominant force in English football.

His reign coincided with the British pop boom, driven in large part by the Beatles and other Merseybeat acts, and before every home game the DJ at Anfield would play the top ten, the terraces ringing with *yeah yeah yeahs*. Into this cauldron came the final magic ingredient, 'You'll Never Walk Alone', played over the public address system for the first time on 19th October 1963, preceding a 1–0 victory over West Bromwich Albion.

How, though, did what might have been just another in a long string of pop pearls become the Liverpool anthem? 'I know how,' says Marjie Thorpe.

Marjie will be eighty on her next birthday, and looks hell of a well on it. A blonde bombshell in a crimson coat, she lives on the next street to Penny Lane and is as ardent a fan as the Reds could hope to find. When the club were relegated in 1954, her brother (an Everton supporter) made a cardboard coffin and laid it on her bed, writing 'Rest In Peace Liverpool FC' across the mirror – 'And what I was more upset about,' she laughs, 'it was me sixpenny lippy from Woolies he wrote it with.' When, in 1962, the sainted year of promotion, her son was born, she called him Ian St John after the striker whose goals ensured Liverpool's return to the top division.

Music, along with football, has always been a great passion with Marjie. In 1956, she and her husband Harry Parkinson went to see the musical *Carousel* at the pictures, and when they came out, Harry was full of the closing number – 'You'll Never Walk Alone'. He was a club singer, performing in Liverpool and the surrounding towns, and decided to put the song in his act.

The years passed. He grafted. Life changed. Music changed. He became a family man. Liverpool bands, Liverpool FC, were on the rise. Then, one particular Saturday afternoon, Harry was standing on the Kop in his usual spot, the third barrier up behind the goal, when he heard – on the PA – a man with a local accent start to sing about walking through a storm.

'Of course the record comes on,' Marjie recalls, 'and Harry with his big Mario Lanza voice, showing off, says, "Oh, I know that!" and he starts singing. So a crowd of lads round about grab hold of him and put him on the barrier facing the Kop with his back to the goal. He starts conducting them and they begin to join in with the song.

'I remember him coming home all excited, banging on the side window, "Marjie, Marjie! You'll never guess what's happened!" Every week then that was the ritual. And as far as I'm concerned, that was how it started.'

Harry died in 1980. His son, Ian St John Parkinson, feels his dad's spirit with him at Anfield whenever 'You'll Never Walk Alone' is sung. It's like that, the song. Memories build up around it in layers, insulating it, keeping it warm and alive.

Karen Gill, for instance, the honorary president of Liverpool FC Supporters Committee, is the granddaughter of Bill Shankly. She remembers him playing 'You'll Never Walk Alone', and 'Amazing Grace', on a huge old gramophone in his home, a modest semi on Bellefield Avenue.

'It makes me cry every single time I hear it,' she says. 'I associate it directly with my grandad, and I can't remember a time when I didn't know that song. I don't know who it was that said, "Football is a religion and Anfield is a church", but this is definitely the hymn, isn't it? Everybody has got a story related to it. It reminds them of a special time or a special match.

'You hear about dads singing it to their sons when they are newly born. It's the words, it's the melody, it's everything about it. It's not just by chance that it's lasted so long and is sung by so many people all over the world.'

Fans of other clubs sing it: Feyenoord, Borussia

Dortmund and especially Celtic. In the east end of Glasgow, and in certain other west of Scotland towns, 'You'll Never Walk Alone' is as deeply felt as at Anfield. It chimes there for the same reasons it does so in Liverpool – there is something in the song that speaks to the character and history of the working class; a sentimentality, a sense of shared struggle, a lingering trade unionism, socialism and religious faith.

Walk into pubs in the vicinity of Glasgow's famous Barras market and you'll be told how much 'You'll Never Walk Alone' means. You'll hear about the great European nights, about how in the late 1960s that song and 'We Shall Overcome' could both be heard at Parkhead, in particular among fans in the legendary north terrace, known as the Jungle.

And you'll hear how, just last month, at a testimonial for ex-Celtic midfielder Stiliyan Petrov, who retired from the game after developing leukaemia, 'You'll Never Walk Alone' was sung with such emotion that the player, and many in the crowd, were overcome.

It is believed that the song was taken up by the Glasgow side in 1966, following the 19th April game against Liverpool FC. 'It would be fantastic to think that that night, which still means a lot to me, was the night that it spread from Liverpool to Celtic,' says Ian Callaghan, Liverpool's most capped player, who is now seventy-one.

Cally, as he is known, has a remarkable story. He was serving his time as a central heating engineer when, in 1960, Bill Shankly signed him as a professional, visiting his parents in Toxteth and promising he would look after the lad. A midfielder, he played in 857 matches, and is the only Liverpool player to have gone from the second division to winning the European Cup. He misses Shankly, still calls him 'the great man' and identifies 'You'll Never Walk Alone' with his mentor.

'It's a song you never get blasé about,' he says. 'In my

day you had thirty thousand on the Kop singing. It's a massive thing on a match day to run out the tunnel to "You'll Never Walk Alone". You're ready for the game then.' He sings it yet, at home games and each Christmas at the annual dinner for former players, where he and the likes of Ian St John and Kenny Dalglish conclude the evening by getting up on stage and belting it out.

You have to belt it out. It's a song about commitment that demands commitment from each singer. Starting low, ending high, reaching for those notes, it's not possible to perform 'You'll Never Walk Alone' in a half-hearted way. Ask anyone. Ask the gang of old Kopites, many of them retired from the Ford plant, sitting chatting over a few halves at a corner table in a bar in the centre of Liverpool.

They've been going to Anfield since the 1950s, since they were kids, right through the Shankly glory years, when 'You'll Never Walk Alone' was the sound of invincibility. These are the men to ask what it's like to sing it.

'It's hard to put into words,' says Terry Rimmer, who is seventy-six years old, six foot three and solid as a brick terrace. 'It's like having your best girlfriend with you, and all your pals, and you're flush with money. You're singing this song with forty-odd thousand others. The happiest moment.'

Ken Johnson, eighty-one, here in his best dark suit, which he has had cause to wear too often, says: 'To me, it's harrowing. It's enlivening when you're watching the games or you're in the Kop but when you're alone at home it's a very sad song. They played that song at my wife's funeral.'

A man across the table nods. This is sixty-seven-year-old Adrian Killen, who keeps in his home what is arguably the largest private collection of Liverpool memorabilia, and in his head what is, inarguably, the greatest collection of Liverpool statistics. He has missed just seven games at Anfield since 1959; one away game he would prefer to have missed was at Hillsborough. 'I'll be truthful with you,' he says. 'I have never sung "You'll Never Walk Alone" since 1989. I cannot. It's too emotional for me now.'

Ken Metcalfe is seventy-two, sang with the Swinging Blue Jeans in their very early days and has a Liver bird tattooed on his right arm. 'The song helped me out once,' he says, 'when I was MC-ing at this working man's club. It was a strippers night. There was about three hundred fellas in, and I thought, what the hell am I going to sing? "You'll Never Walk Alone"! Of course, they were all joining in.'

Some song. An anthem fit for lust and loss, birth and death, victory and defeat. It's bigger than football, but football, itself a conduit for strong emotion, gives it a context and focus.

The modern game, of course, is very different from how it was in Shankly's day. It is moneyed and tamed. It has lost much of its wildness and innocence, a fall from grace caused, in part, by the Hillsborough tragedy. But the song remains untainted, growing ever in purity and intensity of spirit, as if each crowd performance was a fresh distillation.

'The feeling you get is that it's played for you,' says Terry Rimmer. 'It's your song.'

You can't own the club but you can own 'You'll Never Walk Alone'? Big Terry smiles. 'Exactly,' he says. 'Exactly.'

The Sex Shop

WHEN DREW BIGGLESTONE went into his shop, Luke And Jack, on Sunday, water was pouring through the ceiling and swift action was needed to prevent damage to the stock. 'We had to shift the gimp masks and the bondage equipment,' he recalls. 'The leather got moved first, obviously; anything that isn't wipeable.'

Luke And Jack is a sex shop. Well, you'll hear the customers refer to it as such. Drew and his partner Ian Diamond prefer the term 'adult boutique', believing that 'sex shop' has connotations of sleaziness and prostitution and dirty men in dirty macs. Whatever you call it, Luke And Jack can be found on Virginia Street in Glasgow, just off the city's main shopping area. Those walking east along Argyle Street should turn left at M&S and keep straight on for S&M.

You enter through a subtle but classy entrance, passing between stone columns topped by scrolled capitals; this part of Glasgow was, during the eighteenth century, home to wealthy tobacco lords. The shop itself, with its chandeliers and faux flock wallpaper, might at first be taken for a fashion boutique. Dance music plays quietly in the background, drowned out only occasionally by the buzz and thwack of certain items being demonstrated. Downstairs is an art gallery dedicated to erotic work, which, on the day I visit, features a pair of heart-shaped nipple tassels made from Tunnock's Tea Cake wrappers.

Visitors to the sex shop that occupied these premises before Luke And Jack were confronted, straight away as they walked in, by a gigantic bright purple vibrator called

209

the Great American Challenge. It acted as a sort of shibbo-leth, deterring the meek and prudish. Drew and Ian, who pride themselves on being welcoming, continue to stock the Challenge, but keep it round the corner of the shop, behind a partition, giving customers time to grow used to the erotic microclimate before coming face to face – if that is the appropriate phrase – with such potentially daunting objects.

In the first part of the shop, what Drew and Ian call the 'sugary' part, you will find items including erotic art, bespoke corsets in leather and satin, blonde and pink pubic hair dye, G-strings made of candy (further evidence of the famous Glaswegian sweet tooth), a peacock-feather body-tickler, and a wide range of niche magazines such as *Filament* – 'for women who like hot men and intelligent thought'. Ian's mother, when she visits, does not stray beyond this sugary part.

The proprietors are both thirty-eight. They are portly and bearded; using gay slang, you might call them 'bears'. They have been a monogamous couple for nine years. 'There's a presumption that we have tried everything in the shop, but we haven't,' says Drew. 'It would take quite a lot of training to use some of this stuff.' Luke And Jack is aimed at men and women, gay and straight. It is a sort of hub around which several sexual cultures revolve. Visit on any random day and you are as likely to meet a young straight couple as a drag queen in his civvies.

This shop, like every shop, has busy spells and longueurs, but on the day I spend there, a pretty steady stream of customers of both sexes and all persuasions comes through the doors, eyeing the cabinets full of rubber items which, in their colour and dimensions, irresistibly call to mind gour-met black puddings and foot-long baguettes and thus seem more properly to belong in the kitchen than the bedroom.

Here comes Ivor. He's an artist, a petite man in his fif-ties, a bit camp, who sweeps into the shop with the energy of a small localised whirlwind. He used to be married and has two children but is now in a civil partnership.

'I came in to buy some lube,' he says, raising an eyebrow. 'Well, you don't like to buy that in Tesco, do you?'

'Don't you?' I ask.

'No,' he replies. 'Not in Dumfries.'

They get all sorts in here: dominatrices looking to replenish their stock of whips or sending in their 'slaves' to buy them gifts; lesbians examining the heft and fit of various harnesses; guys who are into every sort of kink (except fur coat and nae knickers, which is, of course, the proper province of Edinburgh). The rule is that you can't tell preference just by looking at someone. Folk always surprise you.

Customer service is key. People aren't always totally sure or open about what they want. So sales staff need to be friendly, helpful, give advice and ask questions. The conversation is, necessarily, pretty frank.

'What's the name of that dungeon on Sauchiehall Street?' someone might say. Or: 'Would you like to buy a glass sex toy? There's 20 per cent off and it would look lovely on your mantelpiece.' Or: 'Are there pants to match the corset?' To which comes the reply: 'I know a woman who makes crotchless bloomers.'

Criz, a customer in his mid-forties, has shopped here in the past for riding crops and handcuffs. He has been on a tantric breathing course and once had sex for seventy-two hours. 'I'm a great believer in having a good sex life, regardless of what age you are,' he says. 'As you grow older, you don't want your sex life to be vanilla; you want it to be spiced in some way. In this country, we are slightly prudish about these things, but if somebody has never worn nipple clamps, I would seriously advise them to try.'

Felicity, a mother of three in her late forties, is 'a wee ordinary housewife' who seems quite pleasantly surprised at herself for being in here. 'For me, this is a grown-up shop where you can talk about sex in a grown-up way,' she says. 'The thought of going to an Ann Summers party full of shrieking women fills me with horror.'

Occasionally, the whole idea of being in a shop such as this can be a bit overwhelming for people. They either find it a turn-on and become what Drew calls 'sex-brained', or else somehow wander in by mistake.

There was the man who came in with his wife, took one look at a lime-green corset, and yelled: 'This is a bondage shop!' before dashing out, followed by his mortified spouse. Then there was the guy, so overcome while trying on a pair of leather trousers, that he fell out of the changing room and into the shop, breeks round his knees. 'He was obviously sexually excited and I slid him back behind the curtain,' says Drew. 'I was glad to see he was wearing pants.'

Customers range in age from eighteen-year-old goth girls, newly arrived in the city to attend university, to an octogenarian who has to be helped up the stairs. Whole families sometimes. 'There was a woman came in with her mother, her sister and her aunts,' recalls Chris, the young Irish sales assistant. 'The granny knew exactly what she wanted. She got a couple of bondage ropes and a whip and said, "If I were twenty years younger, I'd be using this on you!"'

Perhaps because the items for sale are intimate, customers often feel a desire to confide in the shopkeepers. Not all those who visit are hedonistic party people. Some are lonely and isolated. Some have problems, sexual and otherwise. The counter can become a confessional, with a sacred and confidential atmosphere that not even the gaudy tubes of bubblegum-flavoured lubricating gel can dispel. Spend a day here and you begin to get a feeling for this. One young man tells me that he lost his partner suddenly in an accident and has been single for a long time; he likes coming into the shop and browsing products which he might, one day, use in a new relationship.

Towards the end of the day, a young woman visits the shop. Debbie is twenty-three and has worked as a model; she is totally open, full of fizz, Glaswegian to the max. Debbie does gallus. 'I've got a dirty weekend coming up,' she announces, 'and I need some new toys to play with.'

Drew leads her round the shop, suggesting items and listening carefully to what she says. They pause at one particular display case full of pink and purple glass toys which, in another context, might pass as abstract sculpture. Looking at them, it's hard to know whether to blush or award the Turner Prize.

'These look exciting. What are they?' Debbie asks.

'This is the highest end in glass,' Drew explains with some pride, pointing to one. 'You can put it in the microwave to heat it up or in the freezer to cool it down.'

Debbie mulls this over with a pragmatic air. 'Is it dishwasher-safe?'

They go round the corner, beyond the sugary and into the spice. Drew shows Debbie a box full of wrist and ankle cuffs. Chris suggests she buy the matching paddle. Her phone beeps. It's her flatmates; they are supposed to be meeting for a drink and she is late. She starts to text them back – 'I'm in the sex shop. I'll be in the pub in a minute' – but it's slow going because Chris, ever helpful, is winding bondage wrap around her wrists. She ends up spending fifty quid and goes out the door, the last customer of the day, thoroughly satisfied, or at least planning to be.

'Have a good weekend,' I tell her.

'Oh,' she smiles, 'I will.'

Iona

A NEW DAWN on Iona. The bright sun bounces off buoys and creels and shines like a benediction on skipper Davie Kirkpatrick's beautiful wooden boat, *Iolaire*, Gaelic for 'eagle', as she leaves the harbour for Staffa.

The sun shines, too, on St Martin's Cross, up by the abbey, a great Celtic cross, fifteen feet high and carved, more than a millennium ago, with biblical scenes: a stone Abraham frozen forever with the knife raised above Isaac. The cross throws its black shadow on Iona, as it has done for more than 1,200 years, through Viking raids, world wars and the industrial revolution; a symbol of constancy on this Hebridean island, a jewel chipped from the south-western coast of Mull, where everything – weather, tide, light – is ever-changing.

'Iona,' says Kirkpatrick, who has lived on the island all his sixty-five years. 'There's *something* here. But I don't know what it is. Nobody knows. Nobody has got the final answer.'

Today, 19th May 2013 – Pentecost Sunday – is thought to be the 1,450th anniversary of Saint Columba arriving on Iona from his native Ireland, establishing a base from which he spread Christianity throughout Scotland. It also marks the seventy-fifth anniversary of the Iona Community, a Christian organisation based on the island, and in Glasgow, that grew out of the Depression and remains dedicated to social justice. In 563, Columba and a dozen followers are said to have arrived by coracle – a boat of hides stretched over wooden ribs – on a rocky bay in the south of Iona. Climbing a nearby hill, the story goes, he satisfied himself that he could no longer see Ireland, turned his back on his homeland, built a stone cairn and decided that on this tiny island – three miles long by one wide – he would build his monastery. 'Unto this place,' he said, 'small and mean though it be, great homage shall yet be paid.'

In the summer of 1938, another boat landed at Iona, the *Dunara Castle*, a steamer that eight years earlier had been used in the evacuation of St Kilda. Now she was bringing a new population. Not monks this time, but a group of young ministers and craftsmen, some unemployed shipbuilders from Govan, led by the Reverend George MacLeod of that parish, on a mission to rebuild the ruined ancient abbey and establish a new ecumenical group, a sort of family, really, in which faith, work and justice, prayer and sweat would intermingle. This was the birth of the Iona Community, which grew from the original Columban mission like lichen over old stone.

These days, the community remains an engaged and engaging mix of Christianity and politics, its 270 members and thousands of friends and associates opposing poverty, sectarianism, injustice and violence. From the early years, when the community was seen, often, as a refuge for radicals and oddballs, it has become an established part of Scottish civic life.

'I think our purpose today remains largely what it was seventy-five years ago, when George MacLeod realised that the Church just wasn't speaking to ordinary folks' lives,' says Peter Macdonald, the fifty-five-year-old leader of the Iona Community. 'George was concerned about the breakdown of community, and I think that has only accelerated over the last seventy-five years. In society and also politically, there's greater individualism, greater materialism. For more people today, the Christian faith is seen as an irrelevance. It just doesn't engage with the things that they're concerned about. So we try in our way to show ways in which faith is relevant to the issues and challenges folk face.'

On the morning I visit Iona, around thirty people – mostly middle-aged, carrying rucksacks and wearing hiking boots – are gathered around St Martin's Cross, heads bent in prayer, waiting to embark on what's known as 'the pilgrimage'.

Iona has a resident population of around 120 but attracts as many as 100,000 visitors each year, many of them drawn by the island's spiritual reputation and its historical significance as the ancient burial place of Scottish kings, including Duncan and Macbeth. John Smith, the Labour leader, is also buried here. 'An Honest Man's the Noblest Work of God', it says on his grave. On the slab, someone has left an offering of pebbles and shells.

The community allows paying guests to stay for a week in the abbey, working and worshipping together. On one day each week, since those early days, guests – and anyone who chooses to join them – have made a pilgrimage around the island, stopping off at its significant places for prayer and reflection, silence and songs, and – this being Britain, albeit a far-flung fragment – tea and biscuits. Everyone will have their own reasons for being here: curiosity, a love of natural beauty, or more likely some deep need for healing and peace.

'You don't stumble on Iona. Iona isn't en route to any-where. Anybody who arrives on Iona means to be there,' says Macdonald. 'You certainly feel, physically, that you're leaving your normal life behind. Iona is the kind of place where you are able to reflect, to form new relation-ships with people, and then change your perspective about whatever it is you're going back to face. The work of Iona begins when you leave.'

The pilgrimage begins at a little after 10 a.m., the rasp of a corncrake, like someone running a thumb over a comb, loud in the nearby field. We head south-west, stopping off at the ancient nunnery, where dandelions grow between graves and tiny purple flowers bloom from cracks in the fallen walls. Spring seems to have arrived here a little earlier than on the mainland, and there is a lovely contrast between the wildness of the landscape and the neatness of the gardens in the village, tulips a vivid red against the blue Sound of Iona, the boilersuits of scarecrows flapping in the breeze. Sheep crop the grass verges by the road, shadows of crows flit across the abbey slates, and a gull perches, blasé in its blasphemy, on the cross on the tower roof.

I fall in with some of the pilgrims and ask what brings them here. One young woman tells me she lost her faith for a time – too caught up with work in London's financial sector and with socialising – but that following the economic crash and a period of redundancy she has rediscovered her religious belief through the liturgy written on Iona.

We walk down to Columba's Bay, on the southern tip of the island, where the saint and his monks are said to have landed. Military jets tear through the sky towards Benbecula. The beach is covered in smooth, round pebbles, including pieces of the distinctive marble, flecked with green, glass-like serpentine, which was used to carve the altar in the abbey. On the beach, sifting the bladderwrack, the pilgrims each choose two stones. The first they throw into the waves, to symbolise something they wish to leave behind; the other they take with them, to represent a new beginning.

Joanne Reid is visiting from Birkenhead. 'Three years ago my home burned down in a fire,' she says. 'I'm on my own with two children. We woke up in the middle of the night and we only just got out alive. I had no insurance and we lost everything.'

It was traumatic. The children were terrified. There was a great sense of loss. 'You feel sad, and then sadder. And then sadder.' Not knowing what else to do, Reid began to pray. She started attending church. She heard about Iona, but could not afford to make the journey. Someone at the church, though, paid anonymously for her to go, and here she is.

As soon as she got off the ferry, she felt anointed, as though someone were dabbing her down with a cool cloth. She feels a little odd saying these things. She is a straight talker, totally Merseyside, yearns even amid the beauty of Iona for a whisky and a kebab, and wouldn't want to be taken for 'one of these Christian loonies'. But she is telling it how it is. Testifying.

'This trip, I feel, is meant to be,' she says. 'What I've felt here, now, within the church and with these people, is that I can go home and be strong. It has given me a stronger heart. I don't feel like I'm a bad person. It's a spiritual feeling when you've been through so much. It's not just the break and no kids. It's something more. It's like a calling. It knows you need to be here.'

This, or a variation on it, is what you hear over and over again on Iona. A sense of homecoming. Anja Jardine is the cook at the abbey. She grew up in East Germany. The Wall fell when she was seventeen and, all of a sudden, she was free to travel. She went for a week to Iona at the suggestion of someone in her church, and then, as the years passed, just kept coming back. Eventually, in 2001, she settled here and is now married to a local man, Mark, himself the son of Community members, who runs boat trips; they have a daughter, Freya, and live by the water.

'Sometimes I wonder whether you're meant to belong somewhere; whether it's meant to be,' Jardine says. 'I felt at ease with the people and the place. You could explain it in a spiritual way, but it just suited me. It's a great place, with all its disadvantages – people have feuds and don't like each other and are pernickety with things. But that's very real. A lot of abbey guests will say, "Oh, what will we do when we get back to the real world?" But Iona is very real. Nobody here is a saint. They are working hard to earn their money. They know how to celebrate and they know how to cry.'

One shouldn't romanticise Iona. Island life can be tough and dangerous, a tide of tears. The *Iolaire* skipper's father, Charlie Kirkpatrick, for instance, was killed in 1955 while working for the Community, unloading timber for the cloisters from a ship's hold.

Iona was never supposed to be romantic. It was supposed to be all about reality. George MacLeod saw the truth of poverty in his Govan parish. He worried that the Church was failing to engage with the lives of working people and those in rags who weren't fortunate enough to be working. His vision was for young ministers to graft alongside craftsmen – labouring for them and learning to use their hands as well as words – before returning to work in impoverished parishes.

MacLeod, who died in 1991 at the age of ninety-six, had been a captain with the Argyll and Sutherland Highlanders during the First World War, fighting on the front line at Ypres and Passchendaele. He won the Military Cross and the French Croix de Guerre for bravery. According to his son Maxwell, a journalist, MacLeod was shaped profoundly by his experiences of the war. He later became a pacifist. 'He was a sensitive young man who was thrown when still twenty into intermittent scenes of terrible carnage. He told me that after the war he spent some weeks walking around Mull visiting Gaelic families he had known, several of which had lost sons, probably under his command.

'He said that one of his chief memories of that walking tour was that he would be put to sleep in the byres and that he was not allowed to take a candle or light there because of the straw. Ater the evenings he had spent with the families, he hated the gloom, but found the experience very cathartic, weeping in the darkness and rushing out at first light to walk in the dawn.'

Darkness and dawn. Life and death. These are the true building bricks of the abbey.

Ian Fraser, a retired minister, first went to Iona in 1939, the year after the Community's founding. He is ninety-five now and still goes back and forth to the island. He was there most recently at Easter. He is an old, old man, but you can still see the strength in his hands and shoulders, and in his eyes.

He is from Forres, in Morayshire, has three children, nine grandchildren, eight great-grandchildren (with another on the way) and enjoys translating the Gospels into Doric, feeling they benefit from the rougher tongue. His father, a butcher, went blind when Fraser was four years old, and so the boy went to work in the business. 'I can tell you,' he says, 'that on a frosty morning, in an unheated shop, one of the worst jobs you can get is to have a pail of half-congealed blood to stir into liquidity for black puddings. Think of a wee lad doing that, then in the kirk on Sunday being asked to sing, "Wash me in the blood of the lamb and I'll be whiter than snow."'

Fraser helped rebuild the walls of the abbey refectory, and recalls that, at a time when timber was scarce because of war shortages, they were able to use wood that washed ashore, having been jettisoned by a ship caught in a storm; and it turned out, miraculously one might say, to be exactly the correct length required. Fraser and his late wife Margaret honeymooned on Iona, and he has a wonderful photograph of the two of them then, in the still ruined abbey, lovers beneath a broken arch. 'She was a head-turner and she had a loveliness that went through her like Blackpool rock,' he says.

Walking across the machair that fringes Iona's main beach, the Bay at the Back of the Ocean, I speak with Sharon Kyle, deputy director of the Community. Originally from Aberdeen, she first visited the island twenty years ago, in her mid-thirties, but moved to Iona from Birmingham last summer with her partner Jen. The pair had been Church of England vicars, but left the ministry as same-sex relationships between clergy were not acceptable. Iona, she says, is a place that allows people to take the risk to be who they are.

'A thin place between heaven and earth. It does feel like that,' she says, pointing towards water the same pale blue as the ring around a gannet's eye. 'The next stop over there is Nova Scotia. This is an island off an island, it is jaw-droppingly beautiful, you get weather by the bucketload, and it is remote. That personal challenge, I think, is what people rise to.

'Iona gives the people time to really think about things, to go off walking, to sit by a beach, to look at the beauty and just reflect on who and what they are in God's creation.'

Joseph McKenzie's Secret

FOR THE LAST thirty-five years of his life, the man known as 'the father of modern Scottish photography' stopped exhibiting his pictures, withdrawing from public life. In the eyes of the world, he had retired, retreated to his home in Tayport, on Scotland's east coast, with its long view over the firth to Dundee. His death on 5th July 2015, at eighty-six, prompted obituaries composed around a minor key of regret – here was a man of great ability whose work had been neglected, nearly forgotten by the public and the arts establishment.

Yet, all the time, all through those decades when his reputation faded like an old photo exposed to sunlight, Joseph McKenzie kept his secret: he was still taking pictures. He just wasn't showing them.

He took photographs right up until a few days before he died. He developed his own work, as had always been his habit, writing title and date on the back of each photo in neat black pen, and adding the new pictures to the great stacks of prints that had come before. The result, as his son Frank puts it, is 'one of the largest single artist photographic archives in the world'. In addition to tens of thousands of pictures, a great many unseen, there is an unpublished autobiography, a diary, poetry and footage of McKenzie talking about his work; all the ingredients for the major retrospective exhibition, books and a documentary which the family hopes will follow.

'We'd like to get recognition for what he achieved,' says Frank. 'We are also going to try to get an OBE posthumously for him. He deserves it.'

Frank is fifty-seven, the eldest of five children. We meet in the Victorian villa where Joseph McKenzie lived and worked and raised a family. Frank leads the way through the kitchen, opens a door, pulls back a curtain, and reveals the darkroom. Here is where all of McKenzie's most celebrated work emerged from its chemical crucible, those moody, melancholy black-and-whites of 1960s street life: pie-sellers and gossip-mongers in cobbled Dundee; petrol-bombed homes in troubled Belfast; the *Gorbals Children* series, in which kids grimed in snot and jam play merrily in the Glasgow slums.

The darkroom has a low ceiling and white wood-panelled walls. McKenzie feels present through his tools. Two old Leicas rest in their case. A magnifier stands on top of an enlarger, and it is easy to imagine the photographer hunched over, squinting into the lens. A pair of white linen gloves sit on a cabinet, one placed neatly on top of the other. His hands, his eyes, his vision. This feels like a shrine, a place of relics and transubstantiation – flesh into film into art. Brown bottles of sodium metaborate stand, sacramental, on a shelf. Listen carefully and you can almost catch Tangerine Dream and Benjamin Britten and recordings of the John Peel show, the music McKenzie used to listen to here, drifting in from the past.

'Joe was a master printer,' the artist Calum Colvin had told me a few days earlier, emphasising how important, almost sacred, the darkroom had been for his former teacher at Dundee's Duncan of Jordanstone College of Art. 'He invested an emotional quality in the printing. They are visual poetry, really. I think he felt that there would be a revealing of his greatness after his death.'

Frank McKenzie nods when asked about this. Did his father wish for his work to be seen once he was gone? 'He always wanted the recognition, but on the other side he was almost frightened of recognition. My personal analysis is he feared rejection. Because he'd had a lot of rejection in the early parts of his life. All the turmoil that he'd been through, I think he felt rejected. Parentally, he felt rejected. He always felt that he was a mistake and his mum didn't really want him. There were some deep psychological fears of rejection.'

Joseph McKenzie was born in the East End of London in 1929. His father was a clockmaker left bankrupt following trouble with a business partner. The family knew real poverty and the sadness that came with it. Material possessions were few. When, aged ten, McKenzie was evacuated to Dorset, he did not even own a bag and had to carry his pyjamas in a pillow-case sealed with tape.

'He felt his life had been a struggle from the day he was born,' says Frank, but it was a struggle which gifted him an empathy for the difficult lives of others. 'Because of my own deprived background I could identify with the children's feelings; there was a rapport between us,' Joseph wrote in the preface to his book *Gorbals Children*. An impoverished upbringing was not, he went on, insurmountable; then, thinking, perhaps, of his own childhood, 'It is the hang-up of being unloved, unwanted, which is a real and permanent disadvantage!'

In 1947, McKenzie was conscripted into the RAF and spent three years as a corporal in the Photographic Corps. While stationed in Germany, he met his future wife, Shelly, who is Dutch and Catholic and inspired his conversion to that faith. In 1954, the year in which he joined the Royal Photographic Society, he began to teach at St Martin's in London. Ten years later, he and his family moved to Scotland, where he headed up the new photography department at Duncan of Jordanstone. That year, 1964, also saw him embark upon his *Gorbals Children* study, inspired by the paintings of Joan Eardley. The show toured in 1965, marking the start of a run of work and exhibitions in which McKenzie was established as a soulful and sympathetic chronicler of the working class.

His work is often likened to that of Oscar Marzaroli, who was similarly inspired by the paintings of Eardley, and who also depicted Glasgow as Weanopolis, a city of golden-haired lasses walking past closes and wee boys in big schemes. But McKenzie's portraits are darker. They lack sentimentality, though not compassion. Marzaroli appears to admire the children he photographs; McKenzie pities them.

In the early 1970s, there came a fork in the road. McKenzie had spent the last years of the previous decade travelling within Ireland, taking photographs – titled *Hibernian Images* – which contrasted the peaceful rural life in the Republic with the sectarian violence of the North. For a show of this work in Aberdeen, he submitted a catalogue statement which he claimed was then altered by the gallery to remove text which the curators seem to have felt was sympathetic to the idea of armed struggle against the British state.

'My father went berserk,' Frank recalls. 'He said, "This is censorship. You have no right to do this." And that's when things really busted up. He just withdrew. He said, "Well, if I can't show my work in the way I want to show it, I'm not showing it."'

This was when McKenzie stopped exhibiting new work in public. Between 1974 and 1980 he turned part of his home into a gallery which could be viewed by appointment, and in 1987 there was a retrospective in Glasgow, but after that – nothing. This feels, looking back, like an act of self-sabotage, even a sort of martyrdom. 'Joe was a great one for thinking about sacrifice,' says Calum Colvin. 'He felt that his integrity had been sacrificed by that incident to do with *Hibernian Images*. He felt that he was suffering, in a sense, for his artistic beliefs.'

Albert Watson, who went on to have a high-profile and successful career in the United States, was a student of McKenzie's in the mid-1960s. He finds his old teacher's decision frustrating. 'He had a lot of self-doubt. But you can't blame the world. You love photography? You pick up a camera and shoot.'

Can't one counter that with the J. D. Salinger argument? We can choose to be frustrated that he wrote stories and then hid them away in a drawer, or we can be grateful that the few books that do exist are exquisite. 'Yes,' says Watson, 'in a way you are right. You can say, "Well, the *Gorbals Children* – he did *that*." And I do think those pictures are terrific. I feel very positive about Joe. But my observation is that he could have done more.'

Anna Robertson, head of Fine and Applied Art at Dundee's McManus Gallery, which owns a major collection of McKenzie's photographs, believes he backed himself into a corner with his decision not to show new work publicly. 'As a very honourable man who lived by a series of beliefs, it would have been difficult for him to come back from that,' she says. 'To say he saw the world in black and white is a trite thing to say about a photographer, but he did. He had a highly developed sense of what was morally right and wrong, and what was right and wrong for him. There weren't shades of grey in his own life, and he felt he had to take these stances.'

It's an interesting thought: the stubborn, awkward, damaged, morally outraged side of his personality which drove him to take such brilliant photographs of poverty and turmoil may have been the very character traits which made him unable, or at least unwilling, to keep on taking and showing them. For, although he continued to work, his photographs were very different from what had come before.

'His work became more introvert,' says Frank. 'He started looking more around the home. He took pictures of family. He took a lot of stuff around the local area. He liked taking walks along the Braes in Tayport, and down the harbour.

'So, yeah, he carried on photographing, but it was closer in. You can see that he went from being a man who challenged the world to a man who imploded – gradually, gradually, gradually until he condensed down to the immediate vicinity, and you can see what he ended up doing. Everything he did in the end was around here in the garden.'

These, then, were the last photographs of Joseph McKenzie – careful, tender, even obsessive studies of flowers and leaves and overgrown paths. Humans are absent, but his own humanity is not. They are in colour, they were taken on digital cameras, and they seem to contain within them an infinite sorrow.

Perhaps, though, it is wrong to see these pictures as sad. McKenzie loved his garden, according to his priest and friend Father Aldo Angelosanto, and he would have regarded photographing it as using the gift God gave him in the service of representing the mystery of God's creation. 'He felt his Catholicism deeply,' says the priest. 'He put his soul into his photographs.'

Father Aldo conducted McKenzie's funeral at Our Lady Star of the Sea in Tayport, a service attended by family, students and friends. Among them was Graeme Murdoch, former chief executive of the proposed Scottish National Photography Centre.

'One of the hymns had the words, "You fear the light may be fading. You fear to lose your way,"' Murdoch recalls. 'I think that was Joe; why he kept taking pictures right up to the end.'

The Bonspiel

THE DECISION, WHEN it comes, is understated, unwelcome, delivered beneath the branches of an old knotted yew, and spreads like a killing frost through the crowds on the frozen surface of the Lake of Menteith. 'Have you heard?' says Jim Paterson of the Royal Caledonian Curling Club, with tears in his eyes and a dram in his hand. 'It's off.'

They call it the Grand Match, or Bonspiel. It would have drawn 2,000 competitors and an estimated 10,000 spectators to the lake, near Aberfoyle, but has been cancelled. It was last held in 1979 but since then Scotland has not been cold enough for long enough to freeze the water to the required depth of seven inches. Until now. Yet, despite this meteorological miracle, the emergency services, concerned about crowds, narrow icy roads and poor access, were not able to give the event their blessing. Without that, getting insurance was impossible.

It seems to the curlers that grim bureaucracy has thrown grit on their dreams, melting them away. 'This country's gone mad,' says one Royal Caledonian committee member.

'We'll be a laughing stock around the world,' says another. 'Scotland's the home of curling and we canna even organise an outdoors match.'

Yet, somehow, it's hard to feel too sad. Not in a place like this. Not on a day like today. Minus seven but sunny, the atmosphere is more like a medieval feast than a wake. There's a certain frolicsome, hedonistic, anything-goes air. The 700-acre lake, covered in a dusting of snow, is solid underfoot, but it still feels joyfully transgressive to step down from the jetty and stroll across its surface.

Today, the whole world seems to be out enjoying Scotland at its most gorgeous and relaxed. A young couple, visiting from Montana, are wearing See-You-Jimmy hats and admiring the sweep of the Menteith Hills. A twenty-something from Australia is pulling his girlfriend along by the hand. She's pretty, in a faux-leopardskin coat, and is standing on two makeshift sledges – trays nicked from BHS. Skiting along, she eventually collapses against her boyfriend for a kiss. If God is choreographing today, he must be a real romantic.

Closer to shore, a retired solicitor called Malcolm Strang Steel strides the ice, pulling behind him six curling stones tied with tartan ribbon. He wears a tweed cap and the happy expression of someone who has never curled outdoors before and is eager to begin. He's here with a dozen or so friends. Even though the official Bonspiel is off, they are going to have a little curling match of their own. 'This is different from all the fancy indoor rinks we're used to,' he says. 'Much more atmospheric.' He gestures towards his party's collection of stones. 'These have been rescued from everyone's garden shed. They're usually used for propping the door open.'

The snow has been brushed aside to form a couple of rinks, concentric rings scored into the ice. The players are very much the green-welly and plus-four set. The women wear big fur hats and pull old-fashioned toboggans on which rest wicker baskets full of whisky, ginger wine and sloe gin. There are mince pies and Scotch eggs. It all feels convivial, though at one point a middle-aged man with extraordinary eyebrows wanders over and exclaims, 'There are rumours that you buggers have got more than sixteen stones! The other rink have only got fifteen and they are moaning.' This is what passes, in certain circles, for the redistribution of wealth.

Andrew Durie CBE, seventy-year-old chief of the Lowland Durie family, wanders over in flat cap and fleece.

'This is magic. Just magic,' he says. 'Even better is curling by car headlight with a bonfire and a bottle of whisky at each end. That's double magic. In the 1960s I did that frequently.'

Durie took part in the 1963 Grand Match on the Lake of Menteith. Back then he was a young training officer with the Argyll and Sutherland Highlanders, barracked at Stirling Castle. In the first round, he and some fellow soldiers used guerrilla tactics to defeat a team from Forfar. 'Our secret weapon was a bottle of cherry brandy,' he recalls. Though it was only 9.30 a.m., the Argylls made sure that the Forfarmen had plenty to drink, which rather affected their curling abilities. 'At the end of the match they staggered off, leaving us the winners, and moaning, "Don't touch the red stuff!"'

Many of the people here today are veterans of previous Grand Matches. The tournament was first held in 1847 and has taken place on only three occasions since the end of the Second World War. Anyone who ever attended seems to remember it as magical, sensuous. 'It was absolutely fabulous,' says sixty-three-year-old Johnny Cuthbert, who was here in 1979. 'It was very cold and everything was beautiful. The whisky smell rose up from the lake, and the stones roared across the ice. Historic stuff.' He looks half-sad at the memory and sets off for the lakeside hotel. 'I'm now going to have a pint of beer to make myself feel better.'

It is such a pity that the Grand Match won't take place. It would have been quite a spectacle – thousands of curlers dressed in tartan. All the pageantry had been arranged. Lord Elgin had agreed to lend his seventeenth-century cannon, which was to be fired at the beginning and end of the tournament. Jim Marshall, seventy-three-year-old president of the Royal Caledonian, was looking forward to arriving at the lake by helicopter. A telegram had been sent to the Queen – patron of the club – and they were anticipating a pleasant reply. Now, cannon, chopper and

Queen are unnecessary, or as Marshall puts it: 'The game's a bogie. The ba's burst.'

There are, of course, plenty of things to do on a frozen lake beyond curling, and all those things are being done. You can play ice hockey. You can teach your toddler to figure-skate. You can skim pebbles just to see how far they'll go. You can even just recline on a pair of deckchairs with a flask of coffee and the sun on your face. That's what Ena and Alec Robertson are doing. A couple in their sixties from near Dunfermline, it's refreshing to meet them as, while most of Scotland has cursed this historic cold spell, they've been revelling in it. 'We've never had a day indoors over the last three weeks,' says Alec. 'On Christmas Day we skated around Loch an Eilein near Aviemore; on Boxing Day, Loch Insh.'

As the afternoon wears on, I walk over to Inchmahome, a small island on which there's a ruined thirteenth-century priory. I've been here before by boat, but it feels important, somehow, to make the journey on foot. Lots of people are doing the same. It's a pilgrimage of sorts, something solemn on a day of fun. 'I'm pleased with myself getting over here,' says an old lady in a pink anorak. 'I was a wee bit nervous but it was something I had to do. I won't see the lake frozen again.'

In the choir of the church, the graves of the local Graham family are covered in snow. One died in 1897, another in 1921, another in 1946. Perhaps they were lucky enough to attend Grand Matches. I hope they had fun during their lives. It feels like a lonely spot to be dead.

Outside the church, David and Angela McLeod from Motherwell are walking their Tibetan terrier, Varin. Angela's fifty, David's fifty-one. She's eye-catching in a big furry coat and hat: 'That's the half-Polish in me.' This place is special to them. 'Last time it was frozen like this was when we got married in 1979. We came here in the winter of that year.'

231

As the sun sets behind the priory and glows pink on ice, I walk back across the lake. It'll be dark soon, the hills nothing more than a dark hump besieged by stars, but for now there is daylight to be savoured.

The skaters and curlers are silhouettes, Lowry by way of Bruegel. In the hotel bar, there are whispers of trying to pull political strings and get the Grand Match to go ahead. There's talk, too, of just going ahead with it unofficially, or holding tournaments on a smaller scale elsewhere.

But whatever happens, whether there's a match or not, there will still be a beautiful frozen lake in a beautiful frozen country, and that in itself is just grand.

The Band Who Gave Glasgow Hope

ESPERANZA MEANS HOPE. Esperanza were the band playing in Glasgow's Clutha bar at 10.22 p.m. on 29th November 2013, when a police helicopter fell from the sky and through the roof, killing ten people. Esperanza are a nine-piece ska group who play joyful, propulsive music that makes anyone who hears it feel a little more alive.

These three facts are not unconnected.

'Did you miss us?' Jake Barr, the frontman of Esperanza, shouts into the mic. 'We fuckin' missed you!' This is what passes for sentimentality in Glasgow.

It is Valentine's Day, 2014, and the band are making their first fully public performance since the crash, supporting British ska legends The Beat at The Arches, a nightclub converted from old railway vaults. A few hours earlier, air accident investigators had announced that both engines of the Eurocopter EC 135 had flamed out – failed – and that the rotor blades were not turning at the moment of impact.

There is, inevitably, some talk about this at the gig. It's in the background, sombre static, but the atmosphere is determinedly upbeat. It feels buzzy, like any other weekend in this city, but with an edge.

A number of the people in Esperanza's audience were in The Clutha that night – one had been pulled from the rubble, crushed but alive – and the thought strikes that this must have been what it was like on that other blighted Friday. Just ordinary. Coming on Christmas. A bunch of pals, mostly middle-aged, Fred Perrys and Docs, out for a few post-work pints and a dance to their favourite local band. This is how tragedy enters lives, shouldering the humdrum aside.

The story of The Clutha, as reported on TV and in the papers, soon began to conform to a particular narrative – this had happened to Glasgow, a wound to the soul of the city; the courage displayed, people rushing into the pub to bring the injured out, was seen as a particularly Glaswegian sort of tender heroism. The truth, though, was that there had been two distinct and specific groups in the pub that night: regulars, and fans of Esperanza. These were friends, a tribe, kin.

Among the thousands of floral tributes left outside the pub was a white polo shirt that has become emblematic of the public response to the disaster. The top button was done up, in approved rude boy style, and across the front, in black pen, were these words: 'Good night friends. Until we dance again! The Glasgow Ska Family.'

This was laid down by forty-three-year-old Frank Brown, a long-time fan of Esperanza. He wrote the words and his six-year-old daughter Emily Jane went over them in pen. 'That's how I see them all, as a family,' Brown says. 'I didn't want to put too much about God because a lot of my friends are atheists. But "Until we dance again" ... because, well, I just hope there is something after, up there, and I hope they're enjoying it.'

The Clutha crash, then, has been a great blow to a particular scene and subculture. Esperanza themselves have, until now, refused all requests to talk to the media because of concerns they might be regarded as exploiting their own heartbreak and that of others to sell themselves. The position they find themselves in is fascinating and unenviable.

Music soundtracks our lives; our pleasures and heartaches. How, then, do a band and their fans move forward when their songs have become linked with the most terrible moment most will ever experience? 'The music is what's carrying us,' says Barr. 'We all strive for each other.'

It was the first time they had played The Clutha, a very small, very old pub on the north bank of the River Clyde, known for its association with poetry and politics. The place was packed with about a hundred people, half of them Esperanza fans. The band had come on at 9.40 p.m. and were approaching the end of their first set. They were performing 'Be Brave' – one of their slower, more reflective songs, a song they have not played since – when it happened.

'There was a bang, an explosion. I thought a speaker had blown, so I took a wee step towards it, thinking, "What's that?"' recalls Gary Anderson, the band's manager. 'It happened so quickly. There was a sort of whooshing sound, and it was like the whole pub got lifted up; a nanosecond pause and it dropped back down.

'Then you got engulfed in dust and debris and it caught your throat. Before I had a chance to work out what the hell was going on, a big Polish guy who was outside smoking and had seen the helicopter come down, he grabbed me and pulled me out.'

Anderson stepped back to the edge of the pavement and saw the state of the roof. He was aware that there might be an explosion. 'But I needed to go back in. I had friends still in there. Inside, it was dark.' He grabbed arms and guided people to the exit, calling others towards his voice. Half the pub was blocked off by the collapsed gantry and ceiling.

'So I went outside again and back through the other doorway, and that was when it hit home just how bad it was. What I saw there really did shock me. People lying unconscious. People who looked like bomb-blast or warzone victims. It was clear that there were some already gone. I was shouting names, trying to account for everybody. I still get flashbacks. You replay it and replay it. You question yourself – "Could I have done more?"'

One of the names Anderson called would have been

Mark O'Prey, known as Ops, a stalwart of the scene, a big guy in his forties beloved for his daft jokes and his love for a party. You could depend on him being at gigs, a totemic presence in oxblood boots, swigging lager and skanking with one finger in the air. Now he was nowhere to be seen. His phone rang out. His sister Barbara, eleven days later, wore his 2 Tone T-shirt to his funeral.

O'Prey, who lived in East Kilbride, was like a lot of Esperanza fans – he'd fallen hard for them, never missing a gig, on one occasion even walking out on his own surprise birthday party to attend a show. Esperanza are brilliant, but they aren't well known or fashionable. They're not trying to make it. They all have day jobs and many are settled with kids. They play for the love of the music, and people love them for it. Their fans are friends, their friends fans.

There isn't much distinction between band and audience. They have a song, 'One Man Down', written a while ago, that has, in the aftermath of The Clutha, taken on a new resonance as a tribute to O'Prey. 'We can't go home, we're one man down' is how it goes. It is a song of abandonment performed and received with abandon.

The ska scene in Glasgow dates back to 1979 and the arrival in the city of the 2 Tone tour – The Specials, Madness and The Selecter on the same bill. Many teenagers who saw that show or who were swept up in the subsequent pop success of those groups fell for ska's sound, look and attitude, and have found nothing else comes close.

There are aspects of that musical culture – socially conscious, working class, hedonistic, exuberantly rough – that suit the local character. In Jamaica, it was the people's music, and something of the same folk spirit has made the journey to Scotland. Unity, solidarity, love – these are the important feelings and ideas, whether in Kingston or in the shadow of the Kingston Bridge.

Glasgow's first ska band, Capone and the Bullets, formed in the mid-1980s and are still going strong. The bands all know each other and share members. Jake Barr plays in Capone but formed his own band Esperanza – Spanish for hope, taken from a Manu Chao song – in 2007. Add in Bombskare, Big Fat Panda, The Amphetameanies and others, and you have an interconnected scene that it would take a family tree to understand properly.

The point is that ska, for these people, is not just a pleasant melody in the background somewhere. It is a sound that they associate with the events of their lives and the people they love. That offbeat is their heartbeat.

Esperanza were unhurt in the crash, at least physically. Some have received counselling. There have been diagnoses of post-traumatic stress disorder. Jess Combe, the twenty-four-year-old bass player, says she is looking forward to being able to sleep again. The band were let back into The Clutha a week after the accident to retrieve their instruments.

Her adored Squier Jazz fretless bass was undamaged but covered in dust. 'I put new strings on it because I just couldn't bear touching it,' she says. 'But it was nice having it back. I felt there was a part of me missing.'

There was some doubt as to whether Esperanza should carry on. Would anyone want to see them any more? Would they be able to play in front of those familiar faces – and in front of crowds lacking familiar faces – without breaking down? 'We had a band get-together not long after the incident,' the bassist explains, 'and I stood up in front of everybody and cried at the thought of losing my family, at the thought of us not going on any more. And then I made them all cry too.'

They agreed to try to continue. Mark O'Prey, they knew, would have been mad at the thought of them giving up. Their comeback show, towards the end of January, was invitation-only – at Pivo Pivo, the pub that hosts the monthly Glasgow Ska Train nights – and opened with a new song, '2 Tone Ain't Dead'.

They knew they had made the right decision, could see it in the smiles and sweat of the crowd, could sense it in the relief and release in the air. 'It was like something was pulling us through it,' recalls the drummer, Jason Good. 'It was exhausting emotionally and physically.'

Playing live again is, for Jess Combe, a 'homecoming feeling'. They are one man down. Always will be. But there is a feeling that, through the power of music so vital, they and their audience are able to channel the anger and pain into something positive: a celebration of a life, of all our lives, which, though brief and full of grief, can be sweetened and soothed by melody and rhythm.

'If they hadn't played again, I would have been devastated,' says forty-nine-year-old Sharon Hart, who – as perhaps Esperanza's most dedicated fan – was in The Clutha that night, dancing down the front as always. 'It's been my sanctuary over the years to be able to go out and see them. There's a crowd of us that love them as people as well as love their music. We're very close, and never more so than after what happened.'

8th March. The Ballerup Hall in East Kilbride. A tribute to Mark O'Prey. His family are here, and a couple of hundred friends: rude boys and girls; grannies, kids, punks, skins, natty cats in pork-pie hats. The mood is up, charged, expectant, a bit drunk. The tablecloths and napkins are 2 Tone check. This, the MC informs us, is to be a night of skanking and pogo-ing; a celebration, not a wake.

Ian O'Prey, Mark's father, comes onto the stage. 'Mark, I'm sure, is with us here tonight,' he says. 'People loved him to bits. We all did. He was an exceptional guy. He was special. I'm so proud to be his dad.' He pauses, choked. 'I'm getting maudlin, so I'd better chuck it. There's only one other thing to do – bring on Esperanza.'

He has been heard in respectful silence but this last remark prompts a proper football-crowd roar. People have been waiting for this. Dancing as catharsis. The band play with a fierce joy, a lust born out of loss. During 'One Man Down', Jake Barr points out into the crowd. 'Ops should be there. Fuckin' there in that wee space there!'

It's an extraordinary performance. Just a little more than three months since that hateful, fateful night, and look at them. Sharon's down the front in her usual spot. Frankie Brown's dancing away. So's Gary. So's Mark's dad, and his sister Barbara. Jess is jumping around like she wouldn't care if she never slept again. It's trite to say that music heals, that a three-minute song can bring any kind of closure, but this band and their fans are supporting each other beat by beat, bar by bar, and it is moving in every sense.

'This is right,' says Jess. 'This is something that needs to keep going no matter what.'

The Biscuiteers

THIS IS A love story from B-road Britain; from unsung towns and unsung lives. Roger Green, a fifty-three-year-old accountant, lives near Pontefract. Karen Carter is a forty-something civil servant from Nottinghamshire. They have been together for the last couple of years, having met during a Half Man Half Biscuit concert at the Holmfirth Picturedrome. This bright cold spring day is a sort of anniversary; the group having returned to the pretty West Yorkshire village for one of the handful of shows they play each year. Bogart and Bergman in *Casablanca* would always have Paris; Roger and Karen will always have Holmfirth. 'Half Man Half Biscuit,' she says, brooking no argument, 'are just the best band in the world.'

This is a minority view to say the least, but those who espouse it do so with remarkable fervour. Half Man Half Biscuit, though ignored by most of Britain for most of their thirty-odd-year 'career', have developed a hardcore band of travelling supporters who buy every record, know all the words, dress up as characters from the songs and attend every show. These Biscuiteers make even the most obsessive Dylan fans, the Bobcats of legend, look like mere dilettantes. Their devotion is more akin to that displayed by fans of lower-league football clubs, struggling along ungritted roads to away games in dismal grounds, breath clouding in the Bovril air. There's something very British about it, something mundanely magical or magically mundane. Man, they've got stories to tell.

Take Mick Bates. He's fifty-five and lives in Leicester. Mick is in a wheelchair, following a stroke and brain

240

haemorrhage he suffered twelve years ago. The music of Half Man Half Biscuit has been vital to his recovery. 'I had lost the power to speak,' he explains. 'That lasted about a month really seriously then it came back gradually. I was in the hospital six bloody month. To keep me going and train my voice again, I was reciting Half Man Half Biscuit songs. That really helped me.'

He was the youngest man on the whole stroke ward. A nurse called Joanne, perhaps taking pity, would sit with him for hours on end as he worked his way through the back catalogue. One song, 'Look Dad No Tunes', proved a particular challenge; once he had cracked that, he knew he had his voice back. His hobby now is making scale models of long-demolished football stadia, and by way of thank you, built one of the old 'Cowshed' stand at Tranmere Rovers for Nigel Blackwell, Half Man Half Biscuit's enigmatic singer-songwriter. Blackwell declared himself 'gobsmacked'.

Mick has a vivid memory of the first time he heard the group. It was not the road to Damascus, it was the A604 near Kettering, but it might as well have been. This would have been the mid-1980s, when HMHB became, for a few glorious months, the biggest indie band in Britain, outselling even The Smiths. Anyway, there's Mick pootling along in his Ford Escort van. 'I was coming home from a race meeting at Snetterton, and Annie Nightingale come on the radio and played "Dukla Prague Away Kit",' he recalls. 'I about crashed when I heard it. I pulled over because I had a real crap radio and got the best reception I could by putting my hand outside and touching the aerial. I thought, "God almighty!" and took the details down by scribbling in the dust on the dashboard.'

'All I Want For Christmas Is A Dukla Prague Away Kit' is one of the band's totemic songs. See also: 'Joy Division Oven Gloves' and 'The Trumpton Riots'. The titles give the unfortunate impression that Half Man Half Biscuit are a comedy group. They are funny, no question, but they are lots of other things too – lovelorn, full of scorn, bookish, hookish, cock-a-snookish. The songwriting, according to the folk musician Eliza Carthy, is 'bitter and very funny, which is very English: pathos disguised by wit and emotional detachment. It's like a camera flying over the country, zooming in and out; like watching a film of England'.

Occasionally a critic, swimming against the tide, sticks up a hand and proclaims Nigel Blackwell the greatest lyricist working today. This is not news to fans. The online Half Man Half Biscuit Lyrics Project ('192 Pop Songs Picked Over By Pedants') offers an ongoing crowdsourced analysis of the references within their thirteen albums and four EPs. 'Thy Damnation Slumbereth Not', for instance, quotes from Thomas Hardy, Richard Wagner and the Child folk ballads. 'Irk the Purists', meanwhile, borrows melodies from the hymn 'Give Me Oil in My Lamp' and Black Lace's 'Agadoo'.

This music breeds obsessiveness in those who take it to their hearts. Consider Steve Harman and Nick Dawes. Pals from London, they have spent the last three and a half years cycling around Britain in an attempt to visit everywhere mentioned in Blackwell's songs. This project is called Half Man Half Bike Kit. They have, so far, managed 102 out of a total 234 destinations, and hope to have bagged the lot by 2020. They worry, though, that Blackwell may have got wind of what they are doing and started adding in far-flung places just to thwart them. The most recent album mentioned – among other locales – Plockton, Skye, Ullapool and Kirkcudbright, all lovely Scottish spots, none of which are easily gettable-to from London. 'As well as going to some beautiful mountainous places, we have to go to some absolute shitholes,' says Nick. 'We went to Tredegar in South Wales and it was terrifying. Everyone stared at us until we left town. On another occasion, we got told off for taking photographs outside a kebab house in Swaffham.'

I meet Nick and Steve in a country pub just outside Holmfirth. They have spent the day crossing the moors. They are both forty-one and cheerfully self-aware. 'I'm in PR, he works for a luxury yacht magazine,' says Steve. 'We are exactly the kind of people who would be satirised in a Half Man Half Biscuit song, and it would be well deserved.'

The essential question, I suppose, is why are they doing this?

'That is the essential question,' says Nick, 'and essentially we don't have an answer.'

'But,' says Steve, 'we're committed to it now. It feels like a very Biscuity thing to do, doesn't it?'

Nick nods. 'There's a real English eccentricity about it. It sometimes feels like we are characters from one of Nigel's songs.'

Nigel Blackwell is a whippet-thin, whip-smart man in his early fifties. He lives in Birkenhead. I meet him, briefly, after the soundcheck. A diffident, shaven-headed figure in a cardigan, he winced at the volume as the band ran through a few songs. He has never given many interviews, and is less inclined to give them as the years go by, so this is more in the way of a chat. He is puzzled, he explains, that so many people spend so much of their lives following his band from gig to gig. 'Don't they get bored? Maybe it's because it's a good day out for them, and we're the not-so-good bit at the end.' Still, such loyalty has its advantages. Blackwell feels physically sick before performing, but when he walks out and sees familiar faces down the front, it calms him down.

'I don't like playing live,' he explains. 'I get nervous and I don't think we're that good, and only put up with having to do it so I can buy food and pay bills.

'I much prefer to simply write songs and put them out, but there's not enough money in just doing that for me these days so I have to psyche myself up and walk onto a stage to perform. It is not a good state of affairs for me, to be honest, but I'm stuck with it as I don't have the skills to do anything else. I'm not qualified in anything and I am shite around the house. I do not possess any tools whatsoever and sandpaper sets my teeth on edge. I buy one scratchcard a week and fill out a fixed-odds coupon at William Hill's every Saturday morning in the vain hope of landing the big one so that I can be in a situation where I don't have to arrange concerts.

'I am not a gig-goer myself, particularly, and the terminology and clichés surrounding that world fair makes me wince ... I always just want to get it all over with and go home as soon as possible. I do, however, endeavour to do the best I can whilst on stage because people have paid hard-earned money for a ticket and I wholly appreciate that.'

This sounds rather more like Eeyore-ish dysfunction than a mulish refusal to conform; can't, not shan't. Half Man Half Biscuit are often portrayed as the ultimate refuseniks; a famous story from their early days has them refusing to appear on *The Tube* because it would have meant missing Tranmere Rovers at home to Scunthorpe United. Blackwell does not like to fly or sail, so they never play outside Britain, and he likes to get home to Birkenhead after each show ('Own bog, own bed') which means that two gigs on the trot are a rarity and touring out of the question.

Despite this self-sabotage, the band is, reportedly, more popular than ever. It's just that their popularity is invisible. Their album *Urge for Offal* topped *The Guardian*'s readers' poll of 2014, despite not having been reviewed in that newspaper.

Nevertheless, HMHB have not been as successful as they might have been, a frustration that Geoff Davies, who runs the Liverpool record label Probe Plus, has grown used to since he signed the band in 1985. Well, 'signed' isn't quite right as he's never had a contract with them. The relationship appears to be tender, avuncular, enabling.

Geoff is tall, slender and dandyish in a flat cap, red shirt, green trousers and yellow jacket, a DIY BFG. He has a strong Scouse accent. I'd been looking forward to meeting him. When we spoke on the phone a couple of months previously, I asked whether he would be with the band in Holmfirth. 'Yes,' he replied, 'if I'm still alive.' This was only half a joke. He is coming up on seventy-three and has not been well. In May 2015, his son, Stephen, died of motor neurone disease; at the next HMHB show, in Wakefield, Blackwell dedicated 'National Shite Day' to his memory. Geoff, in that same year, missed the only two Biscuit shows he has missed since the 1990s. 'I've been in this business fifty years,' he says, unpacking merchandise at the back of the venue, 'and I worry about it more than ever.'

Retirement beckons. But Blackwell has said that if Geoff retires, he, too, will probably pack it in, saying, 'I couldn't do it without you.' So Geoff worries that if he stops, they'll stop, and as he doesn't want to deprive the world of Half Man Half Biscuit, he carries on. One senses that Geoff finds some pleasure in his duty. 'The feeling in the room when the band walk in is just great. I'm so pleased to be a part of it. I will miss it.'

There is a tremendous sense of community, family even, around Half Man Half Biscuit. The fans are a nomadic tribe. At the soundcheck, I meet Jay Coppock, who has travelled up from Maidstone and is leaping about and playing air guitar to 'Bad Losers on Yahoo Chess'. It's his fiftieth birthday this year, he explains, between leaps, and so his wife isn't giving him hassle about travelling to so many shows. 'It's payback,' he grins, 'for me going to *Strictly Come Dancing Live*.'

Some come from even further afield. Gregg Zocchi, a forty-eight-year-old wine merchant from New Jersey, flew to Britain, via Barcelona, four years ago; in the morning, he scattered some of the ashes of his brother, Glenn, a big Beatles fan, in Abbey Road, and then took a train to Oxford to see Half Man Half Biscuit. It was, he recalls, 'a strange pilgrimage' – the most rewarding thing he's ever done in his life beyond getting married and becoming a parent.

Thortsen Köppe, a forty-seven-year-old software developer, thinks he may be Germany's only Half Man Half Biscuit fan. The band, remember, never go abroad, so Thorsten has journeyed from Hamburg to Holmfirth for his third ever show. 'They are special,' he says, when asked what makes this band worth the time and money. 'I don't get a quarter of the things they address in their lyrics, but I can still get the gist. I like their way of extreme understating. They've been flying under the radar for thirty years.'

Thorsten is an anglophile, but his anglophilia is of a particular sort. Not for him the red, white and blue of Carnaby Street and the last night of the Proms. The England he loves is the England of grey skies and bleak moors and social awkwardness. He watches *Happy Valley*, drives an old white Triumph, and is married to a woman who is half-English, which gives him ample reason to holiday in Northampton. Thorsten doesn't believe that German culture has the proper balance of humour and angst to ever produce an equivalent of Half Man Half Biscuit. So no Halb Mensch Halb Plätzchen then?

'*Nee, leider nicht,*' he laughs. 'Or thank goodness.'

Showtime approaches. The Picturedrome, an old cinema, has a capacity of around 650 and is sold out. All day, Holmfirth, a quaint town in a steep valley where they filmed *Last of the Summer Wine*, has been buzzing with Biscuiteers, and now here they are, ready to dunk themselves soggy in the music they love.

The regulars take their cherished spots down the front. There's John, there's Liz, there's Tony. John Burscough is a retired GP, known in these circles as The King of Hi-Vis after the HMHB song of that name. He is wearing a searingly yellow tabard over a black satin tour jacket with detachable sleeves (the title of another song) over a T-shirt bearing a photo of Midge Ure and the accusatory legend 'Milk Thief' (a reference to the refrain of yet another track). John is here with his 'ladyfriend' Elizabeth Stockdale, a retired nurse, whose role is to wait until the band play 'Joy Division Oven Gloves' and then produce from her bag a pair of said gloves printed with a moody photograph of that band, the effect ruined only slightly by the stains from Sunday lunch. These she puts on and waves around with giddy abandon.

'Ah, it's great to be in a gang at the age of fifty-eight,' says John.

'He comes from a family of dresser-uppers,' Elizabeth smiles, as if that explains everything, which possibly it does.

Tony Roberts, meanwhile; well, what can one say? He is sixty-seven. He looks like a wizard, or a member of Wizzard, and he hails from Birmingham way. HMHB are the best live band he's ever seen. The Beatles ran them close, as did Cliff and The Shadows, and Springsteen might have done, 'but he went on a bit'. Tony goes to all the shows. 'My life,' he declares, 'is football, Morris dancing and Half Man Half Biscuit.'

He has an important role, Tony, at these gigs – to stand to the right of Roger Green and protect his note-taking arm from being barged by moshers. Roger is remarkable for his fidelity. He has missed only a handful of HMHB shows since the turn of the century, and has a 100 per cent attendance record going back to 2008. He plans his holidays around them and says he would miss a close friend's funeral or wedding in order to attend, as 'mates would understand'. More, he writes online reviews of all the shows, for which he is not paid, and has, to date, penned precisely 101 of these epics. It is some years now since he swore his oath of fealty. 'I could see other mates were getting married and having kids, and here I was just in this solo world,' he says. 'So I made a deal with meself not to miss any Biscuit gigs.'

In fact, he has found love among the Biscuiteers. He and Karen Carter met at the Holmfirth show in 2014. She had adored them since she was a teenager, in the mid-1980s, and heard them on John Peel, but never saw them live until after her divorce. 'I was in a relationship with someone who didn't like them, and didn't like me putting them on, and would never have come to a gig,' she says. 'So when I found myself single, I thought, "Stuff it, I'll do what I want now. Not what someone else wants me to do."' And she took herself off, on her own, to a show in Leamington Spa.

Unable to see the Biscuits during her marriage, she had enjoyed them by proxy through Roger's reviews. 'I read them and thought, "God, it sounds brilliant." So part of the reason why I started coming was because of Roger, never thinking I would meet him, never mind thinking I would end up going out with him.'

'Or staying in with him,' says Tony with a waggle of his eyebrows.

A lovely story, but sadly there's not a moment to hear more. The house lights are fading, Gershwin's 'Rhapsody in Blue' is striking up, and the band are coming on. Time for a last word from Roger Green. He cannot explain his obsession; all he knows is that this is how he wants to live his life. 'If there's a better night out to be had,' he laughs, 'tell me about it and I'll do that instead.'

Inside Rehab

FOURTEEN WEEKS AGO, Thomas Leith, a sad-eyed grandfather from the Calton, took up a pint glass and smashed it, rim-first, into his face three times, cutting an artery in his forehead and carving his nose like butcher meat. 'I hated myself,' he says. 'I just didn't like who I had become with the drugs.'

The exact circumstances change. The precise blend of intoxication, self-loathing and horror. But this is the sort of state in which addicts often find themselves before they come to live at Phoenix Futures, a residential rehab centre in the north of Glasgow.

Each day in rehab begins with a 'huddle' – residents gathering in the community room and saying in unison the Phoenix philosophy, which begins: 'We are here because there is no refuge finally from ourselves.' They stand in a circle, arms around each other's shoulders, some with eyes closed. Afterwards there is applause and hugging. People congratulate one another on another day clean and wish each other strength for the struggles ahead. Thomas Leith lifts a petite middle-aged woman in a pink velour tracksuit and birls her round for the sheer joy of another morning free of heroin, valium and coke, another morning when he isn't robbing his mother to feed his habit. When he first arrived at Phoenix, he'd have struggled to lift his own head up, never mind anyone else. He was seven-and-a-half stone, a bag of rattling bones, scarred inside and out. 'Coming in here,' he says, 'is the best thing I've ever done.'

Phoenix Futures is a large modern building on Keppochhill Road, an area of warehouses and waste ground not

249

far from the canal. It is one of around twenty residential drug treatment centres in Scotland. The drug problem in this country is huge, with the number of deaths steadily increasing since 1995, when 426 fatalities were recorded. That figure now seems relatively small. There are an estimated 61,000 problem drug users nationwide. Given these statistics, one might think that all rehabs would be full to capacity. Not so. Numbers in many places are in decline. Phoenix has room for thirty-nine residents, but at present only eighteen of the beds are occupied.

According to Rowdy Yates, head of Scottish Addiction Studies at Stirling University, Scotland's residential rehab sector is 'dying'. GPs and local authority care workers are far more likely to put an addict on a heroin substitute such as methadone rather than refer them to residential care. Why? Partly cost. Residential drug rehab in Scotland costs, on average, in the region of £500 to £800 a week. A weekly prescription of methadone comes in at around £28. Yet methadone merely replaces one drug with another, and a life on meth can, in its way, be as miserable, narrow and chaotic as a life on smack. Methadone kills more Scots than heroin. Rehab is an attempt to get people off drugs altogether.

Yet if numbers in rehab continue to decline as they are, Yates says, many centres will be forced to close, meaning that intensive, abstinence-based drug treatment will become available only to those who can afford private clinics. 'All that will be left are the residential treatment equivalents of public schools, which are only really catering for the well-off and the middle-class,' he says. 'The not-for-profit agencies will disappear. They can't continue to operate on those levels of occupancy. It can't go on for much longer.'

To spend a day in rehab, talking to staff and residents, is to understand the severity of the drug problem in a way that the statistics, grim as they are, cannot convey. It is the difference between being shown a photograph of a knife and feeling its edge on your skin. One thing the people here have in abundance is stories. The man who won £100,000 on bingo and blew it soon after. The man who spent nine years living beneath the railway bridge that spans the Clyde on the way into Central Station, climbing up the rivets each night, wearing twelve jackets against the cold, and sleeping on a steel rafter so narrow that had he rolled off he would have fallen to his death.

Phoenix opened in Glasgow in 1995 and is home, at present, to ten men and eight women. Its location in Possilpark is something of a grim joke among residents; they could walk out the door and buy drugs in two minutes if they so wished. 'Kick a Possil dug,' says one man, 'and it could tell you where to score.'

Movement in and out of the house is restricted and supervised. Service users must be resident for four months before they start being allowed out on their own. Phoenix functions as a 'therapeutic community', meaning that all the tasks of the house – cooking, cleaning, maintenance, etc – are carried out by the residents themselves, and that they are there to inspire and support one another. The days are full. Residents meet in groups and have one-to-ones with key workers. It's not just about giving up drugs. It's about confronting the reasons that made you start taking drugs, and finding ways to stay off them in future.

People spend up to two years within the programme, six months in the main house, followed by a further six months of semi-independent living within a nearby tenement; during the final year, service users usually find their own tenancy within the city but remain in contact with support workers. Stephen Kennedy, manager of Phoenix and himself a graduate of the drug treatment programme, estimates that around 40 per cent of those using the service manage to abstain from drugs and alcohol for more than two years.

The first three to six weeks tend to be spent detoxing,

which will usually mean reducing the quantity of methadone taken by four milligrams every three days. Almost everyone who comes here arrives addicted to the heroin substitute. 'We've had people who've been on methadone for more than twenty years,' says Kennedy. 'They are terrified to come off because they've been on it that long. Methadone suppresses your feelings and emotions. You don't feel real when you're on it. The good thing about rehab is you get feelings back. The bad thing about rehab is you get feelings back.'

Among those feelings is guilt. In an upstairs room, cosy with leather couches, I meet Kelly Allan, a thirty-one-year-old from Tollcross. She has a ten-year-old son who has been in the care of her mother since he was five. Kelly's life had become a chaos of drugs and domestic violence. 'I thought I was taking care of him properly, but I was out my face,' she says. 'I can look back now that I'm clean and sober and know that it just wasn't the right atmosphere for my boy to be in. It wasn't fair.'

She had started off taking speed, which she loved for the way it gave her energy to clean the house and prepare her son's breakfast before he woke. She ended up on a large daily prescribed dose of methadone, which she had at first been buying illicitly. Meth, she found, made her calm, numb, able to cope with the pressures of motherhood and a torturous relationship. 'You get a wee kind of glow around you,' she recalls.

After she lost her son, she spent time in hostels, supported accommodation and a women's refuge. She had sworn she would never become an alcoholic as her uncle had died of this. Yet it got to the point where she was drinking nine litres of Frosty Jack cider each day, burned holes in her pancreas and gullet, and took panic attacks when she left the house. 'All my life revolved around was going for my methadone in the morning and then going to the off-licence. I was lucky if I ate one meal a day.'

She knew that she had to change or die. She came to Phoenix at the start of February and credits it with being the reason not only that she is still alive but that she is glad to be so. Kelly knows she has a long way to go, but she is back in touch with her son and hopes, one day, that she can get him back and he will love her. 'A lot of the time people think addicts are worthless and beyond help,' she says. 'But we're not.'

Downstairs, I meet Gary Stewart, who is forty-three and comes from Baillieston. Tall and gaunt with a Scotland tattoo on his right arm, he has survived twenty years of heroin addiction, but not in one piece. 'I ended up losing my leg. Nae teeth. I've no' got a vein in my body.' He has been trying to quit drugs, on and off, since 1994 and has had lengthy periods of being clean. His right leg was amputated twelve years ago after he contracted necrotising fasciitis, the so-called flesh-eating disease, from injecting into a muscle contaminated heroin which had been stashed underground by a dealer; the same batch killed twenty-one drug users. He was, in a way, lucky. Gary remembers being administered the last rites, the soft mist of holy water. Nevertheless, he survived and ended up back on drugs, crucifying himself, plunging the needle into his forehead and the palms of his hands. He has been at Phoenix for four-and-a-half months. 'Aye,' he says, 'some journey.'

Some journey. The same might be said of any of the men and women at Phoenix, rising from the choking ashes of their own lives, or those at Scotland's other rehab centres. It is to be hoped that those centres themselves have a long journey ahead of them. The idea that any of these places might shut for lack of business is, to say the least, sobering.

The Chess Players

IT BEGINS WITH a muted reveille of electronic clocks being set, and before long the thirty-eighth annual Grangemouth Chess Congress is under way. To the players, the tournament is a fight, the latest battle in an endless war against other players and their own limitations; to observers, it has a weird, hypnotic, catatonic charm.

Beneath Grangemouth Town Hall's flickering art deco lights, 117 players are competing for supremacy. Five games are played over the weekend, each lasting up to four hours. The silence is not absolute. A cough goes round the room like a loud guest mingling at a subdued party; a yawn, too, circulates. One player's phone shrills and she scrabbles in her bag then rushes, mortified, for the exit. FIDE, the world chess federation, has a zero-tolerance policy regarding mobiles; if a player's rings during a game, they lose.

Most of the games are taking place in the main hall, amid that unmistakable municipal smell of dust and polish. Each game is contested at a separate wooden table. The symmetry is pleasing. Looking down from the balcony, it could be a frozen frame of a Busby Berkeley musical, albeit one a good deal dowdier than the rest of his oeuvre.

Competitive chess can appear static: steam curls from coffee cups; someone blinks in slow motion; a hand reaches out, birdlike, and pecks up a pawn. The players sit hunched over the green-and-white board, hands cradling foreheads as if to hold in thoughts that have reached escape velocity. Look beneath the table and you begin to get a sense of what's really happening. That's where you see the jiggling feet, the waggling knees, physical outlets for the nervous energy produced by all those birling brains. It is said that during particularly anxious stages of a game, especially during 'time trouble' – having little time left on the clock to complete the remaining moves – a player's heart rate can double.

Daniel Maxwell is a nineteen-year-old Aberdonian, and his purple Nikes are a blur as he plays his way to another victory. 'I get incredibly nervous,' he says later. 'I'm quite literally shaking.' He is a third-year psychology student who spends more time playing online chess – the accelerated five-minute variety known as 'blitz' – than revising. He is also into bodybuilding. There is an idea prevalent within the chess world that physical strength whets mental sharpness.

What makes Maxwell so nervous? 'My expectations of myself. Once you get good results, you want to keep on winning. In the future I want to be a grandmaster.'

Why? 'Grandmaster is the ultimate promotion. Earning the title shows hard work. Just like developing a six-pack shows hard work.'

One becomes a grandmaster by winning enough games to build a rating of at least 2,500 and performing strongly against at least three grandmasters in particular tournaments. Scotland has five grandmasters, sixty-six chess clubs and 2,265 registered competitive players. League matches take place during the week, and there is roughly one weekend tournament each month. The Scottish Championship, first staged in 1884, is the world's oldest chess event, and offers a top prize of around £2,000. In Grangemouth, the prize money of £550 ends up being split four ways by the joint winners; at the apex of the game, godlike beings with ratings above 2,600 can make a very good living from tournament wins, appearance fees, writing and coaching, but most mortal players aren't in it for the money.

They aren't in it for the fame either. Though, thanks to

255

the internet, chess has a global reach (1 million unique visitors from 183 countries were, earlier this month, watching the Chess World Cup live from Siberia), the game is more or less invisible in the UK; its complexity and nerdy image makes it easy for the mainstream to dismiss or revile. 'There's something about British anti-intellectualism that makes us wary of people who want to think in their spare time,' says the Aberdonian grandmaster Jonathan Rowson.

Yet for those acolytes initiated into its mysteries, versed in its secret language of zwischenzugs and zugzwangs, chess can become a passion, even an addiction. 'It's a bug, a wonderful drug,' says one Scottish chess player; or, as the Dutch grandmaster Hans Rees once put it, 'Chess is beautiful enough to waste your life for.'

There is a beauty, certainly, in watching people play chess. We enjoy the sight of athletes playing tennis and dancers performing ballet, and there is something similarly uplifting about examining the faces of those deep in thought. You find a lot written there: serenity, pain, at times a kind of grace. And what chess offers, unlike physical disciplines, is the opportunity for children to take on adults and win. There is something undeniably moving about watching a schoolboy sitting across from an old greybeard, both of them utterly absorbed by the game. One of the players in Grangemouth is Vagif Ramazanov, an eight-year-old from Baku, Azerbaijan, now living in Aberdeen; his father Vasif, also a chess player, works in the oil industry.

Vagif is a cute kid with dark brown eyes and a laser grin. His legs, as he sits and plays, don't quite reach the floor. Those in the know say that he's one of the best players of his age to emerge in Scotland in the last three decades. He learned to play two years ago, while visiting his grandfather in Azerbaijan. The former Soviet republic has a thriving chess culture; Garry Kasparov, regarded by many as the greatest player of all time, is from Baku; for Vagif, Kasparov's example is inspiring. 'I want to be a grandmaster,' he says. 'I like playing chess so much and I don't want to give up.'

On the other side of the room from Vagif, frowning down at his board as if it were an inscrutable foe, is Rudolph Austin, who is seventy-five years old and lives in Edinburgh. His hair is swept back from a face that would make Samuel Beckett appear unlined. The pockets of Austin's suit jacket are full of cigarettes and old scoresheets and coins and newspaper articles. He suffers from hypertension and ringing in the ears, and says that sometimes his mind is in turmoil. Yet, even when he is feeling quite ill, he turns up to tournaments. 'My urge to play,' he explains, 'is very strong.'

He is an anxious man, running on caffeine and nicotine, constantly nipping outside to smoke after he has moved his pieces. Among staff in the Haymarket coffee shop, where he visits and plays chess several times a day on a small portable board, he is known simply as Chessman. One of his rituals is to draw the Star of David on his scoresheet at the start of every game.

Austin's first memory of chess is seeing his parents playing with red and white ivory pieces. This was in Italy during the Second World War. The family had gone there so that Austin's father, a property owner, could take mud baths for his rheumatism. While they were abroad on holiday, Italy entered into an alliance with Germany, and the family from Edinburgh were not allowed to return home for three or four years. It was a traumatising experience, from which he has never quite recovered. They often went hungry. Austin remembers an attempt was made by a German officer to rape his mother and to have his father shot dead.

Through those dark, fearful days, until the Nazis took the board, chess was a consolation and has remained so. 'I have a craving for security, which I think chess provides,' he says. 'Someone once said that the real motivation for playing chess is the wish to create order in a chaotic world. I think that's possibly true.'

What is it about chess that means people *need* to play it rather than simply *want* to do so? For Rowson, the thirty-four-year-old grandmaster who won the British Championship every year between 2004 and 2006, one reason, often overlooked, 'is that the game is utterly beautiful. It has enormous aesthetic charm that is invisible to those who don't play. Once you get into the complexity of chess, you are suddenly transported into this world of geometry and symmetry and asymmetry and flow. There's something about the beauty of how things work, the aesthetics of logic, that lies right at the heart of the game and keeps people coming back for more.'

Rowson, who now works for a think tank in London, first won the Scottish Championship in 1999. The present Scottish champion is Ketevan Arakhamia-Grant, known as Keti, originally from the former Soviet republic Georgia but living in Edinburgh since 1996. The only female grandmaster in the UK, she is forty-three and has been playing since she was six. At twelve, she left her home by the Black Sea to study chess at the Pioneer Palace, in the Georgian capital Tbilisi. A petite, polite woman, she is known as a sharp and aggressive competitor; Keti plays like a man, experienced players say, intending this as a great compliment.

'For me, it was never a question whether I wanted to play chess or not,' she explains. 'In Georgia, there is a tradition of women playing chess. We have had two female world champions, the best players are heroes, and you can read about chess on the sports pages of newspapers.

'I think it suited my personality. I was kind of introverted and capable of sitting for hours and studying play. Also, I am very competitive. For me, chess is very exciting. There is a lot of drama. You have to have very strong nerves. You have to keep control of your emotions. You use a lot of energy sitting at the board. In physical sports, you can express your emotions. In chess, it is all internal and intensive. A lot of players, after a game, they go for a run so they can get rid of the negative. If you lose, the worst thing is when somebody says, "Oh, don't worry, it's just a game." Because, at that moment, it feels like the end of the world.'

One man for whom chess is definitely not just a game is Geoff Chandler, a taxi dispatcher and well-known figure on the Edinburgh chess scene. Chandler is a rangy, restless man of sixty and has been obsessed with the game since he was twelve. He tried to give it up in 1995, feeling he was getting too old to compete, but has since become hooked once more. His flat contains two untidy study areas dedicated to chess, books on the subject – some in Russian – piled up everywhere; above a desk hangs a framed portrait of the great American player Paul Morphy, who died in 1884.

Chandler has allowed a journalist to visit him at home in order to show how a chess player lives. He's a good illustration because, although he is a strong player, rated 2,001, he's not a master; chess is not his living, but it is his life.

As he makes tea, he explains that, much to the displeasure of his wife, he has burned though a number of kettles and saucepans, leaving them on the hob and becoming distracted by chess. 'I don't care what's happening in the world,' he explains. 'I'm just lost completely in a zone of moves and numbers.' He keeps chess boards behind the bars in several Edinburgh pubs.

Taking the mugs through to the living room, Chandler settles on the couch in front of the window, the afternoon sun making a halo of what remains of his bushy hair, and rolls a cigarette. There is a chess board on the coffee table and he often leans forward to move the pieces around in illustration of a particular point. Two black-and-white cats doze on the couch beside him; there is a third around somewhere. Chandler, had he been allowed, would have named them after his favourite chess champions – Fischer, Alekhine and Capablanca.

Chandler has no hesitation in describing himself as an 'artist'. Chess, for him, is a creative act, which is why it can be mentally draining. 'Every time you play it's like giving a blank canvas to Picasso and saying, "Paint me a masterpiece now".' These days he mostly plays blitz online, on the Red Hot Pawn site, for which he is also a blogger. One of the last times he played over the board, he almost passed out with the strain. 'I've not got the stamina for the third hour.'

It is difficult, when considering chess, to arrive at a definite conclusion as to what it actually is. A sport? A puzzle? What? 'Ah,' Chandler grins, 'you're now on the subject of a thousand forum threads. Alekhine said it was an art; Lasker said it was a fight; Botvinnik said it was a science. To me, it's a game.' He chuckles. 'It's the game I love.'

For Chandler, there is no better feeling than grabbing a book and board and playing through the great games of the past, the chess equivalent of covering a classic song. He might, for example, recreate the moves of a game that took place in St Petersburg in 1914, enjoying the feeling of kinship to those Russian players who, though long dead, live on through their ideas. Chess is an ancient game, dating back to at least 600, and Chandler sees himself as part of a lineage of players, one mind connecting to the next, stretching back through the centuries.

Finishing his cup of tea, he suggests we visit the Edinburgh Chess Club, which is on the first floor of a tenement in Alva Street. Established in 1822, it is the oldest club in the UK and arguably the second-oldest in the world, behind Zurich. The club is a narrow, cosy space with a real fire and heavy maroon drapes, the walls decorated with black-and-white photographs of tweedy, bewhiskered players of the Victorian era. There are a dozen tables, each covered by a white tablecloth on which sits a chessboard. The atmosphere is elegant, formal and still.

'This is the place, eh?' says Chandler, unable to contain his excitement. He actually lived in the club for six years, working as the caretaker; his daughter was born in the analysis room.

David Archibald, the club curator, opens a wooden trophy cabinet and brings out a great treasure – the Scots Gambit Cup, won against the London Chess Club during a correspondence match that lasted for four years during the 1820s.

Archibald, who is forty-eight and has a taste for ora-torical flourishes, says, 'Beethoven was writing "Missa Solemnis", Wellington would have been Prime Minister, Catholic emancipation was still a dream of Thomas Moore, and the Edinburgh Chess Club played a match with London by post.'

To spend time at the Grangemouth Congress, and here in this temple of chess with Chandler and Archibald, is to begin to understand just what it is about the game that has captured the minds of so many in Scotland and beyond – it is something to do with its cosmic vastness, its seemingly inexhaustible capacity to delight and to frustrate. Clocks may tick down and hearts may stop, but chess never really ends.

'There are more potential games of chess after ten moves,' Archibald explains, 'than there are atoms in the known universe.'

Both men nod at this. 'That's it,' says Chandler. 'That's *it*.'

The Poultry Show

'THIS,' SAYS NEIL WATSON, 'is the Crufts of the Scottish poultry fancy. This is the one they all want to win.'

Watson, a farmer in his late forties from Plains near Airdrie, is chairman of the Scottish National Poultry Show, a highlight of the year for those fowl-minded folk whose interest in hens, ducks, geese and turkeys goes beyond – way, way, way beyond – eating them.

There are around 400 competitors here, and more than 4,000 birds. As the national and regional flags hanging from the ceiling of Lanark Agricultural Centre attest, the fanciers have come from all over, including as far south as Cornwall and as far north as Shetland. One bus leaves Caithness at 8 a.m. and arrives in Lanark at teatime, disgorging a merry gaggle of Highlanders and islanders, and some 200 birds, all of whom have been quacking and clucking at the back of the bus since it pulled out of Wick in the bleary, beery dawn. It is the purest example of poultry in motion.

Some of the fanciers at the show haven't seen each other for a year, and there is a tremendous sense of camaraderie. 'We are truly birds of a feather flocking together,' is how one puts it. Austin Shaw, a farmer from Larne in his fifties, here with forty-eight bantams, is more blunt: 'This poultry business is just a lot of boys with the same interest talking a lot of bullshit. It's a long hard life if you don't have a hobby.'

A hobby? Well, maybe. A passion is how I would put it, and a kind of sculptural art. Just look at Austin, reaching into a small blue box and lifting out, in a sudden smirr of sawdust, an Old English Game bantam. He cradles the hen gently but firmly, smoothing and moulding its feathers into shape so that, when observed from above, the placid little bird resembles a greetings card love heart. He also wipes its comb with an oil intended to intensify its redness. 'This is like putting lipstick on a woman,' Austin says. 'This is her wedding day. A young bride looks her best on her wedding day, and this one has to look really well, so she does.'

Competitive birds receive the same levels of grooming as a pedigree showdog or a thoroughbred racehorse. They are washed and blow-dried a couple of days before the show, giving them time to preen themselves back into optimum shape. Wandering around, you see the fanciers applying lotions and potions, and clipping claws with the deference and care of a professional manicurist. Everyone is wary of giving away their own particular secret recipe, but rest assured these birds are thoroughly pampered and oiled, and in some instances perfume and aftershave seem to be involved. 'It can smell like a tart's boudoir,' says Neil Watson.

Fanciers are well named. They fall hard for their birds. 'He's pretty special,' says David McVey, a forty-five-year-old from Bute, regarding his Plymouth Rock with a loving eye. This gigantic white cockerel has already been crowned champion at a show in Stafford, and McVey, who works as a gardener at Mount Stuart, has high hopes for him here. McVey was playing rugby in the back row for Glasgow when they won the championship in 1989, and says that poultry is an equally competitive world. He used to take a slagging for being a big rugby player who kept chickens, but he didn't care. 'They didn't understand the excitement. When you walk into your birdhouse and see this fantastic specimen that you bred – what a rush.'

Better even than crossing the line for a try? 'Better than an orgasm.'

One of the most tremendous things about the poultry

show is the noise. You'd think dawn was breaking every second considering the way the roosters keep up the cock-a-doodle-dooing. But in addition to such barnyard clichés, there is every kind of holler, shriek, bray, cackle and crow, ranging in pitch from the guttural to the shrill, and in tone from triumphant to – in the case of certain ducks – deeply sarcastic.

More impressive than the noise, though, is the look of the event. The birds are shown in metal pens, thousands of which are laid out in rows like a cell block. But none of these captives slump prisoner-like and despondent at the back of their confines. Instead, they are up – chests puffed, combs regal, wattles flapping like Communist flags, each bird a dictator in absolute mastery of its territory. When they scratch at the wood-shavings it's like a preening despot stamping his boot.

They are, of course, quite right to be fierce and proud. Some of these breeds are remarkable, flamboyant, exotic. The untrained eye – mine – struggles to make sense of their appearance. Crested ducks look, basically, like an ordinary duck wearing a giant Cossack hat. Faverolles, French cockerels with great feathery feet, are bellicose dandies ready to fight a duel with any other bird they consider to have insulted their dignity. Silkies, meanwhile, are essentially a lunatic cross between a Klingon and an Afghan hound.

'It's like walking into a sweet shop when you come to these shows, there are so many lovely breeds,' says fifty-six-year-old Chris Ward, visiting from Leyton Buzzard with her husband Nobby, and busy applying oil with a make-up brush to the comb of a cockerel. 'I fell in love with the Silver Sebrights so we got a trio of those. Then I fell in love with Golden Sebrights.'

There is a poetry to the names – Leghorns and Langshans, Pekins and Cochins, black Scots dumpies and Rhode Island Reds. Each breed has its acolytes, some demonstrating their allegiance by wearing metal badges carrying a picture of the particular bird pinned to their woolly jumpers or to the front of deerstalker caps. Somehow the judges make sense of this profusion, walking through the halls in long white coats, examining each bird carefully, comparing it with the breed standard, and awarding marks out of a hundred.

To be named Supreme Champion is a massive honour, a wee bit of history. The accolade is all. There is no money in it for the breeders, and no particular reward for the triumphant bird, although some fanciers may, in a moment of ecstatic generosity, reach into their jacket pocket for a small piece of cheese, a foodstuff which chickens – I am told – regard with obsessive desire. 'Cheese is a kind of drug to them,' one old fancier confides.

The first ever champion here was Billy Dalgliesh in 1974, and he's back today, aged seventy-three, to lend a hand with pen-building and judging. A white-haired, twinkle-eyed man in a dark blue boiler-suit, Dalgliesh hails from Berwickshire, and took the top prize with a Black Rosecomb pullet, a type of bantam. 'I couldn't believe it,' he says. 'It's one of these things that comes into your life and makes you feel humble.'

When it comes to bantams, Dalgliesh won all the prizes going, even breeding the all-American champion one year. He keeps the black glossy tail feathers of all his former winners pressed between the pages of a book at home. Though he is an expert on bantams, he will also admit, in passing, 'I ken a guid duck when I see it', and prides himself on being the grandson of Sam Dalgliesh, who won at the Crystal Palace in London in 1890 with some world-class waterfowl. Poultry-fancying seems to run in bloodlines like that.

The initial attraction to the birds was having something to call his own. His father had failed at farming, there was no land to inherit, and so Dalgliesh went to work on someone else's farm as a tractor-man. Having his own flock of bantams was a source of dignity and pride. He called the cocks Jocky, the hens Jenny, and for thirty-four years they brought him joy. He won here for the last time in 1986. 'But when my wife Grace died I put the birds away,' he says. 'My twin girls were only fourteen and I thought that was where my priorities lay. Instead of being out at night looking at my banties, I had to see to them.'

Dalgliesh shakes his head at the memory of those birds, at the memory of his wife, at the aching loss of both. 'Yes, I regret it, but, well, when you're left yersel'...'

It has been quite a day at the Scottish National Poultry Show; a day of beaks and geeks, wings and prayers, spectacle and poignancy. As I leave, I bump into Mike Hatcher, past president of the Poultry Club of Great Britain, a lanky man with long white hair and a long white beard who drifts serenely through the halls like Moses in a polka-dot cravat. He is seventy-four years old, has travelled from Berkshire in the company of some Indian Runner ducks, and is marvelling that poultry-keeping – a fascination since his childhood – is showing no signs of dying out, and is in fact growing more popular all the time.

'Avian flu hasn't stopped us, and the economic crisis hasn't stopped us,' he muses. 'It really is amazing how much we love our chickens.'

A Day in A&E

WATSON MCDONALD HAS blood on his vest, an arm in a sling, a broken collar-bone, and Rizla-thin skin which is difficult to stitch.

He is sitting in the accident and emergency department of the Royal Infirmary of Edinburgh, wearing a tweed bunnet, as insouciant as though this were his local bowling club, and waiting to be discharged into the company of his pal Jock, another bunnet-wearer, with whom he will return to Prestonpans. 'I'll be eighty next month,' he grins, Mr East Lothian Stoicism. 'That's if I make it.'

A few steps away, within a curtained cubicle, a young man in a grey hoodie is pale and sweaty, curled on a hospital trolley, his heart stuttering in irregular rhythms, the result of his having stolen and swallowed the medicine his mother had been prescribed for her psychiatric disorder. Meanwhile, in Resus 2 – one of two large 'resuscitation rooms' dedicated to the treatment of the most serious cases – a woman is crying out in pain as nurses cut the clothes from her body; she has been hit by a car in town and has suffered, at the very least, a broken pelvis. Doctors are concerned that she may have hit her head. 'Did she bullseye the windscreen?' one wonders, using the mix of painstaking tenderness and blunt slang characteristic of emergency room staff.

Three patients. Three cases. A faller. An OD. A trauma. Three strangers whom fate has brought together here. Each is having a bad day, maybe one of the worst of their life, but for the medical team this is just another shift. Your disaster is their routine. Not that you should think they don't care. They do, very much. It's just that they're used to this way of life and have become intensely pragmatic and understated. They talk not of saving lives but 'outcome modification'. They discuss wedding plans while waiting for the ambulance to bring the latest mangled tragedy. They wear Crocs because they wipe clean. 'I've lost two pairs of trainers to catastrophic bleeding,' says Dr Dave Caesar, the thirty-nine-year-old clinical director.

The A&E department of the Royal Infirmary of Edinburgh is the busiest in Scotland. The team treat around 100,000 people each year. Attendances tend to rise sharply from around 11 a.m., and for the next ten hours new patients arrive at the rate of twenty an hour. More difficult to predict are the variations in 'acuity' – the severity of illnesses and injuries; one critically injured patient can divert the staff who might have otherwise been dealing with ten cases, and an incident such as a serious road accident can bring many patients all at once. There are usually around twenty-five medical staff on shift at the one time.

August is the busiest month of the year, as a result of the festival, but midnight on Hogmanay to midnight on New Year's Day is the busiest twenty-four-hour period, thanks to alcohol. Rainy days are busier than sunny days because bad weather causes falls and car smashes, and the wet and cold aggravates respiratory conditions.

Today, there are people with chest pain, folk who have had strokes, and a tough cookie of a school dinner lady with a nasty dislocation to her right elbow which is popped back into place with a loud crack. There is, in the words of one consultant, 'a preponderant number of toxicology patients' – those who have taken an overdose of pills, with the intention of either getting out of their heads or out of their lives. But whether you are a junkie or a granny, or both, you'll get the same level of respect and care. As one doctor puts it, 'People just want to know that you give a shit.'

Late afternoon and the black 'crash' box within the

central administrative area starts to buzz and wail. This is ambulance control phoning to say that the paramedics are on the way. A woman has collapsed. Cardiac arrest. 'Crash call,' says a nurse over the tannoy. 'Resus 1. Ten minutes.'

A team of seven assembles in the room, and the patient arrives soon after, carried on a stretcher by the ambulance crew. She is moved onto a trolley and the work of attempting to save her begins. What's striking is the odd calmness of this scene. There is urgency, but no panic, and certainly no raised voices. It could not be more different from the television dramatisations of such situations. These nurses and doctors know each other and this room so well; it would be rather like a family talking quietly at home, getting on with some mundane task, were it not for the woman lying there, being given electric shocks and chest compressions, the orange traces on the monitor showing her life slipping away. 'The heart's trying,' says Dr Caesar. 'There's something there that's trying to keep going.'

It is no use. The woman cannot be saved. The senior medic asks her colleagues whether they are content to stop, and they are. She gives the PLE time – Pronounce Life Extinct – and everyone steps away from what is now a dead body.

No one wanted this. They did everything they could to prevent it. But it is what happens sometimes. And there are a great many living people just beyond the curtain, all suffering, all requiring attention straight away. If you work in the emergency room, you must be able to go from a fatal heart attack to a cracked rib without breaking stride. That's what it takes. 'You've got to get your game face back on and get back out there,' Dr Caesar explains. 'None of the other patients want to know.'

Screens are wheeled into the corridor so that the body can be moved without being seen. The family of the deceased have to be informed. Alistair Dewar, a twenty-eight-year-old specialist registrar who had pumped air into the woman's lungs as she lay dying, speaks with them in one of the interview rooms reserved for this purpose, known as the 'rellies rooms'. He tells them he has bad news and then he tells them what it is.

'It's never easy to tell somebody that their relative has died,' Dewar explains later. 'You just try to comfort them, and reassure them that the ambulance crew and we have done everything we can to ensure their relative has had the best possible chance. It can be difficult when a patient comes in talking to you and then dies under your care. You feel more responsible at that time. I still get affected by it, even though I've done this for a few years, especially if there's something about the family that you can relate to personally.'

A&E is divided into majors and minors. Patients, as they are arrive, are sifted by a nurse into categories of severity – a process known as triage. Even the quiet days are busy. By half-past ten in the morning, all the cubicles in majors are full and patients are being seen while lying on trolleys in the corridor. There are not enough beds in the main hospital to cope with the sheer numbers of patients in A&E who are out of immediate danger but need further treatment. In majors, one patient has been waiting ten-and-a-half hours for a bed. In minors, seven patients have been waiting between eight and eleven hours.

'To a layperson, and to me, that's unacceptable, but unfortunately I can't manufacture beds,' says Caesar. 'There is no elastic in the hospital system other than in the emergency department. Nowhere else goes over-capacity in an uncontrolled way other than us, which is a daily frustration of mine.'

A&E is a dramatic place. A tragedy or tragi-comedy behind every curtain. You get the sense, walking from cubicle to cubicle, catching dialogue, of passing from play to play – some absurdist, some desperately sad.

Doctor: 'Why did you take the pills?'

Patient: 'Self-pity. He had left me.'

Doctor: 'Do you want to kill yourself now?'

Patient: 'No. Just then. It's hard to explain.'

One fifty-something man is here with his sister. He's been trying to get high on over-the-counter painkillers and has taken them in sufficient doses to give himself internal bleeding. He's chatty, slightly batty; a big fan of TV hospital drama, from which he has picked up a gobful of medical jargon. 'My stools,' he informs the doctor with not inconsiderable pride, 'are normal.'

His sister, scunnered, cuts in. 'Can you not give him something to stop him talking? Not diazepam, though. That's his favourite.'

It is early evening when I leave A&E. This is a place where you see humanity at its frailest physically, but at its best in terms of courage, compassion, humour and love. A woman has died, a family cast into grief, but many others have been saved, or had their pain and distress relieved. A drama, then, which will never come to the end of its run, but which goes on day after day, night after night, testing the character of its protagonists and offering a reward greater than any amount of applause.

'This job,' says Dr Caesar, 'gives you the chance to go home at the end of the day thinking, "We made a difference."'

The Fishermen's Mission

'SMELL THAT?' MURRAY CAMPBELL sniffs long and deep, great greedy lungfuls of the freezing fishy air. 'I like to come down here to breathe it in first thing in the morning. This is where I start every day.'

We are in the fish market by Fraserburgh harbour. Breath clouds the faces of the dozens of fishermen and buyers standing around crate upon crate of haddock and hake, saithe and skate. Cod lie torpedo-like in icy bays. Lumpers – market strongmen in overalls and yellow wellies – use metal hooks to lug the heavy boxes. Selling agents auction the fish in voices so fast and heavily accented that an outsider struggles to catch even a single word; occasionally a recognisable phrase – 'twa hunner poond the bundle' – floats to the surface like flotsam released by the tide.

Campbell, a no-nonsense, energetic sixty-four-year-old, comes here daily, in his white peaked cap and long black coat, in his role as senior superintendent of the Royal National Mission to Deep Sea Fishermen, Fraserburgh branch. That, anyway, is his Sunday title. He is, less formally, 'the Mission mannie fae the Broch'. The Fishermen's Mission, as it is commonly known, is a Christian organisation which, since 1881, has been dedicated to caring for fishermen and their families, providing everything from a warm bed in a cold port to financial and emotional support for the widows of men lost at sea. The Mission mannie thus attends the market each morning in order to sniff out whether anyone might be in need of his help. 'Fit like, ma loon?' is his typical opening gambit. He also comes because he is a former fishermen himself and loves to immerse himself in the culture. That briney reek is his equivalent of a breakfast cigarette. He has been with the Mission for twenty-four years and plans to retire in August. 'I'm moving,' he says, 'to the promised land – Lossiemouth.'

The Mission building overlooks the harbour. Herring gulls strut the roof with a profound sense of ownership. Inside, it's much more cosy, especially the wood-panelled canteen with its framed photographs of local boats and cheery smell of chips. Though the Mission is busy during the day, no one stays here now. The huge reduction in the size of the Scottish fleet has meant far fewer men looking for a bed for the night; the Mission building in Aberdeen closed in recent years and there are plans to sell the premises in Mallaig.

Yet the organisation, which is funded entirely by donations and legacies, is busier than ever. As the industry has withered, poverty and despair have been on the increase, giving the Mission much to do. In addition, fishing remains the UK's most dangerous civilian profession, with fishermen 115 times more likely to suffer a fatal accident than the rest of the UK workforce. In Campbell's four years working in Fraserburgh, he has dealt with fifteen 'tragedies' as he puts it, meaning both individual deaths and the loss of entire boats. He has conducted more funerals than he cares to remember. 'But after the funeral, when everybody's gone, we're still there, and we'll make sure that a cheque goes through that door every month for the wife and the children until they reach the end of their academic life.'

The Mission canteen is the social hub of the harbour. It is a place for fishermen to meet and gossip, exchanging old stories and new information about the most fruitful fishing grounds. Every morning, over tea and rowies, a group of worthies, known as the Parliament, put the world to rights. Most are retired, former shipmates with weather-beaten faces, fading blue tattoos and salt water in their veins. The former skipper of the *Accord*, eighty-year-old Bill McKay, has 'Ina' – his wife's name – inked on his right hand in the fleshy part between forefinger and thumb. He used to put the fear into troublesome members of his crew on the *Accord* by telling them it said IRA.

These men grew up at a time when to be born male in Fraserburgh meant, generally, that you were destined for a life at sea. 'I kent from when I was very young,' says sixty-seven-year-old Ted Nibloe. 'I was that little that this lad here' – he points across the table to his elder brother, James – 'said to me, "When the herring tips its tail it'll haul you over the side." But I was always drawn to the sea. The Bible says, "They that go to sea in ships do see the wonder of the Lord." And that's quite right.'

The Parliament is joined, at this point, by one of its most esteemed members, Ernie Watt, his arrival greeted by mock jeers. 'Here comes Dr Death,' someone says. 'He reads the *Press and Journal* in the morning and then comes down and tells us fa's deid.'

Ernie is seventy-five, all quiff and sinew, Gene Vincent meets Gene Kelly, tough but with admirable masculine grace. He was well-known for his capacity, in the days before motorised pulleys, for hauling in the nets. One night, off the coast of Shetland, he dived overboard and swam a hundred yards through the freezing water, having taken a fancy to find out how much herring was in the net. He's been retired for a decade yet still feels the call of the sea. He feels fit enough to fish even now, and looking at him, I don't doubt he's capable. I've seen lighthouses look more frail.

Over on the other side of the canteen is a group of young fishermen from Peterhead. Chaz Bruce is the skipper of the *Challenger*. Few local men, he says, now leave school and go into the fishing. The oil industry is seen as a safer and more lucrative bet. His dad, grandad and great-grandad were all fishermen, but Chaz, who is twenty-seven, would not encourage his own children – if one day he has them – to go to sea. 'Fishing is awful up and down,' he says. 'Sometimes it's the best job in the world; the next day it's horrible and you're not catching anything. It's very emotional. Just now seems to be harder than ever.'

He feels frustrated by bureaucratic restrictions on where in the North Sea he is allowed to work. 'Personally, I don't think we're doing any damage to the fish stocks. There's more cod than we've ever seen, but we're not being allowed to catch it. It's a shame when there's young guys on our boat wanting to go out there and earn a living rather than staying at home on benefits.'

Out on the harbour, repairing nets in the sun, are some of the foreign workers who are increasingly being used to crew boats in Fraserburgh and elsewhere in the north-east. The majority are from the Philippines. It is thought that there are 120 Filipino fishermen living between Fraserburgh and Macduff, drawn across the world to this cold corner of Scotland by the promise of wages higher than they could ever earn at home. Predominantly Catholic, they are heavy users of the Fishermen's Mission, especially the Saturday night karaoke. Jones Mangdang, who is thirty-nine, tells me that his party piece is 'Unchained Melody'. 'Lonely rivers flow,' he sings in broken English, 'to the sea, to the sea.'

Upstairs in the Mission is the memorial room. It's a small hushed space dedicated to the memory of lost fishermen who came from the towns and villages between St Combs and Banff. Five large boards covered in brass plaques record the names of the dead and the boats on which they worked, going back to 1950. The average age is thirty-six. The youngest, Colin Kay, was fifteen when his trawler, the *Blue Crusader*, went down in a storm off North Ronaldsay in January 1965. His mother, Georgina, now in her nineties, is a regular visitor here. Often, with these drownings, no body was recovered, so the memorial room is a place to come and mourn in the absence of a grave.

Standing in the room, leaning on a stick, and looking intently at the plaques is Billy Stephen. He tells his story quietly, almost whispering. On 1st May last year, Billy, who is sixty-one, was in Norwegian waters as part of the crew of the *Renown*. It was early on a Sunday evening. The net was being put over the side when one of his feet became caught and he was dragged overboard. The crew threw him a rope but the weight of the net round his ankle kept pulling him below the surface. 'I kept going down underneath the water. Before I passed out, I thought, "God, please help me." The last thing I remember is bubbles coming out my mouth and I felt myself filling up with water. Then everything went black.'

He regained consciousness on board the *Renown*. His crewmates had somehow got him out of the freezing water and, though he was blue and limp and broken, performed mouth-to-mouth long after many people would have given up. Later, he learned that his wife, Mary, on hearing he had gone overboard, prayed at the Fishermen's Mission for his safety.

Billy looks around the memorial room, at the names of the lost, with sad eyes. He knew many of these men. 'And I've been to sea with a good lot of them,' he says. 'If it wasn't for the crew, and the answered prayer, I would have been just another plaque on that wall.'

Nessie Hunters

'DO NOT DALLY! Do not dally!' Adrian Shine – naturalist, force of nature and erstwhile monster hunter – is leading the way through the Loch Ness Exhibition Centre, which he designed, and which is home to some of the 'toys' he has used in forty years of exploring this and other lochs, including a tiny home-made submarine. He is a tall man with a hawkish profile and a great white beard, striding the darkened corridors in a three-piece tweed suit and tartan tie, his mellifluous voice sounding in the murk. It is like being led around the chocolate factory by Willy Wonka, or by the Doctor showing off his Tardis.

Shine, who is sixty-four, moved to the Highlands from his native Surrey in 1973, a restless maverick seeking 'fame and glory, even in the cannon's mouth – youth is like that'. He was part of a wave of amateur investigators each keen to find evidence that, depending on their own beliefs, the monster did or did not exist. There was something about that moment, in the late 1960s and early '70s, as the countercultural tide lapped up against the shore of science, when anything – Atlantis, UFOs, Nessie – seemed possible, and Loch Ness became a proving ground for anyone with a working boat and a working theory.

Yet the monster legend predates the hippy era. Accounts of a mysterious creature in the loch go back to around 700 when Adomnán, the Abbot of Iona, wrote that St Columba had once driven away the monster as it was on the point of devouring one of his followers.

However, the birth of the Loch Ness Monster as a global media and tourism phenomenon is about to have its eightieth anniversary. Nessie may be a plesiosaur; she may be a sturgeon; she may even be a he – the theories are endless – but one thing is sure: she will very shortly be an octogenarian.

It was on 14th April 1933, while driving along the north-western shore of the loch, near Abriachan pier, that Aldie Mackay, manageress of the Drumnadrochit Hotel, is said to have spotted an enormous creature with a body resembling that of a whale rolling in the roiling water. 'Stop!' she yelled to her husband, John, who was driving. 'The beast!'

Aldie Mackay made no mention of the now iconic long neck, or at least that did not feature in the account of her sighting which was published in the *Inverness Courier*, headlined 'Strange Spectacle In Loch Ness'. She herself was shy of publicity and was not quoted in the article, fearing that people would say she should take more water in her whisky. It was the then editor, Evan Macleod Barron, who suggested that the creature should be described as a 'monster' – and this story and soubriquet, together, proved so tantalising that they were retold by newspapers around the world, bringing journalists and then tourists flocking to an area of Scotland which had hitherto been rather obscure. 'This,' says Adrian Shine, meaning the whole global phenomenon, 'is Mrs Mackay's legacy.'

The tiny lochside village of Drumnadrochit receives around 300,000 visitors each year; staggering, considering that the local population right around the loch is not quite 3,000. Annual Nessie tourism is estimated to be worth around £30 million – spent on hotels and B&Bs, boat trips, food, monster-branded merchandise – and visitor numbers are said to spike following each new reported sighting. The huge green fibreglass beastie overlooking the A82 from the grounds of the Clansman Hotel is a snarling symbol of the legend's economic importance; as much an emblem of the Nessie industry as the Finnieston crane is of Clydeside shipbuilding.

The grand Victorian Drumnadrochit Hotel, which Aldie Mackay managed, is now the Loch Ness Exhibition Centre, and it attracts people from all over the world. 'We are in search of the monster,' say the Kim family from South Korea – a mum and dad and two young kids.

'It's always at the back of your mind – "Will I be the one to see it?"' says Gavin, who works in the area but is originally from Zimbabwe. He was still living in Africa when he first saw the Ted Danson movie about the monster and grew intrigued. 'You just never know, do you?' says his work colleague, Fredericka, who hails from Ghana. 'My husband lives in New York and he wants to come over here and see the monster.'

The loch, even without the legend, would be remarkable. Loch Ness is twenty miles long, a mile wide, 700 feet deep, a great bleak blackness, stained with peat; a swallower of men, aircraft, boats; insatiable and unfathomable.

On the day I visit, it is gorgeously sunny but bitter cold, minus eight in Drumnadrochit as the sun began to rise over the black fir-serrated hump of hills above the southern shore. Spring has not quite sprung this far north. Lochside trees shake bare twisted talons at the cheerful blue sky.

There have been generations of monster hunters, a sort of cryptozoological papacy full of heroes and villains, defenders of the faith and some who brought it into disrepute. Certain names still ring out in the Great Glen. The late Tim Dinsdale, an aeronautical engineer who led fifty-six expeditions between 1960 and 1987, and who shot an acclaimed black and white film which appeared to show a hump crossing the water. Robert Rines, the inventor, patent lawyer and Broadway composer, who, as a child, played a violin duet with Albert Einstein, and whose sighting in 1972 inspired him to spend the rest of his life seeking the monster, making an elegiac final expedition – in search of Nessie's bones – in 2008, the year before his own death. And then there was Frank Searle, a hugely controversial figure, soldier-turned-greengrocer-turned-self-styled-'Monster-hunter-extraordinary' whose blue caravan and exhibition of photographs was a familiar sight on the loch-side in the mid-1970s. He died in 2005 and is remembered now for his hoaxed pictures and aggressive conflicts with rival investigators.

'He was always offering to knife people,' Adrian Shine recalls. 'Disembowelment was what was proposed for me.'

Shine had been a lazy and unpromising schoolboy, a classic young naturalist of the time, collecting frogspawn and birds' eggs. He came to Scotland because he didn't know quite what to do with his life. He had travelled to India, fascinated by the big game hunter Jim Corbett, and was considering becoming the first man to row across the Atlantic when he chanced upon a book about Morag, the monster said to live in Loch Morar. He decided that he was the very chap to find this beast and headed north, rowing out into the loch at night and spending hours, drifting in the dark, offering himself as bait.

He saw himself as a 'knight errant', out to prove his manhood and make his name. Instead, he came to believe that Morag did not exist and later turned his attentions to Loch Ness with the same sceptical mindset, setting out to prove the absence of a monster by the process of elimination, culminating in 1987's Operation Deepscan – in which a fleet of boats swept the loch with sonar. These days, Shine is more fascinated by the environment of the loch itself than the notion of a mysterious creature.

'It was going to be a very quick route to fame and fortune but didn't quite work out that way,' he says, reflecting on his years here. 'I came here to conquer, to raid, to take home the spoils, but it was me who was captured.'

The loch does, however, still have at least one true believer. Steve Feltham moved here on 19th June 1991, chucking his job and girlfriend, and has entered the *Guinness Book of Records* for his Nessie-seeking vigil. He lives in a converted mobile library at the side of the loch in the village of Dores with an adopted stray cat called Miaow, and makes his living selling small model monsters mounted on rocks washed ashore. He passes his nights reading about Nessie and playing the piano badly. He gets his water from a nearby tap and keeps warm by burning driftwood on a stove sourced on eBay.

I had heard that he recently got married to a local woman, but he explains that it was a ceremony at the Rock Ness music festival, in an inflatable church, which was not legally binding, though it means a lot to them. He spends each day watching the loch, bearing witness, always hopeful that he will see and film the monster. He is fifty now and thinks it quite possible that he will spend the rest of his life on this spot.

He is 'ecstatic' about his continuing adventure and only 'mildly disappointed' that he has not yet solved the mystery. He consoles himself with the thought that when, eventually, he does film Nessie, the length of his stay will lend authenticity to his findings. He does not come across as a crank. He is more like some sort of religious hermit – keeping the faith in the wilderness – albeit one who pops into the local pub for wifi.

Even true believers need a break now and then, of course, and it turns out that Feltham has only just returned from a month in Guatemala. But – and it is a big but – he spent most of his time sitting next to Lake Atitlán, where there is believed to be a monster; so, a busman's holiday of sorts. He is, for me, the guardian spirit of Loch Ness, the keeper of a flame passed from St Columba to Aldie Mackay to Adrian Shine and on down the years. Not that he would put it that way.

'I'm the world champion,' he sighs, 'of sitting on a beach and seeing bugger all.'

Among the Skaters

'SKATEBOARDING IS AWESOME.' Three words. Uttered on a sultry Edinburgh day by Kerr McLachlan, twenty-one years old, a skater since he was nine. Just three words, but they say it all, really, about what skating means to its acolytes and devotees, its whirling dervishes in ragged shoes and baggy shorts. Their certainty about its awesomeness – not *quite* awesome, not *pretty* awesome, just plain awesome – is similar to the way certain religious fundamentalists feel about their holy books. So: 'Skateboarding is awesome.' Amen, Brother Kerr.

The Saughton skatepark in Edinburgh is hoaching when it's hot. There must be well over a hundred folk here this afternoon, crammed into its undulating architecture, some skating, some sitting around in the sun; drinking beer or juice, consuming pizza by the slice, tobacco by the ounce. The air smells of cut grass, hot concrete and sweat. Twenty-year-old Kyle Mowat speeds round the curves, tap aff, with a grace unlikely in one who, not long ago, broke his left leg so badly that the tibia poked through his skin. Fag smoke and dandelion clocks drift dreamily past. Sycamores, shading the entrance, are festooned with dozens of pairs of old trainers, revolving slowly by their laces, flung up into the high branches by skaters who have worn them out in the park and so left them here, in the trees, as a tribute to good times past and a votive offering in the hope of even better times to come.

Thursday is, by long tradition, the big night for skateboarding in Edinburgh. The Thursday session. The sesh. The Thursday club. People start turning up from mid-afternoon. All ages: fresh-faced teenage newbies; leathery weather-beaten veterans with lumps and humps from decades of falls. They greet each other with fist-bumps and proffered cans. Everyone has skint elbows, skint knees, and they complain of being skint because all their money goes on boards and wheels. Still, out here in the sun, in the park, nobody thinks too much about jobs and wages. This, for them, is freedom.

'I had no friends until I started skateboarding,' says Kerr. 'Then this place opened. When I was younger, if I'd had an argument with my mum, or any stress, the best thing to do was just to go skateboarding. Even if you're just rolling, it blanks your mind. I know a lot of people who don't do drugs or drink because they've got skateboarding. It saves people. But it's an addiction. The way I look at Edinburgh is different to someone who doesn't skateboard. The whole city is our playground. The whole world. You're so free. Skateboarding is endless.'

The Saughton skatepark has been open since 2010 and covers around 2,000 square metres. Its concrete surfaces are motley with graffiti, and its areas have been given affectionate nicknames by the skaters: Middle Earth, The Moshpit, The Bowl, Steep Dave. This place is their pleasure palace. Some get the shakes if they are away from it too long. They are hooked on everything about it, not least the distinctive sound of metal grinding against concrete, a sound so adored it even has its own name – shralp.

'It's aw aboot the adrenalin, man,' explains eighteen-year-old Scott Bennie. 'See when you land a trick? It's amazin,' eh? The danger gets you hyped on it. See if I land it and I've not broken my head open? I'm fuckin' cheesin' about it. Only way to describe it, man.'

There's a skatepark etiquette. Every skater takes their turn. Jumping the queue is known as snaking. Even if you've been waiting ages, if you come off at the first wall, your turn is over and you go to the back of the queue. And

if someone is attempting to learn a new trick, it is considered disrespectful for another skater who can already
perform that trick to do so. Generally, it's a supportive
culture. Onlookers are always whooping and hollering
praise, yelling out suggestions for tricks that, to the uniniti-
ated, sound gnomic: 'Bongo! Show us your rock to fakie!';
'Frontside air!'; 'That's sick!'; 'That's rad!'

Bongo is Ali Duncan. He's sixteen and from Selkirk, a
town with a strong equestrian culture but no skate scene,
so he travels to Edinburgh and other parks whenever he
can. He was given a board by his grandad when he was
eight, and when the old man died he used to go out skating
as a way of remembering him. 'I don't know what I'd do if
I didn't skate,' he says. He was, until recently, working in
a mill packaging tartan scarves, and would pass the time
thinking obsessively about tricks. 'When you learn a new
one it's an ecstatic feeling.'

Delam wanders over. Dylan Berrill is his real name.
He's a student psychiatric nurse, covered in tattoos; one,
on his left leg, says Skate Or Die. 'If you're writing about
skateboarding,' he says, 'then you've got to mention
these guys – the modern scourge of the skateparks.' He
gestures behind him to a couple of wee boys, pre-schoolers
on scooters, playing blithely in the concrete bowl. 'Their
mums and dads just drop them off into the park like it's
a crèche. You can't be mean to them because they're just
children. I've hit a couple by accident. I body-checked one
full-pelt, but managed to grab him in mid-air and turn, so
I took the force of the fall on my back. I would have felt
horrendous if he had to be taken away in an ambulance.'

Dylan is one of the older skaters at Saughton. 'If you'd
told me at sixteen that I'd still be skating at almost forty
I'd have laughed at you,' he says. 'We used to think that
you were done after twenty-five. I remember being sixteen
and feeling sorry for a mate who was nineteen; that he was
ancient, past it. But a lot of the guys who got started in the

late 1970s, early '80s have just kept going. I feel physically similar to how I did in my twenties. But there's a little bit more fear comes into it when you're our age. A lot of the guys are joiners or plumbers or whatever, so if they injure themselves they don't make a living.'

At about seven o'clock, in part to escape the kids on scooters, a bunch of skaters head over to the park at Livingston, cadging a lift in Iain Young's big Dodge van, listening to T. Rex and Motörhead as the countryside blurs past. Iain, or Youngo, is – at thirty-eight – an elder statesman of the scene. He is part of Skateboard Scotland, the governing body, and builds skateparks through his company Concreate. He comes from Grangemouth and has been skating since the 1980s, when the scene was still outsiderish and underground – 'You got a lot of shit for riding a skateboard. People would be attacking you and chasing you down the street.' He and his pals would break into abandoned warehouses and build ramps; it was the same with the derelict mills in Dundee.

'Livi', as everyone calls the skatepark at Livingston, dates from 1981. It was one of the first parks in the UK and is known internationally, attracting skaters from far and wide, including famous Americans such as Tony Hawk. It is, therefore, somewhere between a massive public artwork, a historic monument, and a beery hang-out, a kind of Radge Mahal. 'It's the Scottish skating Mecca,' says twenty-four-year-old Craig Benson, a local skater in a red cap and Scotland football top. 'This is our zone.'

Livi was the brainchild of Kenny Omond, now 'seventy-one going on seventeen', an electronics engineer from the area who fell in love with skateboarding while on business in California in 1976. He returned to Livingston determined to build a skatepark, and found that the New Town mindset meant most people in positions of influence were open to the idea. So, in the spring of 1981, Livi opened.

'It was madness on a stick,' says Kenny. He and his wife

Eleanor operated an open-house policy for skaters, putting people up, driving them to A&E with broken wrists and ankles, and even – on occasion – bailing them out of jail. Kenny still skates, even now, and is 'training up' his six-year-old grandson, Kade. He laughs off suggestions that a statue in his honour should be erected at the side of the park. 'It sends shivers up my back,' he says, 'at night, when it's dark, and you hear the noise of wheels on concrete.'

Talking to skaters is fascinating. They don't seem at all like sportsmen; rather more like artists, or even pilgrims of a sort. They speak about skating as a form of creativity, riding a park like musicians playing through a score, each performing in his own unique way, a concept known as 'steez'; they speak about it, too, as a warm meditative feeling, a cotton-wool blankness. It's beyond expression, skating, really. It is what it is.

'If you can put into words what a guid time we're huvin',' says Mark Burrows, a forty-year-old skater from Tranent, as he stands on his board on the lip at Livi, about to plunge down once more, 'then ye're daein' a guid job, right there.'

The Christmas Houses of Port Glasgow

MARY PTOLOMEY, A seventy-nine-year-old widow born and bred in Port Glasgow, shares her cosy semi-detached home with a taciturn son Sam, a talkative green parrot called Blue, and sixty-seven animatronic Santas. 'I just love Christmas,' she says.

The house is on Bute Avenue, a steep street with grand views across the Firth of Clyde to the snowy hills of Argyll. On a fine day, Trident subs can be seen sailing to and from the Gare Loch.

It is hard, though, when visiting here, at this time of year, to lift one's gaze that far. The eye tends to snag on wonders nearer at hand. The seven foot tall inflatable Santa emerging from an inflatable chimney on the front grass, for instance. The illuminated Santa in the privet; the snowmen in the windows; the reindeer on the bench. Stand too long on Mrs Ptolomey's lawn, it is said, and you'll end up wired to the mains.

This part of Port Glasgow is home to a cluster of ostentatiously decorated houses, shining out from the winter darkness like puggies in dim pubs. Seven-year-old Megan Morrison, smiling at an inflatable nativity scene at the bottom of her grandad's driveway on School Road, declares the town 'better than Blackpool'.

Megan has a point. There are so many lights in Mrs Ptolomey's garden, for example, that her home is said to be visible from over the water in Helensburgh. The plugs, snug in a Farmfoods bag, are protected from snow and rain. Traffic slows as it passes, and people make special trips from neighbouring towns. From Erskine, they come; from Greenock, Garvock, Gourock.

Each year, Frank Ptolomey spends three weeks putting up his mother's decorations. 'Aye, it's me that does it,' he says, pointing to his brother Sam, dozing in an armchair. 'He's too fat to get up the loft.'

A friendly fellow of sixty-one with the word 'hate' tattooed across the back of his left hand, Frank sometimes wears a Santa suit while setting out the Santas. He believes that when you're dressed like that, you ought to make a good impression. He remembers taking his daughter, when she was wee, to meet Santa in Coronation Park and noticing how, whenever he reached down into his sack for a present, Santa would take a swig of Eldorado wine. 'See by the time we got to the front of the queue,' says Frank, 'Santa was getting lifted by the polis.'

The Ptolomey lights are switched on at the end of November and stay up until February. 'Once we sober up and get rid of the hangover,' says Frank, 'it's time to get them back in the loft.'

One stormy night, Frank, who lives in Kilmacolm, was woken by his mother phoning, fearful, to say she'd heard someone breaking in through the roof. He sped over, only to discover that the intruder was nothing more than the sixty-seven Santas in the loft, giving it laldy with the 'Ho! Ho! Ho!' having been activated by a clap of thunder. His mother had forgotten to remove their batteries.

Mrs Ptolomey laughs at this. 'My husband, God rest him, he used to say: "See when you go to the shops, would you stop buying decorations?" But I don't smoke, I don't drink and I don't go to bingo. I just buy Santa Clauses. And I'll still be buying them if I live till ninety by the way.'

Over by the window, Blue the parrot squawks, at which the Santa above the cage starts singing 'Santa Claus is Coming to Town'. This, in turn, sets off a toy train – the North Pole Express, which chuffs round the tinselly tree to the tune of 'We Wish You a Merry Christmas' – and a snowman performing 'Jingle Bells' in a warm Bing Crosby-ish baritone. Frank shrugs and grins: 'This is a crazy house. No wonder I take a drink. See if I met the real Santa, I'd probably do him in.'

The association between Christmas and artificial lighting has a long history. Legend has it that the first person to place lit candles on a tree was Martin Luther, in an attempt to show his children how snow had shimmered on firs he saw while walking by moonlight.

The popular use of electric light, however, begins with Thomas Edison who, in 1882, created the world's first electrically lit tree. The trend for decorating the exterior of homes with lights started in America during the 1950s, reaching Britain early in the following decade.

Now, of course, the phenomenon – sometimes known as 'house-bling' – is widespread. We spend many millions of pounds on Christmas decorations each year, and though most of that will be on interiors, there are always some people happy to splurge their savings on a herd of metre-tall reindeer from the garden centre.

Plenty of folk are skint at the moment, of course, but this doesn't seem to have made much difference. Often, the gaudiest homes are in areas which are not at all well-off.

It is too easy to sneer at these so-called 'Christmas houses' or to write them off as simply kitsch. For them to be kitsch, in the modern sense of that word, those who create the displays would be doing so in an ironic, knowing way. But there is nothing ironic about Christmas lights, at least not in Port Glasgow. The thing that makes them most Christmassy is that they are heartfelt and sincere.

John Hurrell, a retired nightwatchman, lives on Cumbrae Drive; most of the streets in this neighbourhood are named after islands. John has 'Merry Christmas' written in lights above his front door and living-room window. He has three illuminated snowmen and a skiing Santa. He has multi-coloured bulbs slung from his gutter and a strobing sledge flying towards his satellite dish. He himself appreciates very little of this as he is losing his sight. Yet Christmas without these lights would be, for John, unthinkable.

He lost the use of his left eye as a child; lost it when someone flung a penny banger in his pram. Glaucoma is now playing merry hell with his right. But this time of year is special to him. He and his wife, Hughina, known as 'Ina', married on Christmas Eve. They were both teenagers and she was pregnant.

'It was 1965 and The Beatles were number one with "We Can Work It Out",' he remembers, fondly, 'and we did work it out. Love doesn't put a loaf on your table, and people maybe say we're not well off, but we've got a roof over our head and food in the fridge and that's all we need.'

Ina worries about the amount of money it costs to power these lights, especially as John sometimes has them flashing from September onwards, but he is unyielding on this issue. 'I'm a person that takes a notion to do a thing and I just do it.'

Patrick McCartney, who is forty, lives on Islay Avenue, just up the road from the Hurrells. Golden bells, snowflakes and crescent moons cast a festive glow on the pebbledash. Stars that would be the envy of Vegas flash in front of the Venetian blinds. Two Victorian-style streetlamps, made from ropelights, stand on each side of the doorstep. Santa shins up a drainpipe. McCartney was one of thirteen children and remembers with fond nostalgia the hectic Christmases of his youth. He has been properly into Christmas lights since his early twenties. It all started with a six-foot snowman he spotted up the town one day, and snowballed from there.

'I wasn't going to do it this year because I've had a tough time,' he says. 'I suffer from cancer and my father's lying ill, too. But I don't know how many people knocked my door and stopped me in the street to ask when I was going to put these lights up. At first I felt I shouldn't be doing this if I'm maybe going to be burying my father. But then I thought: "To hell with it, it's Christmas efter aw'."'

Usually he puts his lights up in the first week of November, combining Bonfire Night and Christmas, setting off fireworks and then hitting the switches. But this year, because of his initial reluctance, he didn't get his lights on until the end of the month.

What most people would consider a bit early, he regards as tardy. He turns them on, each day, at a quarter to four; off at 10 p.m. sharp. On Christmas Eve and Christmas Day they stay on all day and night. He is a stickler for what he regards as the proper ethics of Christmas lights: don't leave them up, unlit, on the front of the house all year round – that's cheating; make sure to create a different display each time; and, whatever you do, don't try to compete with the neighbours: 'See that: "I've got one Santa more than you" carry-on? It takes the goodness right out of Christmas.'

Back down the hill on Bute Avenue, Frank Ptolomey has changed into his Santa suit. There's a party atmosphere. Cans of lager are on the go. Even the paper boy has been asked in to admire the decorations. Frank sits his mother on his knee, as if she's a wee girl after presents, and yanks down his white beard to make himself heard.

'This is nothing, by the way,' he says to me, gesturing round the lights. 'You want to come back up here in the summer and see all her garden gnomes. I'm telling you, it's no' real.'

After Angelika

THE BANNER OF St Patrick's, Anderston, bears an image of the saint ankle-deep in shamrocks. Over the decades, this church banner has toured the world's great Christian pilgrimage sites and been held proudly aloft by people from Glasgow who believe in miracles. On this afternoon of Sunday, 12th August 2007, in a humble room in a run-down scheme, it hangs over the scene of another wonder – a religious community coming back from the dead.

A low, narrow, flat-roofed hall, The Hut forms part of a grey housing association complex. Hidden behind a school, it is not easy to find, but above the roar of Argyle Street traffic it is just possible to detect the sound of singing. Inside, a congregation of around eighty are raising their voices in the hymn 'Hail Redeemer', accompanied by a portable Yamaha keyboard.

The Hut has been temporarily transformed into a church – St Pat's by proxy. The banner is pinned to one wall and a table draped in a white cloth serves as an altar from which Canon Robert Hill, the new parish priest, dispenses Holy Communion. The mood of this makeshift mass is palpably joyful. The congregation, a mix of older people and young families, joke and laugh afterwards, some of the men ducking outside for a cigarette. One exhales smoke with a chuckle and points out a very small man: 'Ye wouldnae believe Mick here was six foot two before he jumped in the water at Lourdes.' This kind of banter is rooted in relief. They know that this is the last time they will be here.

The next service will be held in St Patrick's itself, a five-minute walk away. It will be the first time that most parishioners have entered the church since it closed, abruptly, at the end of last September, when the body of twenty-three-year-old Polish student Angelika Kluk was discovered beneath its floorboards.

In May, sixty-year-old Peter Tobin was found guilty of murder and sentenced to life in prison. I remember him in the High Court in Edinburgh, a bland monster in a lilac jumper; he kept his head bowed in the dock. It looked like a blasphemous prayer.

Tobin had arrived at St Patrick's in 2006, a homeless man drawn by the relief offered by the Loaves and Fishes charity which operated from the church. To hide a previous conviction for a violent sexual attack, he had used the name Pat McLaughlin and won the trust of the then priest, Father Gerry Nugent, who gave him a key and put him to work as an odd-job man.

Father Nugent operated an open-door policy within the church, giving shelter to anyone in need, be they homeless, destitute, addicted to drugs or alcohol, or otherwise troubled; the church would be opened at seven in the morning and kept open as late as the priest could manage. 'For me,' he told the trial, 'the vision was a sacred place where anybody could come ... God's love and mercy applies to everyone and excludes nobody.' This lack of discrimination is regarded as having made the church vulnerable; like a virus, Tobin identified and exploited weakness in his host.

During the trial, the priest claimed to have had a sexual relationship with Kluk, who lived in a room of the chapel house. He also admitted to being an alcoholic. Aneta Kluk in court described him as 'a Jekyll and Hyde sort of person' and said that his claims of romantic involvement with her younger sister were 'outrageous and untrue'. While searching the church for her missing sister, she said, she had found the priest drunk and locked in the section of the church house where Angelika had stayed. In February, the Archbishop of Glasgow, Mario Conti, asked for Father Nugent's resignation.

'The murder hit people really hard,' says Eddie Hart, a regular at St Patrick's for all his sixty-five years. 'Angelika was a girl everybody knew. You thought this couldn't happen in your community. Then the trial, with everything that came out, was traumatic. People felt badly let down.'

St Patrick's will reopen formally next Sunday when Archbishop Conti presides over a mass. Before then there will be low-key services designed to help parishioners get used to being in the church and reflect on the events of the past year. The evening service this Wednesday will be built around prayers for the dead.

'Angelika's going to be the first person mentioned, so our first act will be to pray for her and her family,' says Canon Hill. 'Also, many local families feel one of the sadnesses of the past year is that relatives who died could not be buried from the church which was so much part of their lives. So it's a specific focus for Angelika but it's also for all those whose lives have come to an end in the past year.'

Hill, a genial silver-haired fifty-two-year-old, is obviously very intelligent but not wintry with it; he even makes a pretty good joke about how terrible nuns are at flitting. Appointed as the new priest in late May, he has since held four services in The Hut. They are a way of getting to know his parishioners and keeping them informed of the progress towards reopening.

Speaking to the congregation after Communion, he says: 'With these evening prayers, the idea is to be very low-key. We want to keep the mood sombre. At the big mass on 26th August though, we want the place to be covered with flowers, and candles will be lit. By the time we get to the Gloria we're hoping to get the bells working again so everybody will get the message we're back in business.'

This is what the people have been waiting to hear. Luisa Campbell, a woman in her forties who has been a parishioner for three years, says, 'It's been very strange while St Patrick's has been closed. It felt like everybody disappeared overnight and you never saw people from the parish. It was lonely and isolating, not knowing what's going on. During the investigation they couldn't tell us much.'

Before it closed, St Patrick's had a five hundred-strong congregation, most of whom have spent almost a year at other churches. For St Patrick's, the challenge will be to win the people back. Yet getting bums on pews may not be as difficult as it first appeared. If anything, the parishioners are worried they might not get a seat for the opening mass.

There is a sense that they have a duty to bring the church back to life with their prayer and song. After Kluk's body was discovered, there was speculation about St Patrick's being demolished. The archdiocese insists that this was never a possibility, and the parishioners are horrified at the thought.

Opened in the nineteenth century to cater for a mix of Irish immigrants fleeing religious persecution and Catholics displaced by the Highland Clearances, St Patrick's is one of the oldest buildings in Anderston. Once thriving, the district was decimated in the 1960s by the demolition of housing to make way for the M8 motorway and the Kingston Bridge. In the 1940s, St Patrick's served 20,000 people; there are now reckoned to be only around 2,000 Catholics living in the area. It is a community on life support and the church keeps its blood pumping.

Had it been pulled down, says Eddie Hart, 'Peter Tobin would have murdered more than Angelika; he would have murdered Anderston. But Saint Patrick's will be like the Lord himself – it will be resurrected. We are determined that will happen. You go for your messages in the morning and people say, "It'll no' be long till it's open." Apart from football, that's all people are talking about.'

If the people of St Patrick's need no encouragement to

construe their situation in biblical terms, the reopening programme seems designed to do just that. Next Sunday's mass will begin with the church and congregation being sprinkled with water from the baptismal font, symbolising rebirth. Saturday's service will focus on the journey of the Israelites to the Promised Land, a historic template for a congregation who see themselves as returning home after a period of exile.

For some, the reopening will be nothing less than a blow struck in the battle against evil. Denis Curran, co-director of the charity Loaves and Fishes, says, 'I believe Satan's follower came into the church, and that Christians now have to stand up and be counted. For the benefit of the young girl. What happened to her was horrendous. But it would be worse if the church shut because of that, eh? That would mean he won.'

What will it be like, though, to be inside a church so associated with a violent death? 'I'm nervous,' says Luisa Campbell, 'You ask yourself questions like, "How are we going to cope?" and "How do we start building things up again?" But I'm excited as well. It will be nice to be back.'

The parishioners take some comfort from the fact that Angelika Kluk was killed in the adjoining garage rather than the church itself. Nevertheless, people will be worshipping very near to the scene of a rape and murder and immediately above where a body was concealed. 'Obviously some people will find that difficult,' says Eddie Hart, 'but I've been fortunate over the last weeks to go to the church and volunteer and I've seen the building work going on. The church is completely changed. Parts that were involved with the case are covered up. Where Angelika was found, the floorboards have all been renewed and carpeted. You can't see anything.'

At the time it closed, St Patrick's was in need of renovation. The archdiocese took advantage of the forced closure and carried out necessary repairs, as well as decoration and alterations which draw the eyes and mind away from the murder. 'This is not going to be some shrine to the horrible event that has taken place,' says Canon Hill. 'We will keep it very much as part of our memory, but there won't be anything visible to attract people.

'The parishioners themselves said that while what happened to Angelika was terrible and unthinkable ... the idea of a body in a church? Well, we have that regularly as part of funeral rites. The fact that the body of a deceased person was in the church is not in itself that horrific.'

A native Glaswegian, Hill has been priest to the parish of St Charles in Kelvinside for seven years and will continue both roles while looking after St Patrick's. Though he admits he recently felt a little panicky about the challenge ahead, he never for a moment considered declining the role. He feels sorry for the way Father Nugent has had his reputation destroyed. 'It's a terrible shame because the tremendous good he did outweighs the negative things that have emerged. That's not to downplay the shortcomings that became apparent.

'I think he's the kind of person whose strengths are also his weaknesses – he's quite an instinctive operator. He sees a need and responds to it, appropriately or inappropriately. We're all very smart with hindsight, I suppose, but this instinct meant that he could be approached by so many people. His instinct most of the time was spot on. All of his colleagues admired the way he would get involved with things that needed to be done. But the downside was he couldn't always tell what was a good idea and what was a bad one.'

He hasn't discussed the future of St Patrick's with his predecessor. 'He's not been doing so well,' says Hill. 'He's finding life very difficult and has become a bit distanced from the parish so we haven't spoken about me taking over here. But we're in contact by phone from time to time. He needs to be made to realise the tremendous good that he did. That's what he finds very difficult to take on board. He has never had a high opinion of himself.'

Hill will not be continuing with the open-door policy. 'I don't think it's sensible to have a building anywhere in the centre of Glasgow lying open twenty-four hours a day. St Patrick's got into difficulties because there wasn't enough professional supervision. The building, first and foremost, is a church, and a church isn't really a drop-in centre, so in the light of very painful experience we want to be a bit careful about what's on offer.'

He hopes that the Mungo Foundation, once part of the Archdiocese of Glasgow but now an independent social care organisation, will be able to operate from the church. It is unlikely that Loaves and Fishes will return to St Patrick's.

The charity is now based at the Oasis Café, part of Renfield St Stephen's Church on Bath Street. Loaves and Fishes is thriving in its new location, according to Curran, but he acknowledges the crucial support of Nugent. 'I believe Father Gerry was as good as a man could get because he genuinely helped people,' Curran says. 'A lot of guys used to go in there and sit during the day because it was a place of peace and quiet. Most of the other churches were closed, but he kept his open. Okay, something came of that to haunt everybody, but I can't blame him.'

Curran acknowledges that he introduced Tobin to Nugent and feels guilty about doing so. Indeed, he has had to seek counselling to deal with the whole experience. Loaves and Fishes lost volunteers as a result of what happened and Curran himself considered dissolving the charity. 'I thought, "I don't need this." I had to think and pray hard on it for a long while, but the people we helped spoke about the difference we've made in their lives and that showed me it would be wrong to shut the door ... Not only did Peter Tobin create that horrendous act of murder, he'd have destroyed a section of those people's lives.'

298

And how does he feel towards Tobin now? 'Absolutely nothing. I've no emotions for the man other than I hope he rots in hell.'

* * *

It is 9.30 a.m. on Thursday, 16th August. A band of parishioners – mostly elderly – enter St Patrick's through the back entrance and chain the gates behind them. They are here to prepare the church for reopening. The men will do the heavy lifting, the women will clean the pews and polish the brass till it gleams. A skip lies in the garden, and round the door of the garage where Kluk was killed, blue-purple flowers bloom. Hydrangeas change colour when transplanted into different soil – a symbol of adjusting, moving on, putting down new roots.

A couple of ladies come out to talk. They don't want to give their names, regarding themselves as representing all the women working inside. This is the first time they have been in St Patrick's since it closed. They have found it emotional, but haven't cried. That will keep until the mass.

Why are they here? 'This is my family, really,' says one, referring both to the church and the people within. Like many who go to St Patrick's they can trace their own family back to the 1800s when they came over from Ireland and settled in Anderston. Their ancestors put pennies in the collection plate that paid for the church to be built.

Canon Hill told me that St Patrick's isn't being recon-secrated so much as repossessed, and talking to these parishioners it's clear what he means. This community is taking back something they own – taking it back from Peter Tobin, from Father Nugent, back even from Ange-lika Kluk and the relentless media focus on her violent death.

'I'll never forget that wee girl,' says one of the women.

'She didnae deserve to die the way she did. But we've got to get St Pat's up and running again, as a living parish.'

They turn together and walk through the gates, past the skip and the flowers, back into the gloom and dust of the church, into their past and future.

List of original publications

After the Referendum – *Scotland on Sunday*, 21 September 2014

The Clavie King – *Scottish Review of Books*, March 2017

A Night with the Naked Rambler – *Scotland on Sunday*, 7 October 2012

The Storm – *The Guardian Weekend* magazine, 10 October 2015

The World Crazy Golf Championship – *The Big Issue*, 21 March 2016

The Sikh Pipe Band – *The Scotsman*, 17 August 2015

The Passion of Harry Bingo – written for *Nutmeg: The Scottish Football Periodical*, March 2017. A shorter version was first published in *The Guardian Weekend* magazine, 18 February 2017.

Herring Queens – *Scotland on Sunday*, 29 June 2014

Whaligoe Steps – previously unpublished. The opening paragraphs are adapted from a feature written for *National Geographic Traveler*, September 2016.

Barrowlands – *The National*, 24 December 2014

The Burryman – *Scotland on Sunday*, 16 August 2009

Balnakeil – *Scotland on Sunday*, 25 August 2013

The Circus – *Scotland on Sunday*, 1 July 2012

Behold Now, Behemoth – *Scotland on Sunday*, 31 August 2014

The Bass Rock – *Scotland on Sunday*, 14 August 2011

The Riverman – *Scotland on Sunday*, 13 October 2013

The Wall of Death – *Scotland on Sunday*, 10 March 2013

Ramadan – *Scotland on Sunday* 20 August 2012

The Drag Queen Ball – *Scotland on Sunday*, 11 November 2012

The Eagle's Bairn – *The Sunday Times*, 10 May 2015

In Praise of Small Towns – *Scotland on Sunday*, 23 September 2012

The Scottish Resistance – *The Guardian*, 26 March 2016

A Car-Boot Sale – *Scotland on Sunday*, 22 April 2012

Above Orkney – *Scotland on Sunday*, 29 April 2012

Nihil Sine Labore – previously unpublished. Based on articles published in *Scotland on Sunday* between March 2011 and May 2014

A Grouse Shoot – *Scotland on Sunday*, 15 August 2010

You'll Never Walk Alone – *The Big Issue*, 7 October 2013

The Sex Shop – *Scotland on Sunday*, 18 September 2011

Iona – *Scotland on Sunday*, 19 May 2013

Joseph McKenzie's Secret – *Royal Photographic Society Journal*, December 2015

The Bonspiel – *Scotland on Sunday*, 10 January 2010

The Band Who Gave Glasgow Hope – *The Big Issue*, 8 April 2014

The Biscuiteers – *The Big Issue*, 30 May 2016

Inside Rehab – *Scotland on Sunday*, 18 November 2012

The Chess Players – *Scotland on Sunday*, 2 October 2011

The Poultry Show – *Scotland on Sunday*, 22 January 2012

A Day In A&E – *Scotland on Sunday*, 21 April 2013

The Fishermen's Mission – *Scotland on Sunday*, 6 May 2012

Nessie Hunters – *Scotland on Sunday*, 24 February 2013

Among the Skaters – *Scotland on Sunday*, 2 June 2013

The Christmas Houses of Port Glasgow – *Scotland on Sunday*, 9 December 2012

After Angelika – *Sunday Herald*, 19 August 2007